*A Preacher's Guide
to Topical Sermon Series*

A Preacher's Guide to Topical Sermon Series

24 THEMATIC PLANS

Compiled by Jessica Miller Kelley

© 2026 Westminster John Knox Press

First edition
Published by Westminster John Knox Press
Louisville, Kentucky

26 27 28 29 30 31 32 33 34 35—10 9 8 7 6 5 4 3 2 1

All rights reserved. No part of this book may be reproduced or transmitted in any form or by any means, electronic or mechanical, including photocopying, recording, or by any information storage or retrieval system, without permission in writing from the publisher. For information, address Westminster John Knox Press, 100 Witherspoon Street, Louisville, Kentucky 40202-1396. Or contact us online at www.wjkbooks.com.

Unless otherwise indicated, Scripture quotations are from the New Revised Standard Version Updated Edition copyright © 2021 National Council of Churches of Christ in the United States of America. Used by permission. All rights reserved worldwide.

Book design by Drew Stevens
Cover design by Erika Lundbom

Library of Congress Cataloging-in-Publication Data is on file at the Library of Congress, Washington, DC.

ISBN: 978-0-664-26929-6 (paperback)
ISBN: 978-1-646-98447-3 (ebook)

Most Westminster John Knox Press books are available at special quantity discounts when purchased in bulk by corporations, organizations, and special-interest groups. For more information, please e-mail SpecialSales@wjkbooks.com.

Contents

ix   Using This Resource

BIBLE AND THEOLOGY

3   **Brief: Small Books, Big Gospel**

A six-part series on the Bible's briefest books.

JONAH P. OVERTON

13   **H-E-Double-Hockey-Sticks**

A five-part series on the topic of hell with an emphasis on increasing knowledge and understanding while reducing fears.

BRIAN GERARD

21   **Our Greatest Story**

A four-part series exploring the Greatest Commandment as it pertains to belonging, identity, and our place in the larger story of God's kin-dom.

GAIL SONG BANTUM

29   **Reconsidering Jesus**

A four-part series reexamining well-known passages about Jesus and the lessons they offer.

JIA STARR BROWN

35 **Black Is, Black Ain't: A Celebration of Blackness in the Bible**

A four-part series celebrating the sacred beauty, brilliance, resilience, and diversity of Black identity.

BRANDON THOMAS CROWLEY

43 **A Deconstructionist's Journey**

A six-part series on deconstructing oppressive church beliefs while reconstructing a faith of liberation and hope.

TYLER HO-YIN SIT

SPIRITUAL FORMATION

55 **The ABC's of Spiritual Success**

A three-part series on the building blocks of a sustaining relationship with God.

NAPOLEON J. HARRIS V

61 **Rhythm of Life**

A five-part series on spiritual practices that lead to transformation.

JOSH SCOTT

71 **Rest**

A three-part series on practicing Sabbath.

CAROL CAVIN-DILLON

77 **The Power of Powerlessness**

A six-part series on how Jesus defines power as compassion, not coercion.

BENJAMIN R. CREMER

87 **Sensing Faith**

A five-part series on deepening our faith by engaging the five senses.

RODGER NISHIOKA

CHRISTIAN LIVING

97 All In

A four-part series on what it means to go all in with our hearts, hands, resources, and future as an act of whole-life stewardship.

JOSEPH YOO

105 You Be the Judge . . . or Not

A five-part series about judging other people, how to manage this impulse, and when and how we should (or should not) judge.

COLBY MARTIN

113 Screen Time: Troubleshooting Our Relationship with Technology

A four-part series on mindful and faithful use of devices, media, and AI.

MATT MIOFSKY

121 Ready for It

A four-part series on biblical resilience in the face of personal challenges and unsettling world headlines.

BETHANY PEERBOLTE

129 Imagine the Impossible

A six-part series on imagination and the future of our faith and the church.

ADRIENE THORNE

JUSTICE AND INCLUSION

141 Fight like Jesus

A six-part series on nonviolence as a way of life, exploring Martin Luther King Jr.'s six principles of nonviolent resistance.

MARK FELDMEIR

151 Take Up Your Mat

A four-part series focused on the healing justice ministry of Jesus in the Gospel of John.

AMOS DISASA

159 Faith That Frees

A four-part series celebrating Black history and the role of faith in the stride toward freedom for African Americans.

DIANE GIVENS MOFFETT

167 I Wish You Love

A four-part series for LGBTQ+ Pride month, weaving Scripture with the life and music of Dolly Parton.

SAM LUNDQUIST

SEASONAL

177 Holy Darkness, Holy Light

A five-part Advent and Epiphany series.

SHAWNA BOWMAN

187 In Plain Sight

A seven-part series for Advent, Christmas, and Epiphany using the ordinary stuff of life.

JILL J. DUFFIELD

197 Women in the Wilderness

A seven-part Lenten series on fugitivity, feminism, and the fierce grace of survival.

ROBERTO CHE ESPINOZA

209 What If?

A six-part Lenten series asking the church to embrace the possibility and hope of Jesus's challenging call on our lives.

JOY MARTINEZ-MARSHALL

219 Contributors

Using This Resource

A Preacher's Guide to Topical Sermon Series is designed to equip and inspire your sermon planning with twenty-four creative ideas for series that will educate and intrigue your congregation and help them grow as Christians. You may wish to use these outlines as they are or adapt them for your congregation's needs—or maybe a series included in this resource will spark a different idea of your own.

Contributors include twenty-four experienced preachers from seven denominational traditions offering sermon ideas on a wide variety of themes, from Sabbath to hell to our use of technology. Seasonal series will make for transformative Advent and Lent experiences, while other series are ideal for Black History and Pride months. Some series explore a single book of the Bible, and others draw lessons for discipleship from across the Bible's sections and genres.

Consider this a buffet of homiletical and creative inspiration. Take what appeals to you, try out something new, and plan a menu for years of compelling preaching with your congregation.

What's Included

Each of the twenty-four series plans includes:

- A series overview introducing the overall message of the series.
- A chart outlining the sermon titles and focus Scriptures for each week of the series, along with a very brief description of each sermon's theme.
- Tips and ideas for the series, with suggestions for worship elements, visuals, fellowship activities, and/or outreach efforts that enhance the congregation's engagement with the series topic.

- Sermon starters for each Sunday to summarize the week's message, prompt your research and writing process, and offer sermon illustrations to enhance your preaching.

Making the Most of a Series

Exploring a theme or book of the Bible across several weeks (as short as three weeks and as long as eight in this resource) gives congregants and visitors a memorable handle to latch on to from week to week. Knowing what is being preached on the following week keeps people engaged, coming back, and telling friends. Like a television show or miniseries, preaching in series can create a don't-want-to-miss-it desire to be there for each week of worship.

Maximize the impact of each series with the following tips:

Use consistent visuals. Even if you do not have a dedicated graphic designer in your church, you can create one image or typographic treatment for the series that can be used on your printed materials (bulletins, mailers, posters, etc.) and digital media (website, social media, or worship screen if you use one). Some of the "Tips and Ideas" sections of series plans include ideas for altar displays and other visual elements to enhance the worship space.

Go beyond the sermon. We all know that worship and spiritual growth do not hinge entirely on the sermon. Be intentional about choosing songs and other elements that support the theme. Plan special events at which congregants can discuss or put into practice the ideas being preached on in the series. Many "Tips and Ideas" sections have suggestions for such events.

Spread the word. Visitors may be more likely to give your church a try if they know an upcoming service will be addressing a topic or question they have wondered about. Promotion of the series can be done through social media, special mailings, and church newsletters. The week before a new series begins, introduce it in worship and through email, encouraging members to attend and suggesting they forward the email to family, friends, neighbors, and coworkers who may be interested in the topic.

Get your congregation excited about the opportunity to explore biblical stories and themes in depth across a number of Sundays, and watch their engagement grow.

Bible and Theology

Brief: Small Books, Big Gospel

A six-part series on the Bible's briefest books.

JONAH P. OVERTON

Series Overview   The shortest books in the Bible don't pull any punches. These letters and visions may be brief, but they're fierce—wrestling with justice, power, community, and the gospel's radical call. Some are warm and intimate. Others are weird, wild, or downright enraging. But all of them have something urgent to say. In this series, we're slowing down the quick reads. Each week, we read an entire book aloud—start to finish—then dig in together to ask: What was that? Why is it in here? And what is the Spirit trying to say to us now? These books challenge us to rethink how we read Scripture. They remind us that the Bible isn't afraid to contradict itself, take risks, or make us uncomfortable. And if we let them, these books might just change how we understand the gospel itself—calling us to deeper belonging, sharper discernment, and a holy, liberating resistance to the powers of the world.

	Sermon Title	Focus Scripture	Theme
Week 1	Emails from the Early Church	2 John; 3 John	The gospel spreads through love, honesty, and trusted relationships.
Week 2	Not a Slave, a Sibling	Philemon	True Christian kinship dismantles hierarchy and embraces chosen family.
Week 3	God Takes Sides	Obadiah	Justice demands truth—complicity must be named and reckoned with.

	Sermon Title	Focus Scripture	Theme
Week 4	A Warning for Wandering Stars	Jude	Weird letter, real warning: stay grounded, bold, and loving.
Week 5	When the Church Sells Out	Titus	Whenever the gospel gets too respectable, empire sneaks back in.
Week 6	Salvation Is Not Assimilation	Galatians 3	The gospel transcends culture—liberating, blending, and creating belonging without erasure.

Tips and Ideas for This Series Use email or postcard imagery to represent these short books. Choose script readers who can convey the drama of each text and hold people's attention. Engage artistic expressions of brevity—flash fiction, micro-poetry, or minimalist design. Encourage staff and leadership to consider all their internal communications regarding church life as fodder for the future church millennia from now.

Week 1: Emails from the Early Church
2 John; 3 John

Beloved, do not imitate what is evil, but imitate what is good. Whoever does good is from God; whoever does evil has not seen God. (3 John 1:11)

Welcome to Brief, the sermon series where we dive into the shortest books of the Bible—the ones so quick that, if you blink, you'll miss them. These little messages are often overlooked, but they're packed with heart, theology, and drama. The goal of this series is simple: to give us a taste of what it's like to read whole books of Scripture in one sitting. We're not cherry-picking verses here—we're letting the texts speak as a whole, the way they were written and the way they were first received.

This additional context doesn't mean *everything* will make sense. These are letters from another time, another place—like reading someone else's email thread without all the attachments. But when we let the words wash over us, we start to notice what matters. Themes emerge. And we get to hear the voice of our ancestors of the faith, trying to figure out how to follow Jesus in a world that made it really hard.

This week, we're starting with the shortest of the short: 2 John and 3 John. These read like quick emails from a tired church leader who's trying to hold things together. There's not a lot of theology packed in—just straight-up reminders about who we are and how we're supposed to live. Which, honestly, might be exactly what we need sometimes.

Second John is a love letter and a warning. It says, "Hey church—remember the basics? Love one another. Stick with Jesus. Don't get sucked into teachings that pretend Jesus didn't come in the flesh." This isn't some abstract doctrinal argument; it's about making sure we don't lose sight of the incarnate God, the One who shows up in bodies and stories and messy communities. That's still good advice.

Third John shifts gears. It's more like an accountability email—lifting up one person (Gaius) for being faithful while calling out another (Diotrephes) for being a power-hungry gatekeeper. The early church was dealing with the same kind of internal drama we face today—people trying to hoard power, exclude others, and shape the gospel around their own egos. And the elder says, "Don't imitate that. Stick with what's good."

This introductory sermon gives a taste of what Brief is all about: reading whole books, even the tiny ones, and discovering the complicated, deeply human lives and communities at the heart of them. These aren't abstract doctrines—they're real letters to real people who were trying to follow Jesus together. And the wisdom holds up: stay rooted in love, resist false power, and don't forget that the gospel is embodied. Even when it shows up in your inbox.

Week 2: Not a Slave, a Sibling
Philemon

Perhaps this is the reason he was separated from you for a while, so that you might have him back for the long term, no longer as a slave but more than a slave, a beloved brother—especially to me but how much more to you, both in the flesh and in the Lord. (Philemon 1:15–16)

This letter is short, but it's loaded. Paul is writing to Philemon, a man of status, about Onesimus, who used to be enslaved in Philemon's household and is now with Paul. Somehow, Onesimus has become dear to Paul—dear enough that Paul calls him his own heart. And now Paul is sending him back, but with a new understanding: Onesimus is not property. He's family.

Paul doesn't come out swinging against slavery as an institution here, which is frustrating to modern readers—and honestly, it should be. But what he *does* do is gently (and not-so-gently) dismantle the logic of slavery through relationship. He calls on Philemon not just to release Onesimus but to recognize him as a beloved brother in Christ.

Paul is drawing a theological circle big enough that both enslaver and enslaved are now siblings, and that's going to make things awkward for Philemon if he wants to keep playing master.

And Paul knows it. This letter is soaked in passive-aggressive grace. "I could command you," Paul says, "but I won't. I'll just appeal to your better nature. And also, remember, you owe me your life. No big deal."

Paul is using all his tools—emotional connection, spiritual authority, communal accountability—to push Philemon toward doing the right thing. It's a master class in pastoral pressure and using the resources you have to make powerful people feel uncomfortable about their sin—in public, no less. And it's based in Paul's deep conviction that, in Christ, everything changes. The old hierarchies don't hold. The gospel reshapes how we treat one another, especially across lines of power.

We don't get to hear how Philemon responds. Maybe he frees Onesimus and welcomes him home as a sibling. Maybe he doesn't. But the letter itself stands as a challenge to anyone who has benefited from systems of domination: Are you willing to be transformed by love? Are you willing to release your grip on status and control to embrace someone as family?

This isn't just a sweet story about Paul doing Onesimus a favor. It's a radical disruption, a call to repair what empire has broken. And it still speaks—loudly—to every system of oppression we've inherited and upheld. Who have we treated as less than? Who are we willing to see with new eyes, not as someone beneath us, but as our own heart? And how is the gospel advocating for our own freedom from oppression?

The gospel demands righteousness of us in our relationships. Are we willing to risk comfort, control, and even reputation to live out the truth that we are siblings in Christ?

Week 3: God Takes Sides
Obadiah

On the day that you stood aside,
  on the day that strangers carried off his wealth
and foreigners entered his gates
  and cast lots for Jerusalem,
  you, too, were one of them. (Obadiah 1:11)

Obadiah is the shortest book in the Hebrew Bible, but it is intense. This is one long, furious rant—poetic, prophetic, and deeply political. Obadiah is mad, and God is too.

The target? Edom. It is a neighboring nation, kin to Israel by blood (descended from Esau), whose people stood by—or maybe even participated—when Jerusalem was ransacked and its people were exiled. Obadiah is calling out Edom's betrayal, their smugness, their opportunism in the midst of Judah's suffering. This is the cry of someone who watched their people get crushed while their so-called siblings cheered or looted in the aftermath.

And here's the thing: God hears that cry. God is not neutral here. God is *not* shrugging and saying, "Well, that's just geopolitics." God is promising justice, promising reckoning, promising that the very empire Edom tried to cozy up to will eventually fall—and take Edom down with it.

This book reminds us that God takes sides. Not petty, tribal sides, but the side of the trampled, the displaced, the ones whose wounds were laughed at. And God remembers betrayal, especially betrayal that props up systems of violence and supremacy.

Now, if you're thinking, "Oof, this feels personal," it should. Because while Obadiah is a sharp rebuke to Edom, it's also a mirror to anyone who has stood by and benefited while others suffered. It asks us: When empire is stomping through the city, are we helping people escape—or are we just keeping our heads down, hoping to come out ahead?

The warning to Edom is sobering. But it's also hopeful, because it means the story isn't over. Empire doesn't get the last word. God does. Obadiah ends with a vision of restoration: that the devastated people of God will return, reclaim their land, and build something new. That's the part we sometimes miss in these fire-and-brimstone passages. The point isn't just punishment—it's the promise that justice is possible. That betrayal can be named. That solidarity matters: that the kingdom of God is rising, even while empire looks unbeatable

So maybe this book doesn't have a lot of verses—it's doing big theological work. It's calling us to pay attention to who we align ourselves with; to reckon with our participation in injustice; to remember that God isn't interested in neutrality and that God never forgets the ones who've been crushed. Most of all, it reminds us: Human empires may feel eternal, but God's justice is *coming*. And it starts with truth-telling.

Week 4: A Warning for Wandering Stars
Jude

These are blots on your love feasts, while they feast with you without fear, feeding themselves. They are waterless clouds carried along by the winds; autumn trees without fruit, twice dead, uprooted; wild waves of the sea, casting up the foam of their own shame; wandering stars, for whom the deepest darkness has been reserved forever. (Jude 1:12–13)

Jude is weird. There's no way around it. It's got angels arguing with the devil, fallen beings chained in darkness, and references to ancient texts that didn't even make it into our Bibles. If 2 and 3 John were short and sweet emails, Jude is more like a panicked group text from someone who's *really* mad and starting to spiral out of control.

But beneath the chaos, there's something real here—something ancient and urgent. Jude is worried. He's watching the early church get pulled apart by charismatic teachers who are using grace as an excuse to do harm. These folks aren't just misguided—they're predatory. And Jude is not having it.

This letter is a warning, and not a polite one. It's more like someone slamming the brakes and yelling, "Wake up!" It's a reminder that the early church was not some perfect utopia. From the very beginning, there were power struggles. There were liars and manipulators. But there were also people willing to stand up and say that this is not what Jesus meant.

Jude is one of those people. He pulls from all kinds of ancient sources—1 Enoch, the Testament of Moses, apocalyptic stories that his readers would've known well—to paint this intense picture: God sees what's going on. And God is not OK with it. The people twisting the gospel for their own gain and leading others into exploitation and destruction will face judgment.

Now, depending on your baggage with judgment language, that might feel either deeply satisfying or deeply uncomfortable. But for Jude, judgment isn't about wrath for wrath's sake. It's about protection. This is a shepherd throwing rocks at the wolves, not the sheep.

What's most striking, though, is how Jude ends. After all the fire, all the rebukes, all the weird cosmic drama, he tells the faithful to stay rooted. Build yourselves up. Pray. Stay in love with God. Be merciful. Save others when you can—but don't get dragged under by the chaos. There's wisdom in that balance. Jude knows that confronting corruption is exhausting and that sometimes the best thing we can do is stay grounded, stay loving, and help one another hold on to what's good.

So, yes, Jude is weird. But weird doesn't mean irrelevant. It means human. It means that this ancient letter understands what it feels like to watch your community fray under the pressure of bad leadership, bad theology, or plain old bad behavior—and still choose to stay, to speak up, to hope, and to love.

Maybe that's Jude's real invitation: not just to call out what's wrong, but to fiercely protect what's worth saving—even if you have to use big, dark, wild imagery to get their attention.

Week 5: When the Church Sells Out
Titus

Urge slaves to be submissive to their masters in everything, to be pleasing, not talking back, not stealing, but showing complete and perfect fidelity, so that in everything they may be an ornament to the teaching of God our Savior. (Titus 2:9–10)

OK, let's just say it: Titus is a mess. Not just because it's boring (which, honestly, it kind of is) but because it feels as if it's straight-up preaching the opposite of Jesus's good news. It says enslaved people should be extra obedient so that the church looks good. It says women should stay home, stay quiet, and stay out of sight so that the church looks good. It says church leaders should behave respectably so that, you guessed it, the church *looks* good.

But if we scratch the surface, we start to see what's really going on here: respectability politics. A once-radical movement is trying to go mainstream, and in the process, it's selling out the heart of the gospel.

This letter is attributed to Paul, but most scholars agree Paul didn't write it. It was probably written a few decades later, by someone in Paul's tradition, trying to preserve the Jesus movement by making it look more Roman, more respectable, more friendly to the empire. You know, the same empire that executed Jesus.

This shift isn't subtle. In earlier letters (like Philemon), Paul is pushing toward equality and radical love. By the time we get to Titus, the writer isn't challenging hierarchy; they're reinforcing it. Slaves, obey. Women, submit. Leaders, behave yourselves so that nobody gets mad. And here's where it gets extra slippery: They're still calling it gospel.

That's what makes this letter dangerous. It claims divine authority. It signs Paul's name. But it uses that authority to water down the gospel, to make it more palatable, more acceptable, more aligned with empire. It puts on sheep's clothing, but its teeth are sharp.

So what do we do with a text like this? First, we get honest. We name the harm it's done, especially in modern churches where texts like Titus have been used to justify patriarchy, slavery, and silencing dissent. Second, we read it in context. We remember that Scripture was not magically downloaded from the mind of God—it is a book written by people living in a specific time, trying to solve specific problems, with very human fears.

And third, we treat it like a cautionary tale. Because this right here is how a movement gets co-opted. First it's "tone it down a little," then "don't rock the boat," then "submit to empire so that no one gets the wrong idea."

But Jesus didn't come to make us respectable. Jesus came to make us free.

The good news is: We still have the real gospel. We still have Jesus. We still have Paul, the radical mystic, if we're willing to separate his voice from the voices that tried to tame him. So read Titus—not to obey it, but to learn from it. To see the warning signs. To ask: Where are we choosing palatability over truth? Where are *we* sacrificing liberation to protect our own reputation?

And then choose the gospel instead.

Week 6: Salvation Is Not Assimilation
Galatians 3

There is no longer Jew or Greek; there is no longer slave or free; there is no longer male and female, for all of you are one in Christ Jesus. (Galatians 3:28)

NOTE: This is the only sermon in the series where we won't read the whole book aloud. Instead, read all of Galatians 3—and encourage everyone to read aloud the full letter (which takes about twenty minutes) with someone this week. The principle still holds: Reading larger chunks of Scripture, especially in community, opens us up to deeper meaning and surprising clarity—even in familiar texts.

Galatians is Paul turned all the way up. He's fiery, defensive, urgent—and completely unwilling to let the gospel be hijacked. Which is exactly what's happening in Galatia. Paul preached radical freedom, but now others are saying: "You can follow Jesus . . . as long as you also follow all the Jewish laws." And Paul is not having it.

The fight is about circumcision on the surface, but beneath that it's about belonging. Do you have to become Jewish to follow Jesus? Do you have to adopt someone else's culture to be accepted? Paul's answer is a resounding no.

The gospel, he says, is bigger than any one culture. Christianity was already syncretic—Jewish faith, Greek language, Roman infrastructure. The danger isn't cultural blending; it's supremacy. The danger is calling your culture the gospel and requiring everyone else to conform. That's what happened in colonial missions—Christianity enforced as a White, Western identity. But Paul's message in Galatians rejects that. The Spirit shows up in every culture. Jesus doesn't erase our distinctiveness. He honors it.

According to Paul, salvation doesn't come through rule following, purity codes, or cultural conformity—it comes through trust in the love of God, a trust that transforms and bears fruit: love, joy, peace, patience, kindness, generosity, faithfulness, gentleness, and self-control.

So if you've been told you don't belong until you conform, Paul has something to say. And if you've ever felt as if your ancestors or rituals or ways of knowing God didn't "count," Galatians is good news for you. You belong just as you are. This is the gospel. It goes by many names, in many tongues, across many cultures. And in every one, it sets people free.

As we close this series, may we carry forward the habit of reading whole books, seeing the big picture, and digging for deep truth—even in small texts. May we keep finding freedom in unlikely corners. And may we live as if the gospel is as wide and wild as God's love.

H-E-Double-Hockey-Sticks

A five-part series on the topic of hell with an emphasis on increasing knowledge and understanding while reducing fears.

BRIAN GERARD

Series Overview   There are a lot of misconceptions and fears surrounding hell, many of which exist because of the inaccurate and sometimes theologically dangerous ways people talk about the subject. That needs to change.

The purpose of this series is not to prove hell does or does not exist. Instead, it is to help relieve fears about this topic by helping people understand what the biblical concept of hell is, what it isn't, and why no one needs to lose any sleep worrying about it. Because, in the end, we worship a loving God whose grace knows no bounds.

	Sermon Title	Focus Scripture	Theme
Week 1	Hell 101	Matthew 8:11–12; 25:41	With study, we can understand what hell is and isn't.
Week 2	What in the Hell?	Psalm 9:17; 55:15; 89:48; Job 14:13	That word may not mean what you think it means.
Week 3	Why in the Hell?	Matthew 25:31–46	Scripture offers at least three reasons for why hell exists.
Week 4	Who in the Hell?	Matthew 7:1–2	Your list of who's in hell may not mirror God's.
Week 5	Hell No!	1 John 4:16b–18	God's love drives out all fear, including that of hell.

Tips and Ideas for This Series

There is more to this topic than can be covered in any sermon series, so consider providing opportunities for deeper study and conversation. Given the fear and religious trauma that exists around hell, be sensitive to your audience and the experiences they may have had around this topic. Offer reassurances and, when appropriate, inject some humor. The suggested sermon titles are meant to provoke but also to disarm, an approach that has proven effective in multiple settings.

Week 1: Hell 101
Matthew 8:11–12; 25:41

Then he will say to those at his left hand, "You who are accursed, depart from me into the eternal fire prepared for the devil and his angels." (Matthew 25:41)

Hell does not exist in Scripture. Well, at least it doesn't exist as a clear, singular concept conveyed by a Hebrew or Greek word. Derived from the Old English word *hel/helle*, the word *hell* wasn't even around at the time the Bible was written. Instead, there are four words that, while often translated as *hell*, carry different meanings. Those words and their meaning will be covered in the second sermon of this series.

Even if these four words were more accurately translated, there would still be a lot of misunderstanding and confusion about this topic. After all, the Bible is not very clear when it comes to describing the place of eternal torment, which many people call hell.

For example, some passages use the image of fire to describe hell. In Matthew, Jesus says, "Then [God] will say to those at [God's] left hand, 'You who are accursed, depart from me into the eternal fire prepared for the devil and his angels'" (Matt. 25:41).

In another part of that same Gospel, Jesus describes hell in this way: "I tell you, many will come from east and west and will take their places at the banquet with Abraham and Isaac and Jacob in the kingdom of heaven, while the heirs of the kingdom will be thrown into the outer darkness, where there will be weeping and gnashing of teeth" (8:11–12).

How can hell be a place of both eternal fire and darkness? And, if hell is a literal place, then which of these descriptions is meant to be metaphorical? Speaking of hell as a literal place, is it? Some people believe that hell is very real and that deserving people go there to experience punishment and torture. Others believe that hell is not a literal place and that ultimately God will draw all humankind into God's self in heaven.

What do you believe about hell? Do you believe it exists, and, if so, what is it, where is it, why does it exist, and who is going to be there? Does your understanding of hell come from Scripture or from other sources like Dante's *Inferno* or the Left Behind series? Perhaps you learned about hell from a religious tract or from a movie you were made to watch at a church lock-in. Maybe it's a combination of things that has left you so confused you can't remember what came from where.

The good news is that with a little bit of study, we can come to a more informed understanding of what hell is and what it is not. Doing that will not only alleviate our fears around this topic but also remind us of the good news—that in the end, God's love and grace are enough. Of that, you can be certain.

Week 2: What in the Hell?
Psalm 9:17; 55:15; 89:48; Job 14:13

Let death come upon them;
  let them go down alive to Sheol,
  for evil is in their homes and in their hearts. (Psalm 55:15)

While it is commonly believed that hell is some kind of fiery underworld, what Scripture says is more complicated than that. If the devil really is in the details, then we need to pay attention to them when it comes to this topic.

When the word *hell* is found in Scripture, it is being used in the place of four other words, each with specific meanings. Unfortunately, those words are often conflated, and that has created a lot of confusion. One way to ease our fears about hell is to understand what these words are and what they mean.

The word *Sheol* is found in the Hebrew Scriptures. In its original form, it means a pit, grave, or realm of the dead. It is important to note that Sheol is a place where both righteous and unrighteous people can be found. While some English Bibles leave the word untranslated, some use one of the definitions above, and some use the word *hell*. A good example of how Sheol is translated in different ways can be found in the King James Bible. In Psalm 9:17 and 55:15, Sheol is translated as *hell*. In Psalm 89:48 and Job 14:13, it is translated as *grave*.

Looking at these passages, you will notice a pattern. When talking about the wicked, the translators used the word *hell*. When talking about the righteous, they used *grave*. While that is not a universal pattern of translation in the King James version, it is more than just a coincidence. It has also shaped the way people understand hell.

Another word often translated as hell is *Hades*. This Greek word is found in the New Testament and is close enough in meaning and use to Sheol that we won't dive into it any deeper. We'll also skip digging into the Greek word *Tartarus*, which is used only once (2 Pet. 2:4, WEB) and appears to be a temporary confinement for fallen angels until their final judgment.

The most common Greek word translated as "hell" is *Gehenna*. While its use can point toward a place of eternal torment, it is important to note that Gehenna was a very real place. The word comes from the Hebrew *ge-hinnom*, which means the canyon or valley of Hinnom. That valley was located outside the southwest wall of Jerusalem. Terrible things, including the burning of children in sacrifice, took place there. When this word was used, people knew that historical context. Many modern readers do not know that history.

As accurate as some English translations of the Bible may be, they often miss the mark. This is certainly the case when it comes to the words explored above. Unfortunately, the conflation of these words into a singular understanding of hell has caused confusion and unnecessary fear around this topic. Knowing what in the hell is actually going on will help ease those fears.

Week 3: Why in the Hell?
Matthew 25:31–46

"Then he will answer them, 'Truly I tell you, just as you did not do it to one of the least of these, you did not do it to me.' And these will go away into eternal punishment but the righteous into eternal life." (Matthew 25:45–46)

If hell exists, what is its purpose and why would a loving God create such a place?

This is one of the more complicated topics in this series, and it has spawned a lot of debate throughout history. Instead of trying to cover every possible answer to the question above, we are going to focus on three of the most common beliefs about why hell exists.

The first answer is likely the most familiar. Hell exists for the purpose of punishing the deserving through eternal conscious suffering. One of the Scriptures used to defend this understanding of hell is Matthew 25:31–46. This passage, sometimes called the judgment of nations, ends with these words, "And these will go away into eternal punishment but the righteous into eternal life" (Matt. 25:46).

While the idea of hell as a place of eternal suffering is a commonly held belief, some argue this understanding cannot be correct because it is not just. After all, submitting someone to eternal suffering for something they did in a comparably short earthly life falls outside the standards of biblical justice (e.g., an eye for an eye). This justice-oriented argument points to another possible reason for hell's existence: the annihilation of the unworthy.

Annihilationism is based on the idea that the souls of those who deserve hell are not kept there for all eternity but, after a period of suffering, are destroyed. Passages like the following are used to support this idea: 2 Thessalonians 1:9, Philippians 3:18–19, and Matthew 10:28.

Our third reason for why hell exists is often referred to as ultimate reconciliation. This purpose for hell is based on the idea that it provides a cleansing fire that causes the impurities of the unrighteous to be refined in ways similar to that of precious metals. After being purified in this way, the soul can be reconciled with God. Scriptures used to support this include Isaiah 48:10 and Zechariah 13:9.

It's also worth noting that in the ancient world, brimstone (a sulfur-like substance) was burned as part of the process to purify something. So images of fire and brimstone aren't just about punishment but about purification.

While the three answers above assume the reality of hell, this message is not meant to support that assumption. As a reminder, the purpose of this series is not to prove hell does or does not exist but to provide knowledge of the topic in ways that increase understanding and decrease fear. The final message of this series will explore some of the arguments against the existence of hell. In the meantime, it may be helpful to let people know that is coming. It may also be comforting to wrap up this sermon with a reminder of the reassurances we have through the love of God and the grace of Christ.

Week 4: Who in the Hell?
Matthew 7:1–2

"Do not judge, so that you may not be judged. For the judgment you give will be the judgment you get, and the measure you give will be the measure you get." (Matthew 7:1–2)

If hell exists, then who's there? My guess is that a lot of people have some thoughts on this, and a few folks may even have a list. But what does Scripture say?

According to some, Scripture is clear on this matter. Non-Christians are among the first who will be found in hell, even those who are good people or have never heard of Jesus. John 3:18 and 14:6 are sometimes used to support this belief.

But does that mean that all Christians will avoid eternal punishment? "Once saved, always saved," as the saying goes? While some people believe this, there is little support for it in Scripture. In fact, Jesus even says that not everyone who calls him Lord will enter heaven (Matt. 7:21–23).

Scripture also lists some common behaviors that could land someone in hell, no matter the faith they proclaim. For example, calling someone a fool (5:22), looking at someone with lust (5:27–30), and lying (Rev. 21:8) will land you in hell. So will failing to give drink to the thirsty, food to the hungry, or clothing to the naked. Refusing to welcome the foreigner or stranger, failing to take care of the sick, and not visiting those in prison will also come with an eternal cost (Matt. 25:41–46).

If we're going to take Scripture literally about what causes people to go to hell, we're all in trouble. Of course, our faith teaches us that no one is perfect and that grace will make up for our shortcomings. The problem is that, all too often, people proclaim a faith based on grace for me and judgment for them. Either way, we'd all do well to remember Jesus's commandment not to judge, because by the measure we judge others, we will receive the same judgment from God in return (7:1–2).

While there are Scriptures that talk about what can land a person in hell, there are many that provide a more reassuring message. For example, in John, Jesus says that as the Good Shepherd, he lays down in life even for sheep who "do not belong to this fold" (John 10:14–16). Jesus also proclaims that when he is lifted up from the earth, he will draw all people to himself (John 12:31–32). Not some people. All people. In Colossians, we are told that through Jesus, God reconciled all things to God's self (Col. 1:19-20). Again, not some things, but all things.

Passages like these are often used to argue that salvation can be given to everyone through the reconciling grace of God in Jesus Christ, even those who don't believe in him. Taking that belief one step further is the concept of universal salvation, which holds that there is no hell, except the ones we sometimes create or experience here on earth, and that everyone—without exception—will end up in heaven.

All of this is ultimately up to God. The good news is that we worship a God of perfect love, something we will celebrate in the next sermon.

Week 5: Hell No!
1 John 4:16b–18

There is no fear in love, but perfect love casts out fear; for fear has to do with punishment, and whoever fears has not reached perfection in love. (1 John 4:18)

While there are some Scriptures that people use to stoke fear about hell and about God, the overwhelming biblical witness counters that practice. A prime example of this is found in 1 John 4:16b, where we find these words: "God is love, and those who abide in love, abide in God, and God abides in them."

Can we sit with that for a moment? God is not fear. God is not anger. God is certainly not hate. God is love, and Jesus was the embodiment of that love. The Bible is clear on this. And yet, somehow, so many people lose sight of that.

The passage continues by addressing the idea of judgment: "Love has been perfected among us in this: that we may have boldness on the day of judgment" (v. 17). When it comes to the day of judgment, whatever we understand that day to look like, we do not need to worry. We can walk into it with boldness because God's love is not about condemnation; it is about grace and reconciliation.

The last sentence in this passage reassures us of that: "There is no fear in love, but perfect love casts out fear; for fear has to do with punishment, and whoever fears has not reached perfection in love (v. 18).

God's perfect love casts out fear, even the fear of judgment. A fear-based religion forgets the promise that, in Christ, God was reconciling the world to God's self, "not counting their trespasses against them, and entrusting the message of reconciliation to us" (2 Cor. 5:19b).

A fear-based religion denies the hope found in these words:

> Who will separate us from the love of Christ? Will affliction or distress or persecution or famine or nakedness or peril or sword? . . . No, in all these things we are more than victorious through him who loved us. For I am convinced that neither death, nor life, nor angels, nor rulers, nor things present, nor things to come, nor powers, nor height, nor depth, nor anything else in all creation will be able to separate us from the love of God in Christ Jesus our Lord. (Rom. 8:35–39)

These, and other passages like them, reassure us that God's love is so great and that there is nothing that can separate us from God. And if nothing can separate us from God, then surely God is not going to condemn us to a place of eternal isolation and suffering. God's desire is to reconcile with us, not forsake us.

It is heartbreaking when people distort the gospel in ways that cause others to fear God, that cause people to be afraid of what God is going to do to them or to those they love when they die. Where's the hope in that? Where's the grace in that? What's the goal of that?

Unfortunately, for some, the goal is to scare the hell out of people. To that, I offer an emphatic, "Hell no!"

Our Greatest Story

A four-part series exploring the Greatest Commandment as it pertains to belonging, identity, and our place in the larger story of God's kin-dom.

GAIL SONG BANTUM

Series Overview

This series is a call to expand our notions of belonging, identity, and story, undergirded by the two greatest commandments: to love God, and to love your neighbor as you love yourself. The series begins with the idea of our lives as stories and, in turn, explores our relationships with God, the author of our story; our self as created in God's image; and others whom God created and calls us to love. Matthew 22:36–40 should be read each week in addition to the week's unique Scripture passage to call attention to the ways love between God, others, and ourselves flows in each story.

In the diversity of our stories, both individual and collective, there may be pain and ill-formed memories in our origin stories and when it comes to our faith in God. The preacher's vulnerability in telling their own story is a way of demonstrating that we are all on this journey together to find that nothing is ever wasted in the economy of God.

	Sermon Title	Focus Scripture	Theme
Week 1	The Story I'll Tell	Matthew 22:36–40 (for the whole series); 2 Kings 4:8–21, 32–37; 8:1-6	Life has many full-circle moments.
Week 2	Between Never and Now	Matthew 22:36–40; Acts 10:1–20	Nothing is impossible in the economy of God.
Week 3	Who Made You?	Matthew 22:36–40; Exodus 3:9–12; 4:10–12	Shifting our perspective on self as image bearers of God.
Week 4	Love Is a Decision	Matthew 22:36–40; Luke 10:25–37	Love is not about feeling but *doing*.

Tips and Ideas for This Series

Invite your community to offer pictures of themselves or meaningful images that signify belovedness and belonging that can then be displayed throughout the series.

Have the diversity of voices and bodies within your community share in various elements of worship that they may not otherwise have opportunities to participate in—for example, serving Communion or reading Scripture. Include opportunities for people to give testimony, sharing how they've discovered or practiced loving God, self, and others in this season.

Consider offering a class or panel discussion around a challenging social issue in your community to more deeply explore what it means to put love for others into action. Invite a trauma-informed therapist to facilitate a conversation or class around story, self-awareness, and healing to nurture the image of God in ourselves.

Week 1: The Story I'll Tell
Matthew 22:36–40; 2 Kings 4:8–21, 32–37; 8:1–6

Now the king was talking with Gehazi the servant of the man of God, saying, "Tell me all the great things that Elisha has done." While he was telling the king how Elisha had restored a dead person to life, the woman whose son he had restored to life appealed to the king for her house and her land. (2 Kings 8:4–5a)

This is the foundational sermon for the whole series—the why. Living out what Jesus named as the Greatest Commandments in Matthew 22 can feel challenging and abstract until we put it in the context of our own life story. Our story is the sum of our experiences, ideas, feelings, and actions. When tapping into our unique story and witnessing God's presence within it, we are reminded that while we may not know the whole story, we know God is still writing our story; our story is still being told.

Life, no matter what our social location, has a way of reminding us that we all share in the common human experiences of pain, loss, disappointments, and doubt. Especially in challenging social and political times, every one of our stories, individual and collective, informs our identity and our desire for belonging and connection. Our stories lead us to ask where God is and to perhaps see God at work.

This is why the story of the Shunammite woman in 2 Kings is compelling here. Her faithful tending to Elisha, her longing for a child being realized, the devastation in the death of her son, and his resurrection to life—all her dramatic and traumatic experiences—had an impact that she never imagined and that she would not see until years later. Little did she know how her story would transpire while in the midst of her greatest need. Second Kings 8:5 says that while Gehazi was telling the king how Elisha had restored a dead person to life, the very woman whose son he had restored to life showed up and made an appeal to the king for her house and her land. Her *need* collided with God's *provision*, and her *past* collided with her *future* at just the right moment. What a full-circle moment! The fullness of the woman's story in chapter 4 is waiting for her in chapter 8. Would the restoration of her home and land have happened if her son had not died and been restored to life? Why would Gehazi tell the king about a random woman who had a baby? What would be unique about that? It was the fact that her child died and was revived that made her story worth telling.

What are the stories we tell of God, of ourselves, of others? Are we telling just the story of brief snapshots of life—the doubt, the pain, the loss? Or are we looking at the full-circle moments, the chapter 8 of our life? Are we seeing a period where God has put a comma, or a final chapter where God has written a cliffhanger? The Shunammite woman's story bears witness to the way that life in God's economy is never linear but full circle. Perhaps not always (or ever) in the timing or manner that we believe is best, the redemptive work of God is always moving and present with us, holding us in a great web of love.

Week 2: Between Never and Now
Matthew 22:36–40; Acts 10:1–20

Then he heard a voice saying, "Get up, Peter; kill and eat." But Peter said, "By no means, Lord, for I have never eaten anything that is profane or unclean." . . . While Peter was still thinking about the vision, the Spirit said to him, "Look, three men are searching for you. Now get up, go down, and go with them without hesitation, for I have sent them." (Acts 10:13–14, 19–20)

Narrowing the series theme here to our relationship with God, this sermon is an invitation for the preacher to be vulnerable in sharing a story of God's transformational work in the midst of their own moments of doubt and uncertainty. Where have you witnessed God's full-circle and redemptive moment in your own story? We live in a time when people in our pews are deconstructing their faith and contemplating leaving faith or the church altogether. People are questioning how God can still be good when God's people seem to be everything but. The preacher's vulnerability here, especially if describing a way they (like Peter) have reconsidered past beliefs, is a powerful way to welcome others to participate in reflecting on their own story with God.

In Acts 10, Peter is sitting on the roof of the tanner's house when he sees a vision of a blanket filled with "unclean" animals and hears a voice saying "kill and eat." He says, "I would *never* . . ." because it went against everything he knew as a Jew (see Lev. 11). Everything he saw on the blanket went against the specific dietary restrictions God gave the people of Israel so that they would be set apart. But for Peter, this was about more than changing his diet; it was about the formation of his faith and his frame of reference about his identity. God was pushing him to rethink his "never" and listen to God now.

I know there are many things that I have said "never" to God about: "God, I *never* want to be a pastor," or maybe, "I would *never* change my belief about that." All these nevers come from aspects of my larger story and formation. But as life unfolds and progresses, my now tells a different story, a transformed story. Have you, like me, ever found yourself wondering how it all changed? What happens when a *never* in your story becomes different in the *now*?

I am reminded of something Renita Weems wrote regarding the space in between never and now. She says,

> That is faith, I suppose, learning how to live in the meantime, between the last time we heard from God and the next time we hear from God. And if during that time we have an insistent sense inside that we are being asked to forgive someone we never meant to forgive, to trust a stranger, to open our heart to someone or something we normally shut ourselves off from, to give up our right to punish those who have wounded us, then *that* is quite likely the beginning of our long-awaited encounter with God. When God does appear, if ever God does again, it will be to leave us not with intimate knowledge about God but with a painful, exquisite insight into what it means to be human before a loving God.[1]

It is rarely comfortable when God transforms our *never* with new insight for *now*, but what a gift it is to live in loving relationship with God, listening, learning, and growing in our potential for love.

---

1. Renita Ann Weems, *Listening for God: A Minister's Journey through Silence and Doubt* (Touchstone, 1999), 174.

Week 3: Who Made You?
Matthew 22:36–40; Exodus 3:9–12; 4:10–12

"The cry of the Israelites has now come to me; I have also seen how the Egyptians oppress them. Now go, I am sending you to Pharaoh to bring my people, the Israelites, out of Egypt." (Exodus 3:9–10)

The pressures of life and the messaging we receive all around us can dictate what we believe about ourselves and affect our actions in turn. How can you write a good story when you don't know or like your main character? This sermon offers a critical reminder that we will be hard pressed to embody the second greatest commandment to love others rightly, that is, "as ourselves," when the perception of our own selves as God's image bearers (Gen. 1:26) becomes maladjusted. There is a reason why the command to love our neighbor is directly placed alongside our love for self.

There are at least three different images reflecting back at us at any given time: (1) how others see us, (2) how we see ourselves, and (3) how God sees us. How our story goes often depends on which reflection we believe.

Throughout Scripture, we see people doubting themselves when God has called them to do great things. Abraham and Sarah are one example, when God promised to make of them a great nation and yet they had to wait many more years to have even their first child (see Gen. 15:1–6). Similarly, Mary the mother of Jesus questioned God's intentions for her, saying "How can this be, since I am a virgin?" (Luke 1:34). The Israelites who return from having scoped out their enemies not only felt like grasshoppers next to the giant Canaanites but also insisted that the Canaanites saw them as but insects as well! (Num. 13:31–33). Perhaps the most relatable example is Moses's protests at the burning bush in Exodus 3 and 4, when he heard God calling him to challenge Pharaoh and lead the Israelites out of Egypt. Moses wondered why Pharaoh would listen to him and pointed out his poor speaking skills before God reminded him that it was God who created his mouth with the power of speech.

Moses's very real fear and insecurity feel like plot points we see in our own stories. His self-doubt is honest and real, and chances are most of us can relate to it. This is an opportunity for the storyteller in you. What could it look like to place yourself as preacher in the moment? Imagine putting forward the words of YHWH in response to Moses's questioning: "Who made man's mouth?" (as many translations phrase Exod. 4:11; see, for example, the World English Bible). Oop! It is a promise within a call—a promise that God does not ask us to do things God hasn't already equipped us for! This sermon is an opportunity to offer hope and encouragement in a time when the noise of the world and its expectations of us can cloud the truth of who we are and were created to be. This is an opportunity to remind us all that the God who created us is always within us.

In *The Color Purple*, a novel by Alice Walker, there is a character named Shug who says to Celie: "Celie, tell the truth, have you ever found God in church? I never did. I just found a bunch of folks hoping for him to show. Any God I ever felt in church I brought in with me. And I think all the other folks did too. They come to church to share God, not find God."[2] Indeed, everywhere you go, wherever your body shows up, you are sharing God. Because God is *in* you. You are an icon, an image of the living God.

Week 4: Love Is a Decision
Matthew 22:36–40; Luke 10:25–37

"Which of these three, do you think, was a neighbor to the man who fell into the hands of the robbers?" He said, "The one who showed him mercy." Jesus said to him, "Go and do likewise." (Luke 10:36–37)

When Jesus said, "Love your neighbor as yourself," we already know that this term *neighbor* represents more than those people who live in your neighborhood—it means everyone in the orbit or ripple effect of your life. And because Jesus said the second command is like the first, we have to take this seriously—that to love your neighbor is a priority for Jesus.

The more I look at my own heart and the more I look out at the world, the harder Jesus's command becomes. The more our communal story is wrought by injustice and division, desperate for acts of justice and liberation, the more profound this command to love your neighbor seems, the more revolutionary it feels, the more essential it becomes.

The one thing to highlight in this command, that is actually a requirement for loving your neighbor, is the discipline of doing. In the words of Grace Lee Boggs, a Chinese American civil rights activist who supported the Black Power movement in Detroit, Michigan: "Love isn't about what we did yesterday; it's about what we do today and tomorrow and the day after."[3]

---

2. Alice Walker, *The Color Purple* (Harcourt, 1982), 193.
3. Grace Lee Boggs, *The Next American Revolution: Sustainable Activism for the Twenty-First Century*, updated and expanded ed. (University of California Press, 2012), 97.

We often confuse the word *like* with *love*. *Like* involves an emotional attachment to something, but *love* requires action. In our text today—the Great Commandment of Jesus—the Greek word for the word *love* there is *agape*. Its verb form is *agapeo*, and it has to do with a decision. Like starts with an emotion because it is how we feel about something, but agape love may or may not include an emotion. That is why Jesus can command us to love our enemies. Jesus is not telling us to feel good about somebody who hates you. Jesus called it a commandment, and we cannot command our emotions, but we can command a decision. Love is not just what we say or what we think, it is what we do. Jesus is just naming a decision that will need to be made. This love is a decision.

Most parishioners will be familiar with the story of the Good Samaritan, Jesus's answer to someone uneasy with Jesus's command to "love your neighbor as yourself." To help people imagine how this famous story can be applied in our own stories, consider these three questions around the decision to practically engage in actions as a response: (1) Do we even recognize that there is a need? If so, what is it? Two people in the story did nothing and crossed the street. (2) Knowing that we all have different stories and experiences, when we recognize a need around us, are there any obstacles, hinderances, or barriers that keep us from doing justice? (3) Understanding that love can often be costly, what will it cost me? What will I need to sacrifice? What might I lose as a result? The Samaritan used his own medical supplies, his own transportation, and even paid for the man's hotel.

The word *sacrifice* may sound daunting, but to quote Boggs again, "We never know how our small activities will affect others through the invisible fabric of our connectedness. In this exquisitely connected world, it's never a question of 'critical mass.' It's always about critical connections."[4] The connection between ourselves and our neighbors, as the Greatest Commandment reminds us, is an extension of the connection between God and ourselves, a product of finding our own wholeness in the image of God.

---

4. James and Grace Lee Boggs, *Revolution and Evolution in the Twentieth Century* (New York University Press, 1974), 44.

Reconsidering Jesus

A four-part series reexamining well-known passages about Jesus and the lessons they offer.

JIA STARR BROWN

Series Overview This four-week series will reexamine some well-known passages about Jesus and his ministry in order to see our Savior from a new angle. Exploring four different roles Jesus embodied in his teachings and ministry, this series provides an opportunity to reconsider what—and how—many of us have been taught about walking in Jesus's footsteps. From confrontational messiah to self-sacrificial friend, Jesus defies expectation and always offers us more to learn. While the final week of the series focuses on a traditional Easter text, the trials of our death-dealing world cry out for a study of the resurrected Jesus that is not bound to a calendar date or season.

	Sermon Title	Focus Scripture	Theme
Week 1	Jesus: Son of God	John 10:22–31	Jesus was not "meek and mild," especially when discussing his identity and relationship to the Father.
Week 2	Jesus: Teacher	Matthew 6:5–13	Rabbi Jesus provides a template—not a script—for prayer.
Week 3	Jesus: Friend	John 15:12–17	Jesus our friend raises the bar for our standard of agape love.
Week 4	Jesus: Risen	John 20:1–18	Resurrection takes place in the dark of night, not in the brightness of day.

Tips and Ideas for This Series

Images that contrast the Western, whitewashed versions of Jesus and and his ministry with more accurate or unique depictions would be helpful in symbolizing the significant shift in interpretation and retelling.

Urging Sunday school and study groups to pair the weekly texts with articles about current events in your local community or in our nation would provide opportunities for discussion surrounding justice-centered application and ministry.

Week 1: Jesus: Son of God
John 10:22–31

So the Jews gathered around him and said to him, "How long will you keep us in suspense? If you are the Messiah, tell us plainly." (John 10:24)

Language deeply impacts our interpretation of Scripture—not only words but punctuation and pronouns as well. Every faithful translation, developed to make the gospel tangible and relatable to the people of the age, incorporates the cultural lens of its authors. In this particular passage, we find Jesus at the temple, walking in the beautiful and polished portico of Solomon—a partially enclosed walkway with a roof attached to the outside of a building with spaced columns. When reading that the Jews gathered around him to inquire about his identity as Messiah, the image that springs forth is often a gentle one of curiosity and confirmation as community members come to gain clarity.

The Greek translation uses the word *ekyklōsan,* meaning "encircled" or "surrounded," to highlight the tone of the Jews coming to Jesus in the portico. Found in other parts of the Bible, this word was also used in descriptions of armies advancing, with strategy and tones of hostility. (See, for example, Luke 21:20.) With this lens, the tone of the conversation certainly shifts from peaceful discussion to intimidation and interrogation. This is reinforced by John 10:31, where we read that once the tense exchange was concluded, the Jews picked up their stones *again* to stone him. With the portico a part of the extraordinary rebuilt temple, it was unlikely that stones large enough for killing and punishment would have been found on the grounds; they must have brought them, which denotes intent of violence and harm.

In this light, an angry, torch-carrying mob seems to be a more fitting image for this passage, rather than the meek and mild illustrations that we often refer to. Drawing on recent history, cross burnings on the front lawns of African American homes carry a similar tone. Charged. Angry. Deadly.

Jesus's use of language in verse 28 regarding his identity and connection to his followers (his sheep) aligns with the energy of the scene. After demanding he speak directly and practically daring him to say that he is the messiah, Jesus doesn't seem to smile warmly or shy away from the matter at hand; rather, his charged response mirrors theirs. Jesus tells them that his action speaks for itself: "My sheep hear my voice . . . No one can snatch them out of the Father's hand" (28b–29).

The fact that Jesus was surrounded on the portico meant that he would not have had many opportunities for exit. This would have been the understandable time for him to respond calmly and try to diffuse the situation, for his own sake. Yet, our Lord is bold, direct, and *not* backing down—all for us, his sheep. His love for us is so vast; Jesus is willing to stand firm against institutional powers to defend his vulnerable followers. What does this new information mean for our theology and teachings? To know that we serve a God who does not cower in the midst of fear and intimidation, how does this apply to our zeal for justice on behalf of others and all?

Week 2: Jesus: Teacher
Matthew 6:5–13

"Do not be like them, for your Father knows what you need before you ask him." (Matthew 6:8)

We live in a microwave society, programmed to seek immediate gratification. We want get-quick schemes—get rich quick, get happy quick, get saved quick, nice and easy. We want God or someone to tell us what to believe and what to say to get to easier, better, brighter. So many of us are taught to see prayer as a magic fix. We come to believe that by saying specific words, reciting a chant, or entering a secret code, the doors of heaven will open for us. But God is not a ventriloquist, and we weren't created to be puppets, relying on rote liturgy and public prayers with all word and no heart.

In the middle of his Sermon on the Mount, in which Jesus offers extensive guidance on how we are to live faithfully, Jesus teaches us how to pray. He makes clear that our motivation is what guides our prayer journey, not our words. Jesus tells us in verse 8 that God already knows what we need before we even ask. So if it is not the words, then it must be what is behind them. The good stuff is the real stuff that's on the inside, where nobody sees and nobody hears. It's the truth that we keep hidden deep down in the depths of our being that God wants to hold with us. Our connection to the Divine is not predicated on uniformity or conformity but solely on grace—costly and undeserved.

Jesus teaches us that the content and timing of our prayers are not the point; we should read to model, not necessarily to recite. The Lord's Prayer, possibly more appropriately named "Our Prayer to the Lord," is not intended to be a script but a template. James 2:19 and Luke 4:9–11 remind us that even demons know God and can quote Scripture, illuminating and affirming Jesus's sentiment in this passage that what distinguishes us from the worldly measures is our posture in prayer. It is our heart that matters.

"Pray, then, in this way" (Matt. 6:9) leads to a prayer guide that highlights relationship, submission, acceptance, and hope. Heart is in all these elements, going far deeper than simply speaking the words. Asking God to forgive us as we forgive others is a holy math equation that calls us to account. We are called to share the love and grace (and forgiveness) that we receive from God with others in similar fashion and consistency. By praying "May your kingdom come. May your will be done on earth as it is in heaven," we are committing to participate in the transformation of earth to embody God's vision. Thus, it behooves us to consider not only what we are asking but what we are *doing* as well. Let us follow the lessons of Jesus our teacher.

Week 3: Jesus: Friend
John 15:1–17

"No one has greater love than this, to lay down one's life for one's friends." (John 15:13)

We find four different types of love in the Greek language: *eros* (romantic), *philia* (friendly), *storge* (familial), and *agape* (godly, unconditional). The type used in this passage references agape—unconditional love. This selfless, altruistic love takes time and intention to cultivate—like trust, it takes time to form an authentic friendship. Studies show that it takes approximately ninety hours within a six-month period to form a casual friendship, and two hundred hours in the same time period to cultivate a close bond, a relationship that is not riddled with hierarchies or conditions but that is mutual, intentional, and invested. In a Westernized culture where the term and title of *friend* is used loosely, these numbers may cause some shock for many.

Jesus is not interested in surface or performative connections; rather, he spends an extraordinary amount of time and energy—most of his ministry, in fact—in community with others, establishing trust on the path toward agape friendship. The twelve disciples with whom he was closest no doubt spent enough time with him to form a close bond; they have abided with him like fruit on a vine and been immersed in his words. They are true friends, privy to all the wisdom Jesus imparts. As Jesus's friends, they will sacrifice their own well-being, even their lives, for him and for one another.

Likewise, we are commanded to love God and love one another, to the point of sacrifice, of it costing us something. Sacrifice is not a simple or transactional event. Loving others should cost us something. Jesus tells us that there is no greater love than to give your life for your friends. This may mean standing up for oppressed or marginalized people, even putting your body on the line to demand justice.

Jesus's crucifixion certainly models sacrifice of life for others, and there are certainly many other examples of Jesus standing between the vulnerable and the threat of empire. There are no shortage of accounts of Jesus putting himself in harm's way to protect or heal another. Agape love is not choosy, case dependent, or time sensitive. It is abundant, virtuous, and integral to our personal relationship with God. Everyone is both unworthy and worthy, including us.

The lyrics of the familiar hymn "What a Friend We Have in Jesus" center characteristics of agape friendship that we can both embrace and model. Just in the four main stanzas are notes of sincerity, restoration, empathy, generosity, reliability, loyalty, agape, and relationship. In true relationship, we would never ask for anything that would compromise the integrity of a connection we value; rather, when our hearts are invested and love is shared, we seek support, conditions, and resources that maintain and nurture that bond. We can direct our spiritual gaze toward the other, trusting that Jesus's holy gaze is fixed on us.

Reflecting on our own relationships through this honest lens, let us consider how we form them and how we maintain them. How can we grow to model Jesus's posture in our daily relational lives?

Week 4: Jesus: Risen
John 20:1–18

Early on the first day of the week, while it was still dark, Mary Magdalene came to the tomb and saw that the stone had been removed from the tomb. (John 20:1)

Easter is globally observed by Christians as a time of celebration, rebirth, and renewal. Taking time to engage the resurrection story apart from Easter Sunday allows us to wrestle with some of the more complex aspects of the risen Christ.

While Easter is typically celebrated after daybreak, the stone that preserved and imprisoned Jesus's body was not rolled away in the morning but in the middle of the night. While many White-majority churches are still employing "light/dark" metaphors for good and evil, the holy magic of the resurrection happened in the thick of the night—during the hours of weeping, mourning, and endless pacing. This means that during the times when grief and wailing may be abundant, God is still on the move! Holy is happening.

Both can be true: holy and traumatic. For the persecuted "least of these" who have historically been denied the right to abundant life, due process, and perceived innocence before guilt, the closure of a burial of a loved one who was unjustly executed is a high priority. After witnessing the brutal torture and murder of an innocent loved one, finding the stone rolled away and the body missing would be nothing short of traumatic. Considering all the funeral plans, the heartbreaks, and the repast preparations, Mary must have felt an additional layer of grief when she saw Jesus's body missing.

I am reminded of Mamie Till, mother of Emmett Till, the Black teen who was kidnapped, beaten, tortured, and murdered because of an untrue accusation that he whistled at a White woman in 1955. Like Jesus, he also surfaced on the third day; Emmett had been thrown into a river with a fan tied around his neck. Reeling from the panic of a missing loved one, I imagine Mamie and Mary Magdalene shared similar dread as they screamed out into the void.

Upon learning of the unspeakable murder of her innocent son, Mamie chose to have an open casket to highlight the horrible torture and abuse inflicted on her son, which rendered him unrecognizable. With so many funeral attendees saying they would not have even known it was him, I find the possible parallels with Mary Magdalene's experience quite remarkable. Unrecognized by Mary when he revealed himself to her, it has been suggested that Jesus's very appearance had changed after resurrection. Later verses of John 20 indicate that the resurrected Jesus had wounds in his hands and side, but we do tend to envision his body as otherwise pristine. While this may have been the case, I offer the possibility that Jesus—with blood dripping, flesh hanging, eyeballs bulging, muscle and bone exposed—may have been beaten unrecognizable too.

These are the complexities and realities of Easter that must be engaged alongside the anticipated joy of the season. All are a part of the gospel story, and the good news. We must learn to tell the truth—all of it—so that it can change us and set us free.

Black Is, Black Ain't: A Celebration of Blackness in the Bible

A four-part series celebrating the sacred beauty, brilliance, resilience, and diversity of Black identity.

BRANDON THOMAS CROWLEY

Series Overview Inspired by Marlon Riggs's powerful documentary *Black Is . . . Black Ain't*: this series affirms the rich diversity and complexity of Black identity, which is divinely crafted and celebrated in Scripture. Each sermon explores a different facet of Black life, such as beauty, desire, blessing, creation, and wisdom, revealing that Blackness is not a deficit to be fixed but a gift to be celebrated. From the bold self-love in Song of Songs, to the divine affirmation of the Ethiopian eunuch in Acts, to the brilliance of the queen of Sheba in Chronicles, these messages reclaim Blackness as sacred. The series speaks against racism, colorism, patriarchy, and homophobia and lifts a theology of inclusion, resilience, and joy. Above all, it proclaims that Black lives are fearfully and wonderfully made and that to honor Blackness is to celebrate the image of God.

	Sermon Title	Focus Scripture	Theme
Week 1	Black Is Beautiful: A Womanist Homily on Self-Awareness, Pleasure, and Love	Song of Songs 1:1–7	A Black woman's powerful declaration of selfhood, beauty, and agency.
Week 2	Black Is Blessed: A Homily on Apostolic Affirmation	Acts 8:28–40	The church's call to embrace the marginalized through inclusion, affirmation, and liberation.

	Sermon Title	Focus Scripture	Theme
Week 3	Black Is Fearfully and Wonderfully Made: A Homily on the Divine Creation of Black Lives	Psalm 139:13–18	The divine intentionality of Black identity as royal, resilient, and deeply beloved by God.
Week 4	Black Is Brilliant and Wise: Claiming Our Divine Design in a World That Tries to Deny It	2 Chronicles 9:1–12	Black brilliance as embodied by the Queen of Sheba, who models discernment, dignity, and divine intelligence.

Tips and Ideas for This Series

Watch *Black Is . . . Black Ain't* by Riggs.[1] In keeping with the documentary's metaphor of gumbo, host a "Gumbo and Grace" fellowship night with Black cuisine and storytelling. Utilize vibrant Afrocentric imagery in graphics, such as kente cloth patterns, Black art portraits, and stained glass featuring biblical figures from African American history. Incorporate spoken word, African drumming, or freedom songs into worship. For week 1, display bold images of Black women and offer a mirror moment where worshippers affirm, "I am Black and beautiful." Week 2 might include a baptism. In week 3, feature baby photos. Week 4 can highlight local Black musicians and artists.

Week 1: Black Is Beautiful: A Womanist Homily on Self-Awareness, Pleasure, and Love
Song of Songs 1:1–7

I am black and beautiful,
  O daughters of Jerusalem,
like the tents of Kedar,
  like the curtains of Solomon.
Do not gaze at me because I am dark,
  because the sun has gazed on me. (Song of Songs 1:5–6a)

This sermon should open the series by drawing the congregation into a sacred reimagining of identity, desire, and divine beauty through the voice of the Black woman in Song of Songs. The preacher should

---

1. *Black Is . . . Black Ain't*, directed by Marlon Riggs (Signifyin' Works, 1994).

name the historical discomfort that surrounds this text. The Song of Songs is often spiritualized or avoided altogether because of its sensual themes. Yet the preacher must resist that impulse. This sermon should take seriously the raw physicality of the text and treat the woman's voice as a theological proclamation. The preacher should introduce the womanist lens by centering the voice of a Black woman who knows herself and claims her space, emphasizing the woman's bold agency. She does not wait for permission or validation but declares, "I am black and beautiful."

This act of self-definition reflects the core of womanist thought, which uplifts the voice and power of Black women. This sermon should delve into the profound, theological significance of that statement. In the first move, this sermon should explore the importance of the words *I am*. These words echo the divine name revealed in the book of Exodus. When the woman says *I am*, she is not just describing herself. She is embodying the presence of someone who knows she was created with a purpose. The preacher should encourage the congregation to find strength in simply declaring their existence without apology. *I am* is a complete sentence. *I am* is a form of resistance. *I am* is a form of praise. It is a model of sacred self-love and holy defiance.

In the second move, this sermon should unpack the significance of the phrase, "I am black." Provide historical context, noting that in the world of the text, darker skin was often a marker of labor and social exclusion. The woman in the text has been made to work outside. Her skin has been darkened by the sun. Yet she claims her Blackness with pride. She does not allow her labor or her suffering to diminish her dignity. This sermon should connect her declaration to the lived realities of Black people today who have been told their skin is a problem. It should teach that Blackness is not a stain to be scrubbed away but a mark of sacred presence. This sermon should also address the social critique embedded in the text. The woman speaks of being overworked and unprotected by her family. Yet, even after being mistreated, she retains her sense of self-worth. The preacher should name that this is the lived experience of many Black women who are burdened with responsibilities but often denied tenderness and rest. Still, she dares to love and to be loved. Her desire becomes a form of resistance.

In the third move, this sermon should celebrate her final claim: "I am beautiful." The preacher should draw attention to the translation. She does not say, "I am black but beautiful." She says, "I am black *and* beautiful." The preacher should guide the congregation in understanding that beauty and Blackness are not opposites. They are companions. This sermon should reject the false binaries of worth and beauty and help the community embrace a theology where Black bodies, Black stories, and Black desires are part of God's good creation. Ultimately, this sermon should convey that self-love is a sacred act. The woman in the text is not ashamed of her body or her desire. She is in love with herself and with the One who delights in her. This sermon should call the people to do the same.

Week 2: Black Is Blessed: A Homily on Apostolic Affirmation
Acts 8:28–40

As they were going along the road, they came to some water; and the eunuch said, "Look, here is water! What is to prevent me from being baptized?" He commanded the chariot to stop, and both of them, Philip and the eunuch, went down into the water, and Philip baptized him. (Acts 8:36–38)

This sermon affirms the sacredness of Black life *and* queer identity by exploring the apostolic affirmation of the Ethiopian eunuch in Acts 8. The Spirit sends Philip away from the thriving revival in Samaria to a wilderness road—an opportune moment for the pastor to teach that divine purpose often leads us away from comfort into radical encounters. Walk the congregation through the geographical, cultural, and theological significance of the road from Jerusalem to Gaza, highlighting its danger and solitude. Then exegete the identity of the Ethiopian eunuch, showing how race, gender, sexuality, and power intersect in one individual. He is a dark-skinned African official of great wealth, a sexual minority, and a seeker of God. The preacher should draw on biblical scholarship that connects this figure to African lineage. Invite the congregation to imagine the boldness of someone who is both Black and queer asking, "What is to prevent me from being baptized?"

This sermon should then center Philip's radical response. Philip does not interrogate the eunuch's body, background, or beliefs. Instead, he listens to the Spirit and simply joins him. This should lead to a teaching moment about how ministry requires presence more than performance and compassion more than critique. Use this to challenge church traditions that withhold affirmation until after rigid doctrinal vetting. The sermon should insist that the Spirit prompts us not to gatekeep God but to get in the chariot and ride beside the marginalized.

Note how verse 37—Philip's solicitation of a particular confession of faith and the eunuch providing it—is missing in many manuscripts, which suggests that the act of baptism did not hinge on verbal confession but on visible desire. The eunuch's yearning for full inclusion was enough. This should be connected to present-day affirmations of Black

LGBTQ+ people who are too often asked to justify their existence before being embraced. This sermon should declare that the gospel is not a checklist of conditions but an open invitation to belovedness. It should end by proclaiming that Black is blessed because God says so and because God's Spirit has already gone ahead to prepare the waters. Philip's job was not to save but to get out of the way and baptize. So, too, must the church baptize without barriers, affirm without hesitation, and proclaim without apology that God's yes is already on the record.

Week 3: Black Is Fearfully and Wonderfully Made: A Homily on the Divine Creation of Black Lives
Psalm 139:13–18

For it was you who formed my inward parts;
  you knit me together in my mother's womb.
I praise you, for I am fearfully and wonderfully made.
  Wonderful are your works;
that I know very well. (Psalm 139:13–14)

This sermon should affirm the inherent sacredness, intentionality, and beauty of Black lives by drawing deeply from Psalm 139. It should begin by declaring that every Black body is divinely crafted and lovingly known by God. Use the poetic richness of the psalm to remind the congregation that the Black body, so often politicized, criminalized, and devalued, was first spiritualized and humanized by the Creator.

Exegete the Hebrew poetry that speaks of God forming inward parts and knitting the psalmist together in the womb. Linger on the language of intricacy and divine intention. These images are powerful tools to dismantle narratives of inferiority, shame, or accident. The sermon should proclaim to every Black child, teenager, adult, elder, woman, man, and nonbinary person that they are not random or flawed. They are not the result of oppression. They are the result of a holy imagination.

Note how, in verse 14, the word *fearfully* does not mean afraid but rather reverent, majestic, or awe-inspiring. God took great care with every coil of Black hair, every hue of Black skin, every cadence of Black voice, every stride of Black gait, and every creative impulse that flows through Black thought and culture. The sermon should affirm that Black is not only beautiful but also sacredly designed, despite how often society declares the opposite. Schools, hospitals, courtrooms, news headlines, and even some pulpits have preached that Black life is expendable. But the psalm teaches that before there was a system to oppress Black people, there was a God who blessed them. Before there was a culture that feared them; there was a God who formed them. Before there were chains, there was a choice made by heaven to create them with purpose.

This sermon should also reflect on verse 16, where the psalmist says that God beheld their unformed substance and wrote every day of their life in a book before they were born. Remind the congregation that Black futures matter to God. That despite premature death, systemic poverty, or erasure, God has already envisioned the fullness of Black flourishing. Each Black life has a holy narrative that cannot be canceled by injustice.

End by guiding the congregation through verses 17 and 18, highlighting the magnitude of God's thoughts toward them. The preacher should encourage every listener to resist internalized hatred or social narratives that demean them. They should leave knowing that to be Black is not to be cursed. It is to be counted. It is to be seen. It is to be wonderfully made.

Week 4: Black Is Brilliant and Wise: Claiming Our Divine Design in a World That Tries to Deny It
2 Chronicles 9:1–12

When the queen of Sheba heard of the fame of Solomon, she came to Jerusalem to test him with riddles, having a very great retinue and camels bearing spices and very much gold and precious stones. When she came to Solomon, she discussed with him all that was on her mind. Solomon answered all her questions; there was nothing hidden from Solomon that he could not explain to her. (2 Chronicles 9:1–2)

This sermon should explore the story of the queen of Sheba as a model of Black intelligence, discernment, and divine dignity in a world that often misrepresents or undermines Black brilliance. Begin by affirming that wisdom is not only a spiritual virtue but also a vital tool for cultural survival and strategic advancement within Black communities.

The preacher should remind the congregation that before she was mythologized by the West or exoticized by historians, the queen of Sheba was a real African ruler whose legacy deserves theological recovery. The exegesis should underscore that she did not come to Solomon out of infatuation or flattery but rather to test the limits of his wisdom through rigorous questions. She approached with wealth, confidence, and intellectual curiosity. This was a woman of means, culture, and sovereign power who carried questions in her mind and honor in her step. Her journey to Solomon was not about submission but investigation.

This text should be framed as a story of one great mind meeting another, not of seduction but of strategic alliance. The text explicitly notes that the queen posed challenging questions, and Solomon was able to answer them all. Their exchange affirms the power of dialogue and discernment rooted in mutual respect and intellectual seriousness.

The sermon should also address how the queen of Sheba has been historically misrepresented, particularly by Western scholars who have sexualized her visit and overlooked her intellectual contributions. This distortion mirrors the ways Black women are often reduced to their bodies or style while their brilliance and leadership are dismissed or devalued. This sermon must reclaim the queen of Sheba not as a myth or seductress but as a stateswoman, a sage, and a symbol of divine Black intellect. Reflecting the broader theme of divine design, note how her brilliance is not accidental but God-given. She models what it looks like to lead with questions, honor the sacredness of wisdom, and make investments that bless entire nations.

The sermon should encourage the congregation to see themselves as thinkers, leaders, and decision-makers, capable of asking hard questions and negotiating with clarity and courage. It should affirm that to be Black and wise is to reflect the image of God. This sermon should end by calling the people to become stewards of wisdom. Encourage them to invest wisely, to test truth before embracing it, and to value intellectual integrity in their decisions. Wisdom is not just about the accumulation of facts but about discernment, justice, and service to the greater good. Through Sheba, God shows us that Black wisdom has always existed, has always mattered, and continues to have the power to shape history. Preach this so that young Black children know that they come from brilliance, not a lack of it. Declare that to be Black is not only beautiful but also brilliant and wise.

A Deconstructionist's Journey

A six-part series on deconstructing oppressive church beliefs while reconstructing a faith of liberation and hope.

TYLER HO-YIN SIT

Series Overview

Like a fever burning out a virus, deconstructing oppressive theology is about breaking down harmful internalized beliefs. Just as important as deconstruction, though, is reconstruction. Even after the fever breaks, a healthy system must take over or that person will be prone to illness again.

This sermon series is for people who were hurt by the church but, miraculously, still find themselves drawn to it. Specifically, this series is for people who have been taught beliefs that they now find oppressive: women who were told that they could never preach, for example. Or straight people who were scolded for having gay friends. Or queer people of color who kept finding churches that accepted one of their identities but not both.

This series moves through both deconstruction and reconstruction while acknowledging that everyone's journey will require different timelines, reach different depths, and flow nonlinearly. This sermon series is in no way a replacement for therapy (which is also often helpful for deconstructionists!). Rather, it is a chance for the church-curious to find sprouts, buds, and saplings where they thought there was only desolate land.

	Sermon Title	Focus Scripture	Theme
Week 1	The Deconstructionist's Journey	Romans 1:16–17	Exploring the need for deconstruction and reconstruction.
Week 2	Reconstructing Faithful Sexuality	Romans 1:26–27	Healing the damage church has done to the LGBTQ+ community.

	Sermon Title	Focus Scripture	Theme
Week 3	Reconstructing Salvation without Abuse	Romans 5:6–11	Seeing the cross in a new light.
Week 4	Reconstructing Peace with Our Bodies	Romans 8:1–8	Discovering an embodied faith.
Week 5	Reconstructing a Line between Church and State	Romans 13:1–7	Understanding Christian nationalism and Jesus.
Week 6	Reconstructing the Belief That God Actually Loves Us	Romans 8:31–39	Accepting how loved you really are.

Tips and Ideas for This Series

Create worksheets that people can use to continue their deconstruction journey with these prompts: I once believed . . ., I empathize with my younger self . . ., I forgive . . ., Now I believe . . ., Because of this belief, I am . . .

For example, someone might write: "I once believed that I should treat sex with shame and distrust. I empathize with my younger self, who was feeling confused about her body and looking for guidance. I forgive myself and my pastor who started this belief. Now I believe that sex is a way to affirm the body. Because of this belief, I am striving to treat my body and my partner's body with respect."

Week 1: The Deconstructionist's Journey
Romans 1:16–17

For I am not ashamed of the gospel; it is God's saving power for everyone who believes. (Romans 1:16a)

The first sermon in a series should accomplish the same thing that the first song in a musical does. You need to introduce the main characters, make people feel invested in the tension that will drive the story, and, most importantly, create the world in which everything unfolds. For this sermon series, you're inviting people to wrestle with previous, painful chapters of their lives for the sake of creating a more peaceful life and world. The top priority for this sermon is creating the safety and stakes for people to buy into that.

It may be surprising to some that this series revolves around the book of Romans. Romans is perhaps the most weaponized book in the Bible; it has been used to justify homophobia, body shame, nationalism, slavery, and all sorts of horrors throughout history. I started with this acknowledgement so that my justice-minded community could have a shared starting place ("oppression is bad!") while making a case for why we must reexamine Romans, even if it's a book where some do not wish to linger. And, as we'll discover, Romans is actually an incredible book that has many subversive and liberative messages!

Next, the main argument: *how* you deconstruct your church hurt matters. If you want to dismantle a house, you don't just pick up a sledgehammer, walk into the middle of the house, and start swinging. You might hit a load-bearing wall, and the roof could cave in. Neither can you sledgehammer your beliefs without things crumbling away so fast that nihilism caves in, and then nothing matters at all.

So, the five-question flow named in the "Tips and Ideas" section above is a way to guide people in their deconstruction while showing kindness to themselves. I walked through each of the questions in understanding Romans 1:16, citing references from our community:

I once believed . . . that Paul is a judgmental colonizer and that I should be too, that this text is about forcing people to accept Jesus.

I empathize with my younger self . . . for wanting to have something to be *right* about, to be moral.

I forgive . . . myself and my teachers for pushing me to "save" non-Christians in my life and doing it in a way that was emotionally manipulative and culturally callous.

Now I believe . . . that Paul was writing as a member of an oppressed people group and that this text is about creating community between disenfranchised subgroups within the community.

Because of this belief, I am . . . trying to build community between feuding people groups, just as Paul did.

To conclude, a metaphor that is more beautiful than a sledgehammer in a house: Imagine you're an environmentalist who hears that grass lawns are bad for the environment. They're water-intensive, they require fertilizer that pollutes runoff water, and so forth. Now imagine that, hearing about this harm, you rip up all the grass, leaving the soil under it bare in the sun. Soon, it will dry out, and you'll be left with dust. You removed the harm, but nothing is growing in its place. This is not God's dream for our spiritual lives. Instead, God wants a *garden*, a life blossoming and buzzing with an abundance that is so much more than the absence of harm. This is the future that is possible with deconstruction *and* reconstruction. May it be so, for all of us.

Week 2: Reconstructing Faithful Sexuality
Romans 1:26–27

Their females exchanged natural intercourse for unnatural, and in the same way also the males, giving up natural intercourse with females, were consumed with their passionate desires for one another. (Romans 1:26b–27a)

Most of the people I've met on the deconstruction journey broke away from their church because of its treatment of the LGBTQ+ community. The loudest question in their heads when they're listening to you preach (and when they're perusing your social media) is whether this will be a deconstruction series that is LGBTQ+-affirming, not affirming, or another bait-and-switch tactic where a pastor seems to be affirming of LGBTQ+ people and then—surprise!—the pastor still condemns LGBTQ+ people. This sermon comes early in the series so that you can clear the air.

When addressing the harm churches have done, and especially passages like Romans 1:26–27 that are often used to clobber LGBTQ+ people, try to leverage preaching illustrations that have some gravity with your listeners. For congregants who grew up in sexual purity culture and read *I Kissed Dating Goodbye*, author Joshua Harris's subsequent apology to the LGBTQ+ community may be of particular interest. For survivors of ex-gay conversation therapies that promised to rid a Christian child of gayness, the shuttering of Exodus International is a powerful counternarrative. And yet for others, denominational or traditional identity may be the key. Organizations like Pride in the Pews, which collaborates with historically Black congregations, provide resources that don't require racial code-switching.

Often people who are deconstructing still maintain reverence for what their church tradition considered authoritative, even if they no longer agree with that church tradition. Some folks will need to hear you engage the Greek, while others will want to hear how Augustine, Calvin, Luther, or Wesley would have arrived at this conclusion if they lived in our time.

This is a challenge for progressive preachers, because our training and conscience may be pressuring us to preach on this topic in a way that is aligned with the broader LGBTQ+ discourse but might fail to meet the congregation where they are. Preachers who read the "Centering Marginalized Voices" chapter of my book (*Staying Awake: The Gospel for Changemakers*) sometimes tell me they feel guilty if they're not preaching on each and every form of intersectional oppression. The underlying logic goes like this: "LGBTQ+ people are oppressed; and Black, disabled, undocumented, transgender women are the most oppressed. My congregation has no framework for engaging those intersectional identities, but if I don't start with that, I am not in solidarity. If we gloss over profound suffering in order to focus on palatable suffering, we lose our integrity." Then, they preach a sermon that is ideologically perfect but completely fails to connect with the congregation.

On the other hand, though, I meet preachers who are *too* incremental about their approach to LGBTQ+ oppression. Their thinking is, "This Sunday, I will mention that gay people exist, then in three years I'll talk about wedding cake discrimination, and I'll discuss transgender oppression the Sunday before the Second Coming of Christ." Meanwhile, they have youth in their congregation who are actively questioning their gender identity and developing opinions of the church that they will carry for the rest of their lives.

I bet God is giving you some intuition on how much pressure to apply to your congregation. For the purposes of deconstruction, what matters is that you give people legitimate counternarratives that disrupt harmful theology, explain your posture clearly, and create emotional safety by letting people ask questions.

Week 3: Reconstructing Salvation without Abuse
Romans 5:6–11

Much more surely, therefore, since we have now been justified by his blood, will we be saved through him from the wrath of God (Romans 5:9)

This might be a good sermon to begin with a trigger warning, because the focus question is simply this: Is God abusive? I explicitly give people permission to go to the lobby, get a drink of water, or pace in the back of the sanctuary. When I first started offering trigger warnings, it felt foreboding ("Wait, what is he about to say?!"), but now it is so normalized that people gladly move around as they need.

The depiction of God and humanity in Romans 5 is, at first glance, a troubling one. Especially for people who grew up in damaging church cultures, the message seems clear: Humans are terrible. We're so bad that Jesus had to die so that God—who, remember, is our parent—doesn't torture us forever.

This sets the paradigm for every other Christian belief. God—*our parent*—has a rage that will brutalize us—the children—by condemning us to a torture chamber that we can never escape. Jesus saved us by diverting God's beatings to himself. And if that is the nature of God, we have to do everything we can to make sure we don't get on God's bad side. We must believe the right thing, do the right thing, and sacrifice our lives in just the right way to save us from a God who, apparently, has an anger management problem.

For preachers like me, who believe this is an upsetting misrepresentation of God, it's easy enough to skip this passage. We tend to focus more on the ministry of Jesus, dash a little "God is love" in there (1 John 4:8), and call it a day.

For many who are deconstructing, this is plainly insufficient. If a daughter grew up in a household with an abusive father and ran away, she would (rightfully) be skeptical about whether she wanted to move back in. And a pastor saying, "But your father is so loving now!" doesn't really change that. And so we must name the abusive elephant in the room; we must look at texts that seemingly cast God as a rampaging father who can't wait to hurt his children.

When I approach this topic, I first clarify that *blood* would have had a connotation of ritual rather than one of violence. As we read throughout the Old Testament, animal sacrifices were a ritualistic way for priests to account and apologize for the wrongdoings of the society. In that regard, the blood of Christ is more similar to the waters of baptism than the wounds made by a ferocious God. The Passover story (Exodus 12) shows us that blood has a connotation of liberation, of *escaping* Pharaoh's abuse.

Second, inspired by Howard Thurman and many others, I clarify that it was the empire who killed Jesus. The nails that crucified Jesus were forged by the Roman Empire, hammered in by people executing the decisions of a faulty justice system. The crucifixion is an important part of our faith because it shows us just how unjust society can be, not how unsafe God is.

Which, I name lastly in this sermon, is why we still *need* Jesus. Sometimes deconstructionists start thinking, "Well, if I don't need Jesus to be saved from God's wrath, I don't need Jesus at all!" This is the quintessential mindset of a survivor of abuse. In a healthy relationship founded on love, we discover that we *need* our beloved not because of the absence of harm but because love is the only thing that makes life worthwhile. God loves us into existence, and when we love God back, we realize how foolish it would be to give our lives to anything else.

Week 4: Reconstructing Peace with Our Bodies
Romans 8:1–8

For those who live according to the flesh set their minds on the things of the flesh, but those who live according to the Spirit set their minds on things of the Spirit. (Romans 8:5)

Too often, churches are where people learn to distrust their bodies:

- "You want to have sex? That's an impulse that is dangerous and must be controlled."
- "You feel exhausted from volunteering? That just means you don't believe hard enough."
- "You think you're queer? Probably not. But if you are, you are called to a life of celibacy."
- "It's a wife's job to keep her man satisfied (even if she doesn't want to), so he doesn't stray."

Over time, messages like these generate a deep distrust of our innate intuition. And, too often, there are implicit messages underneath: that skinniness is morally superior to fatness, able bodies are favored over disabled ones, and women must always try harder than men.

Many of these arguments are rooted in Paul's use of the word *sarx*, here translated as "flesh." If Christians don't want to "set their minds on the things of the flesh" (Rom. 8:5), that means rejecting sexuality and, by extension, any sort of physicality. It all comes down to self-control, to not doing the thing that your body really, really wants to do.

Indeed, people who are deconstructing often have an overdeveloped ability to police themselves. Self-control has gone from being a fruit of the Spirit (Gal. 5:23) to an idol of the empire, and this sermon is your chance to cast a different vision of what it really means to reject *sarx*.

For my congregation, I've gotten particular traction in referencing work like Resmaa Menakem's book *My Grandmother's Hands*. An increasing number of antiracism practitioners and researchers are finding that racism isn't just an intellectual opinion. Racism, reinforced by systemic oppression, creates muscle memory. Racism is *physically* present in our nervous systems, in our breathing, and in our heart rate. And so, if racial justice (or any type of justice) is going to be realized, people of privilege must work on their physical response as well as their intellectual one. This unlocks a new understanding of *sarx*. Following Jesus doesn't require us to suppress God-given intuitions, but it *does* require us to find new ways of showing up to our society.

If embodied antiracism is too unfamiliar of a framework for your congregation, center the sermon on the tools that we have to discern God's truth in our lives. For example, in United Methodism we frequently reference the Wesleyan Quadrilateral of Scripture, tradition, reason, and experience. One of the ways to discern the difference between a God-given intuition and *sarx* is putting Scripture, tradition, reason, and experience together.

Either way, you are giving people the tools to discern what is providence and what is a socialized pattern. Equipped with a new paradigm, deconstructionists will then have a way to start trusting their body again.

Week 5: Reconstructing a Line between Church and State
Romans 13:1–7

Let every person be subject to the governing authorities, for there is no authority except from God, and those authorities that exist have been instituted by God. (Romans 13:1)

I titled this sermon to use a term that people are familiar with (the separation of church and state), but of course, I do not prioritize Thomas Jefferson over Jesus! This sermon starts with the biblical imperative and moves toward an understanding of how Christians relate to society, not the other way around. Specifically, this sermon is your chance to proclaim your church's relationship with Christian nationalism.

Many people who are deconstructing theology grew up in churches where the Bible and the U.S. Constitution were connected by a golden thread. I'm not just talking about a United States flag in the sanctuary—I mean a deeply reinforced narrative that the United States is God's favorite, and it is a country that can uniquely manifest God's redemption in the world. And if that is the case, then Christians have an obligation to subject themselves to U.S. law. In that paradigm, crime isn't just breaking a law, it is a *sin*, something that is stopping the United States from continuing its holy mission.

For this sermon, then, it would be worth reciting all the people in the Bible who broke the law because God required it. Shiphrah and Puah (Exod. 1) did not make themselves "subject to governing authorities," and Paul himself was arrested (Acts 16:16–40). As we established in week 3, Jesus was crucified by the governing authorities!

One of the freedoms you can offer to someone who is deconstructing is to name the Christian responsibility to oppose unjust laws and support just ones. That means that when the United States is furthering a world of peace, justice, and belovedness, it is acting in keeping with the Holy Spirit! But when the United States is oppressing someone, the Holy Spirit is on the side of the person who is being oppressed. In other words, there is no political party that perfectly embodies God's will, and there certainly is no country that does either.

After all, "there is no authority except from God" (Rom. 13:1b), which is to say, no pharaoh, emperor, prime minister, or president is higher than God. For a Christian, the U.S. president isn't the highest ranking officer, because God is our number one authority. And, as we read particularly in the Old Testament, God moves in and out of favor with leaders all the time. If the president disobeys God's will, then God's authority passes on to the first person who *is* willing to do God's will.

This remains true regardless of which political party is in power, and it's important that congregants witness their church leadership applying the same rigor of discernment to elected officials regardless of party affiliation. Otherwise, Christianity becomes yet another political strategy, which is exactly what most deconstructionists are trying to escape.

Week 6: Reconstructing the Belief That God Actually Loves Us
Romans 8:31–39

For I am convinced that neither death, nor life, nor angels, nor rulers, nor things present, nor things to come, nor powers, nor height, nor depth, nor anything else in all creation will be able to separate us from the love of God in Christ Jesus our Lord. (Romans 8:38–39)

This sermon doesn't have to be last in the series, but I placed it here because it creates closure. Love deserves the final word, don't you think?

Deconstruction and reconstruction are back breaking work, after all, and your congregation should know what it's all for. The goal of this series isn't to have beliefs that fit with a social justice discourse, and it isn't to be able to win a debate with religious family members. The goal is to receive God's love and to offer love back to God, like vapor rising up and raining down in a perpetual cycle of affection. Indeed, the greatest violence of harmful theology is that it convinces us that God's love "just isn't for us," when in actuality God's love is the *only* thing for us.

This would be a good sermon to begin and end with a personal testimony, since you want to be clear that you're speaking out of your own life and not trying to seize control of theirs. If you have been on a deconstruction journey yourself, you can tell (with appropriate vulnerability) how you encountered God in the midst of it. And if you haven't been on a deconstruction journey, just be honest about why you became a preacher in the first place. Testimonies remind congregants that they're engaging a person, not a philosophical construct.

With your testimony starting and ending the sermon, the middle is open for you to address whatever heights or depths might be separating people from the love of God. What keeps your congregants up at night?

Every October, I survey my community about where God is calling the church to go in the next year. The survey has broad questions like: How many friendships have you made at church? What type of transformation would you like to see in your neighborhood, city, or society? And, most importantly for this sermon, What do you worry about? The results ranged from "I'm afraid I'll be single for the rest of my life" to "I worry I'm not putting enough money into savings."

Worry, which is a form of fear, is a giant flashing sign that shows us the heights or depths that we believe are greater than God's love. In that regard, fear is a great friend, because it shows us the parts of our lives where we could use reassurance. Fear is sometimes helpful, but it shouldn't drive our lives. Love doesn't always get rid of our fear. Love shows us how to be courageous amid fear for the things we love. If your sermon can shift how someone relates to fear, that is a huge win that makes God dance.

Romans 8:38–39 is a fantastic passage to reiterate often with your congregation, a message they can hold on to through all the ups and downs of life and faith. No matter what they used to believe or still fear may be true, they can rest assured that no belief or behavior, no nagging voice in their head, can separate us from God's love.

Spiritual Formation

The ABC's of Spiritual Success

A three-part series on the building blocks of a sustaining relationship with God.

NAPOLEON J. HARRIS V

Series Overview — Visit any modern bookstore and you'll find countless books on success. Yet, much of what society defines as success is fleeting and unfulfilling, leaving many who attain it still frantically searching for more and always asking, "What's next?" Spiritual success, however, is different. It is lasting, rich, and deeply fulfilling. Best of all, it's within reach. Achieving it comes down to three key steps of faith: acknowledging God, believing God, and committing our ways to God. This back-to-basics three-sermon series explores these essential steps, guiding us toward a deeper connection with God and the kind of success that truly endures: spiritual success!

	Sermon Title	Focus Scripture	Theme
Week 1	Acknowledge	Proverbs 3:1–12	The key to achieving lasting spiritual success is in acknowledging God.
Week 2	Believe	Hebrews 11:1–3, 6	The key to achieving lasting spiritual success is believing God.
Week 3	Commit	Proverbs 16:1–7	The key to achieving lasting spiritual success is committing our ways to God.

Tips and Ideas for This Series

This sermon series, like all good sermons, is rooted in the sacred act of teaching. Its title naturally evokes images of the classroom, offering a unique opportunity to embrace a more overt teaching style. Consider using whiteboards or blackboards as visual aids and incorporating ABC blocks in marketing and worship graphics. Dressing in a stereotypical grade-school teacher or professor style can enhance the theme, while name tags for congregants may foster connection and invite fellowship after the sermon. Embracing a classroom-inspired modality allows the message to be more engaging, memorable, and interactive for the congregation.

Week 1: Acknowledge
Proverbs 3:1–12

Trust in the Lord *with all your heart,*
  and do not rely on your own insight.
In all your ways acknowledge him,
  and he will make straight your paths. (Proverbs 3:5–6)

I want to start with a question. What do you call a peanut butter and jelly sandwich made without bread? A mess! Here's another question: What do you call a life full of temporal success but bereft of spiritual success? The same thing: a mess.

Unlike bread, spiritual success isn't just an important part of life; it is the essential element of life. Without it, no matter how much temporal success we accomplish, no matter how many goals we achieve, we will still be woefully incomplete. Life will lack meaning and purpose. Spiritual success anchors us in life. It keeps us from being tossed by the ups and downs of our circumstances. It gives us purpose. It allows us to live abundantly. It is the measure of who we are rather than just what we have.

A group of kids showed up for basketball tryouts. One kid looked as if he had it going on with brand-new Jordans and Nike gear from head to toe, but he was the first one cut. Why? Because he had gear but no game. Life is the same way. We can amass all the material success the world offers, but without the essential element—without spiritual success—our lives will lack true purpose and fulfillment.

But here's the good news: God doesn't leave our spiritual success up to chance. Proverbs 3:5–6 teaches us that the first step to spiritual success is acknowledging God in all our ways.

To acknowledge God is to recognize God in every moment of life—the good, the bad, and everything in between. It means thinking of God in every decision, seeking God's guidance, and allowing our experiences to teach us more about who God is.

Today's Scripture gives us three ways to acknowledge God:

1. *Humility before God:* Proverbs 3:7 says, "Do not be wise in your own eyes; fear the LORD and turn away from evil." Spiritual success begins with humility. When we think we have all the answers, we cut ourselves off from God's wisdom. But when we humble ourselves, we make room for God's direction.
2. *Honoring God with Our Resources:* Proverbs 3:9 says, "Honor the LORD with your substance and with the first fruits of all your produce." Giving isn't about God needing our money; it's about keeping our hearts in the right place. Jesus said, "For where your treasure is, there your heart will be also" (Matt. 6:21). When we give to God, we acknowledge that everything we have comes from God.
3. *Embracing God's Discipline:* Solomon reminds us that "the LORD reproves the one he loves" (Prov. 3:12). Just as a coach pushes an athlete to be their best, God places parameters around us—not to harm us, but to grow us.

Friends, if we want spiritual success, we must begin by acknowledging God. And when we do, God promises to direct our paths and lead us into the fullness of life!

Week 2: Believe
Hebrews 11:1–3, 6

And without faith it is impossible to please him, for whoever would approach God must believe that he exists and that he rewards those who seek him. (Hebrews 11:6)

Imagine a couple in a relationship. They both keep their phones locked—and not just with passwords, but with biometrics so that their partner cannot access their phone. Moreover, whenever one gets a call or text, they instantly grab the phone and go to another room. Even when they're out to eat, they leave the table and take the call. Making matters worse, they both get calls and texts at all times of the night. Both parties have been known to stay out all night, coming home to the other with rationales and excuses that don't hold water. Furthermore, both have been known to follow and tail the other, like spies right out of comic books, and there isn't a week that goes by where one doesn't show up at the other's job unannounced and cause a scene. In fact, this same couple doesn't even bank together; they opt to keep their finances hidden from each other.

Can I ask you an honest question about this couple we're imagining? How many of you would stay in a relationship like that?

I bet none of us would. In fact, none of us would even admit to being in a relationship like that (at least publicly), because the relationship we just imagined together is a relationship devoid of any trust. A relationship without trust just isn't much of a relationship, because to be in a relationship with another person is to trust them and to be trusted by them.

The same holds true with regard to our relationship with God!

To be painstakingly clear: There is no spiritual success without a relationship with God, and we can't have a relationship with God when we don't trust God.

The writer of Hebrews tells us today that without faith—without belief—it is impossible to please God, to be in a mutually satisfying relationship with God.

To have faith or belief in God is to do more than just agree to the idea of God. It is more than just cognitively accepting and collecting facts and stories about God. It's entrusting our lives to God! It's not just believing *in* God but *believing* God. Children believe in Santa; children believe in the Easter Bunny; we believe in the democratic process and the justice system (sometimes). But when it comes to God, don't just believe *in* God—*believe* God!

Like the so-called couple we imagined earlier, we cannot be in relationship with God without trusting God, living in confidence that we can count on God and God can count on us. Without seeing, believe that God is God. Believe that God exists and rewards those who seek him. Believe that God is present with you right now and everywhere you go! Believe that God is powerful! Believe that God is passionate and compassionate toward you! Believe the promises of God. Believe God!

Week 3: Commit
Proverbs 16:1–7

Commit your work to the Lord,
and your plans will be established. (Proverbs 16:3)

Have you ever been in a relationship where one person was doing all the right things—showing up, spending time, even saying the right words—but something was missing? The other person could feel it. "When will you commit to me?" they ask. "What do you mean?" the other responds. "I'm here, aren't I?" But presence is not the same as commitment. Doing the right things isn't the same as giving your whole heart. And while this sounds like the conversation of a couple at a crossroads, it is also the conversation God is having with us.

"Thou shalt have no other gods before me, I said, but you're playing the field! When will you commit?"

God is not interested in hollow routine. God is not impressed by empty ritual. The question is not whether we show up once a week but whether we are *all in*. No divided loyalties. No competing affections. Just an undivided, unwavering, unflinching commitment to God. And that same call rings out to us today. Who or what captures our hearts? Where do we expend the most energy? Who gets our best ideas, our deepest devotion, our first and final thoughts? Is it God? Or is it easy to pass on God's work, to neglect God's call, to reach for something or someone else when we're in need? If we want spiritual success, if we want to grow in God, we must commit ourselves to God. "Commit your work to the Lord," says Proverbs 16:3.

Commitment is not just about personal piety; it is about justice. Proverbs 16 tells us that commitment to God is demonstrated by walking in God's statutes, and the Hebrew word used, *hoq*, refers to laws that establish justice. God has always been clear about what matters most: "What does the Lord require of you but to do justice and to love kindness and to walk humbly with your God?" (Mic. 6:8). Justice is not an accessory to faith—it is at the heart of faith. To be fully committed to God is to be fully committed to justice, because justice is what God desires.

And justice is not a trend, not a hobby, not a soundbite; it is a way of life. It means standing up against oppression, fighting against systems of inequity, calling out everything that dehumanizes and destroys. It means showing up, whether we're confronting public policy, mass incarceration, voter suppression, racism, sexism, homophobia, transphobia, or economic injustice. To be wholeheartedly committed to God is to work tirelessly for the world God desires.

Proverbs repeatedly instructs us to *keep* God's commandments, and the word here means to build a hedge around them, to secure them like a fortress. Not to keep others out, but to keep *us in*—fastened to God, tethered to his truth, anchored in his word, committed and connected to God.

And why should we commit to God? Because God has already committed to us. While we were still sinners, Christ died for us. God's love has never wavered. God's devotion has never faltered. God's heart has always been ours. And it's easy to commit to someone who's already committed to you. So the only question left is, when will we?

Rhythm of Life

A five-part series on spiritual practices that lead to transformation.

JOSH SCOTT

Series Overview

Most Christians are familiar with the idea of spiritual practices—intentional actions or rhythms of life that cultivate a deepening relationship with God and that empower us to experience transformation in our lives. Too often, these practices can become about performance and induce guilt and shame when we don't seem to measure up to the expectations of ourselves or others. What if we could engage these practices free from the shame-inducing "shoulds" or anxiety about performing them a certain way? This series focuses on spiritual practices that empower us to do four key things: (1) exercise our spiritual muscles and build muscle memory; (2) open and enlarge our hearts, keeping them soft toward God, others, and ourselves; (3) expand our awareness; and (4) invite us to experience transformation.

	Sermon Title	Focus Scripture	Theme
Week 1	The Rhythm of Experience	Genesis 28:10–16; Exodus 3:1–5; John 9:24–25	Our experiences can be transformative and shaping if we practice awareness and intentionality.
Week 2	The Rhythm of Rest	Genesis 2:1–3; Exodus 20:8–11	Scripture begins with a creation story that establishes a rhythm for everything and everyone in creation—a balance of work and rest, creating and ceasing.
Week 3	The Rhythm of Ritual	Joshua 4:1–9	Engaging in meaningful, intentional ritual can help us experience the transformation for which we long.

	Sermon Title	Focus Scripture	Theme
Week 4	The Rhythm of Prayer	1 Thessalonians 5:17	Prayer gives us an open-ended posture toward God and the world.
Week 5	The Rhythm of Forgiveness	Matthew 5:21–24	Forgiveness isn't just something we give to others but a spiritual practice that keeps our own hearts soft and open.

Tips and Ideas for This Series

When designing graphics for this series, focus on an aesthetic that creates a feeling of calm—muted, soft tones. Additionally, as you plan worship, think of ways you can implement the theme of each week into the gathering through additional time set aside for the practice. For example, perhaps on the rest week you take some time for stillness and silence, or during the week focused on prayer, think about creative ways to give people time and space to pray. Consider putting together short-term small groups that spend time discussing and practicing the theme of each week. Finally, make this personal and practical. If you have stories of struggle or success with these practices, it would be helpful to share them with your community as you feel comfortable. We aren't experts but fellow practitioners. Letting our community see that we are working things out like they are can be encouraging for them.

Week 1: The Rhythm of Experience
Genesis 28:10–16; Exodus 3:1–5; John 9:24–25

Then Jacob woke from his sleep and said, "Surely the LORD is in this place—and I did not know it!" (Genesis 28:16)

Many of us have been taught not to trust ourselves or our experiences. That's why it's so important to begin this series by affirming that God has always worked to shape and form us through the ordinary experiences of our everyday lives. This isn't a departure from Scripture but the very norm we find on page after page, story after story. God has always met people in the ordinariness of their lives and called them to join God in the transformation of the world.

Our first text from Genesis 28 focuses on an encounter the patriarch Jacob had with God at a critical moment in his journey. When we meet Jacob in this passage he is on the run. After tricking his older brother, Esau, out of his birthright, Jacob had to leave home to avoid his brother's retaliation. On that trek, he stopped at "a certain place" (v. 11), essentially nowhere and anywhere, just an ordinary place. Yet, it was in that anywhere that God met Jacob in a dream and shared God's vision and promise for Jacob. He awoke and realized that God had always been with him. An experience gave him a new window into his relationship with God and the meaning of his life.

In Exodus 3, Moses's experience in the midst of an ordinary, everyday moment as a shepherd gave him an understanding that the ground on which he stood had always been holy and that God was calling him to partner with God in the work of liberation. Finally, it was a healing encounter with Jesus that led the man in John 9, with no knowledge of who Jesus was or even how he was healed, to express faith in his experience.

Again and again in Scripture we find this pattern: unexpected experiences that lead to transformation and growth. Learning to pay attention to the experiences of our lives, how God meets us in the ordinary, is an essential part of our growth and transformation. This truth raises some important questions for us: How do we evaluate our experiences? How do we know the experience we are evaluating is from God, inviting our growth?

Considering the testimony of Scripture, there are three questions we must ask ourselves as we weigh the meaning of our experiences: First, does the experience call us to be better humans? In Scripture, we find God calling people to a more just and generous way of being in the world. Second, does the experience expand our hearts—does it increase our capacity for love, empathy, generosity, and compassion? Third, does it lead to human flourishing? Does it call us beyond our individualism and into a more robust humanity that joins God in the healing and transformation of the world? If an experience does these things, we can have confidence and conviction that we are being invited by God to take another step on the path of transformation.

Week 2: The Rhythm of Rest
Genesis 2:1–3; Exodus 20:8–11

For in six days the LORD *made heaven and earth, the sea, and all that is in them, but rested the seventh day; therefore the* LORD *blessed the Sabbath day and consecrated it. (Exodus 20:11)*

It's interesting that the Bible begins with a story of creation that culminates in a particular pattern, a rhythm that grounds creation in a consistent tempo of work and rest, creating and ceasing. And yet, for many of us, the consistent answer to, "How are you doing?" is some version of, "I'm good. Just really busy!"

It's almost like busyness is a badge of honor. It's how we prove our worth, that we matter, that our lives have contributed something meaningful to the world. And yet, at the same time, most of the people I talk to will say, in their most honest moments, that they are actually a bit exhausted. Are we wearing ourselves out trying to prove something that we never really needed to prove?

Scripture begins with a rhythm of work and rest, and that becomes a rhythm for God's people. There's a period of activity and then recovery. We work, and then we rest and play. This pattern, according to Scripture, is not a bug or flaw but how we were created to live.

Rest is a reminder of our humanity. The story of creation in Genesis 1 insists that being human is a good—very good—thing to be. Rest is an invitation to ground ourselves in our humanity, in our limits. We aren't machines. We aren't human doings but human beings. We aren't here to simply produce things. It's the exact opposite, actually. Yes, we have work to do, but we are also here to love, enjoy, laugh, and experience the goodness of life. We aren't designed to eat every meal in the car in transit from one thing to the next thing. We need moments for slow, long meals; taking in sunsets; and taking deep, grateful breaths that remind us that being alive in this world is a gift.

As a spiritual practice, rest enables us to recover and recharge, it opens our hearts to the gift of being alive, and it reconnects us with the rhythm of the Divine that is already found within the intention of our humanity.

Rest is about self care, which is also part of our tradition. When asked what is the Greatest Commandment, Jesus called our attention to the importance of loving not only God and our neighbor but also ourselves. Self-care is bound up in the way we love others. Similar to the instructions we receive on an airplane, putting our oxygen mask on first is not selfish but part of how we can better show up to love and serve others.

Finally, rest is about recognizing the holy that is all around us, all the time. By setting aside time for rest, we acknowledge the holiness of all time. Slowing down and being intentional about how we allocate the brief time we have creates the kind of awareness that empowers us to see that the bush is always burning, that all ground is holy ground, even if we are just waking up to that truth.

Week 3: The Rhythm of Ritual
Joshua 4:1–9

Joshua said to them, "Pass on before the ark of the LORD your God into the middle of the Jordan, and each of you take up a stone on his shoulder, according to the number of the tribes of the Israelites, so that this may be a sign among you. When your children ask in time to come, 'What do those stones mean to you?' then you shall tell them that the waters of the Jordan were cut off in front of the ark of the covenant of the LORD." (Joshua 4:5–7a)

There's a story about a woman who, when she made a roast, would always cut the ends off before placing it in a pan to cook. Eventually her daughter, who had watched this practice for years, asked why she always trimmed the ends off the roast before cooking it. The mom's response was, "That's how your grandma has always done it, so that's how I do it too." Curious, they called Grandma and asked about this now two-generations-old approach to preparing a roast. "I cut the ends off," Grandma said, "because my pan was too small."

That's how many people have experienced ritual—as something we do because we're supposed to, not necessarily because it adds meaning or value to our lives or enables our growth. Like many aspects of faith and theology, ritual means different things for different people. For some people, the word *ritual* carries the connotation of something boring and rote, activities that are more about habit or tradition than meaningful transformation. When this becomes our primary experience of ritual, we can find ourselves feeling disconnected, even frustrated, by the lack of connection and meaning.

For others, ritual has been used against them as a tool for controlling and mediating belonging—determining who is in and who is out by only allowing those with the "correct" beliefs to participate. In these cases, the access to the important rituals shared by a community is blocked off by the gatekeepers of the community. These problematic ways of experiencing and viewing ritual have left many wondering why they should even bother.

However, when we dismantle the boundaries and remove the rigidity of our ritual practices, they can be a source of deep meaning and connection, forming a type of community memory that makes transformation possible.

In our text from Joshua, the Israelites had just completed forty years of wandering in the wilderness and entered the land of promise. To mark the immensity of that moment, the tribes of Israel were told to stack stones, to essentially create a kind of monument or marker that would be a reminder of their experience and would help future generations hold on to that collective memory. In other words, they were given a ritual to ground and process their story. Similarly, Communion and baptism are rituals of the Christian tradition that hold deep meaning for many people, that express important convictions of our faith, and that ground us in both the memory and hope of our tradition.

Ritual, through this lens, is not about magic but about meaning making. It serves as a way to remember, reflect, and recommit to our values and build belonging together. Further, rather than being reserved for extraordinary circumstances or settings, rituals can be found in the everydayness of life—sharing meals with friends, sipping a cup of coffee at sunrise, walking the dog, playing pickleball . . . you get the idea. What makes a ritual meaningful and helpful is that we find it to be meaningful and helpful. It does not have to be dictated or controlled by religious institutions; it can be personal, communal, and even spontaneous.

As part of this sermon, consider inviting your congregation to think about their own day-to-day lives and the rituals that, even if they are unaware, help them feel grounded throughout the day. To do that, begin by sharing some of the rituals that you find personally meaningful and transformative.

Week 4: The Rhythm of Prayer
1 Thessalonians 5:17

Pray without ceasing. (1 Thessalonians 5:17)

Prayer is a challenging topic to address, because people are usually not neutral about what prayer is or means. For many, prayer is central and essential to their lives. On the other hand, others feel frustrated by prayer, experiencing it as another opportunity to feel guilt and shame over not praying right or enough. These words from Paul in 1 Thessalonians don't really help that, either. How does one "pray without ceasing" anyway? That depends on what we think prayer actually is.

It's important to begin by acknowledging the ways that some approaches to prayer can be or feel problematic. Offering a few examples of what prayer should *not* be can make people in your congregation feel seen and safe to really explore what prayer can become for them.

First, prayer is not a substitute for action. Instead of taking meaningful action in the fact of suffering, we offer clichés like "thoughts and prayers." This has increasingly diminished the value of prayer for many people. Second, using prayer requests as an excuse to share private information is just gossip. Prayer should never be used as a weapon of shame, as when someone says, "I'll be praying for you" in the context of disagreement, especially over a theological issue.

My last caution or challenge relates to prayer as intervention. There are many opinions and understandings of how or if God responds to prayer. Believing that God will answer our prayers if we just say or do the right thing can create many problems, however, whether or not things end up the way we'd hoped. For prayer to be helpful, it has to be about more than seeking the occasional miracle.

For prayer to be a meaningful spiritual practice that helps us pay attention to our relationship with God, our neighbor, and ourselves, we must first name that prayer isn't always about saying specific words with our eyes closed.

Prayer is a posture, a way of focusing and opening ourselves up to God. Instead of being about how we pray—eyes open or closed, kneeling or standing, how often or for how long—this understanding of prayer sees Paul's call to "pray without ceasing" as a posture of the heart, an attitude that shapes how we show up in the world every day. As such, prayer can be a different experience for everyone.

Prayer can be about naming and being present to our feelings, making us aware of the things we think and feel about which we were previously unaware.

Prayer can be an act of solidarity, raising others to the top of our hearts and minds. Praying for others is an act of love, and as we think of them and their well-being, it can even move us to action like checking on them and showing up for them.

Prayer can be about hearing as well as being heard. The hallmark of any good and meaningful conversation is that it includes listening as well as talking, and two-way communication nurtures connection to and intimacy with God.

Prayer can be about aligning our hearts and minds with the vision and values of Jesus. For example, in the Lord's Prayer, Jesus teaches us to pray that our lives will be aligned with the values of the kingdom of God and to participate in making that reality come to the world.

Week 5: The Rhythm of Forgiveness
Matthew 5:21–24

So when you are offering your gift at the altar, if you remember that your brother or sister has something against you, leave your gift there before the altar and go; first be reconciled to your brother or sister, and then come and offer your gift. (Matthew 5:23–24)

We don't often think of forgiveness as a spiritual practice. It's usually framed as something we're just supposed to do, a box we at least pretend to check in order to be a good person. According to Jesus's steaching, however, forgiveness isn't a solo sport, and it's not just about the other person. Forgiveness has the power to shape and transform the forgiver.

In this text from Matthew, Jesus is not minimizing the law but deepening it. He's saying that murder doesn't start with a physical act—it starts in the heart, with anger, dehumanization, and contempt, so we need to address those inner issues before we ever get close to the point of violence. Jesus is saying something like: Be careful. When we harbor anger and unforgiveness, it has the potential to be as transformative as forgiveness can be, just in the other direction. If forgiveness expands and softens the heart, then a refusal to forgive does the opposite; it shrinks and hardens our heart.

Jesus then makes this radical suggestion: Tending to the fractures in our relationships is so vital that it would be better to pause worshipping God in order to go attempt reconciliation. For Jesus, human relationships are sacred. The rhythm of forgiveness and reconciliation is as vital to our spiritual health as worshipping and offering our gifts to God. Just as many of us make communal worship a regular rhythm of life, so should we tend to our human relationships.

Forgiveness is a journey, not a quick fix. It's not a thirty-minute sitcom where everything happens and is resolved by the end of the episode. It's a messy process, which means it takes time.

Forgiveness shapes us. It's not just a surface-level act. It has the capacity to work on us and in us at the deepest level, changing the way we show up in and see the world.

Forgiveness is about setting ourselves free. It's not just about the person who hurt us. It's about our own transformation and healing too. It's about refusing to let the resentment fester and shape who we become.

Forgiveness doesn't always equal reconciliation. Sometimes, relationships can't or shouldn't go back to what they were. In those cases, we can set firm boundaries and at the same time release bitterness and experience our own healing. Forgiveness doesn't mean forgetting (we often can't forget nor can we control what pops into our brain) or excusing the harm that has been done. We also cannot force others to reconcile with us. While meaningful and important when possible, forgiveness does not depend on reconciliation or the other person.

Forgiveness makes a new reality possible. When we choose forgiveness, we step out of cycles of retribution and into new possibilities for the future. We also become more compassionate, more generous, and more free. Like the other spiritual practices we've explored, forgiveness is a doorway to personal and communal transformation that brings sustaining rhythm to our lives.

Rest

A three-part series on practicing Sabbath.

CAROL CAVIN-DILLON

Series Overview

We live in a culture that tells us our worth lies in what we produce, what we achieve, how busy we are, or how much money we make. Our technology makes us feel as if we must always be available and working twenty-four hours a day, seven days a week. No wonder that *rest* feels like a pipe dream or luxury, and the biblical concept of *Sabbath* seems even more elusive. Spending several weeks with the concept of rest is a simple but invaluable reminder to congregations that our worth lies not in our activity and output but in our very being as children of God. This series emphasizes that rest is not only God's intention for us but a countercultural stand against the forces that would use up our bodies and discard our souls. Far from another task on the to-do list, rest is a different way of seeing the world.

	Sermon Title	Focus Scripture	Theme
Week 1	Rest by Design	Genesis 1:26–2:3	Rhythms of work and rest are built into the pattern of creation.
Week 2	Rest as Resistance	Exodus 5:1–9	Sabbath rest resists the voice of "Pharaoh," who would tell us we cannot stop working.
Week 3	Jesus as Sabbath	Matthew 11:28–12:14	The ultimate resting place of our lives is in relationship with Christ.

Tips and Ideas for This Series

Invite your congregation to commit to a Sabbath practice for the three weeks of this series, for example, taking a walk, spending ten minutes in silence, reading sacred poetry, fasting from technology for a set time every day, etc. They can share their experiences in small groups or keep a journal. For worship, you could offer a restful image to go on the bulletin covers or in your newsletter graphics for the three weeks of this series, with the phrase, "I will give you rest." You could also carve out time for silence each week in worship, perhaps after the sermon or during the time of invitation at the end.

Week 1: Rest by Design
Genesis 1:26–2:3

Thus the heavens and the earth were finished and all their multitude. On the sixth day God finished the work that he had done, and he rested on the seventh day from all the work that he had done. So God blessed the seventh day and hallowed it, because on it God rested from all the work that he had done in creation. (Genesis 2:1–3)

There is a popular area of research and marketing today that focuses on sleep. Sleep experts tell us that good rest is essential for good health and quality of life, but that is not news to the people of God. Our Scriptures tell us that, from the very beginning, we were created both for work and for rest, for doing and for being. Rest is essential to life.

Rest is also essential to our relationship with God. In the creation story of Genesis 1, God declared creation good and then chose to rest on the seventh day. In other words, God designed creation with a regular pattern of rest. And if God can stop working and creating and producing in order to rest, what makes us think we can't?

Throughout the Old and New Testaments, we are reminded of the importance of keeping the Sabbath. The Fourth of the Ten Commandments tells us to "remember the Sabbath" and allow ourselves and those for whom we are responsible to rest. This Fourth Commandment is the linchpin between the commandments toward God and the commandments toward others. In some ways, keeping Sabbath—finding patterns of rest—is central to our relationship with God and with neighbor. In Leviticus 25, God even commands us to let the land rest every seventh year. We are invited to look at the earth as something to be tended and enjoyed, not worked to death and exploited for our own consumption.

The way our culture is structured today makes it hard for many to take a whole Sabbath day, especially one that falls every week on a

Sunday. Many professions call on people to work on Sundays. However, we are called to find regular patterns of rest, when we stop producing, stop working, stop checking email, stop being on, and simply allow ourselves to be. Rather than be legalistic about keeping the Sabbath, how can we hear a gracious invitation to rest?

Taking time to rest is a spiritual practice that helps us put our trust in God. We trust that God will keep the world running while we take a break. It's a reminder that we are not in control and are not the center of the universe. Rest is not only good for our bodies; it is essential to our souls.

Week 2: Rest as Resistance
Exodus 5:1–9

But the king of Egypt said to them, "Moses and Aaron, why are you taking the people away from their work? Get to your labors!" (Exodus 5:4)

As we consider God's invitation to rest throughout the Scriptures, it is helpful to ask ourselves, "What keeps me from resting? What are the voices in our heads, in our culture, in our systems, and in our world that try and tell us that we cannot rest?" We live in a culture that tells us our worth lies in what we produce, what we achieve, how busy we are, or how much money we make. Our technology makes us feel as if we must always be available and working twenty-four hours a day, seven days a week. We often internalize this pressure and are afraid that if we take time off to worship and rest or if we turn off our devices and make ourselves unavailable, we will be considered lazy. Even worse, we will not know who we are.

How do we resist society's pressures and set aside time to rest and be present to God?

In the fifth chapter of Exodus, the Hebrew people are enslaved in Egypt, and the heavy hand of their oppressors is getting heavier. Moses approaches Pharaoh and asks that the people be allowed time away to worship their God, but Pharaoh refuses. By examining Pharaoh's reaction, we can hear the voices that pressure us today. First, Pharaoh asks, "Who is this God?" Pharaoh is threatened by the Hebrew people's allegiance to Yahweh. The Hebrew people longed for time away from their work to worship God. But their faith in God was a threat to Pharaoh, who set himself up as a god. If the people worshipped Yahweh, it meant that they were not worshipping Pharaoh. Here we see the economy of God and the economy of Pharaoh in opposition, and Pharaoh's economy does not allow rest.

Rest

As the conversation between Moses and Pharaoh continues, Pharaoh complains, "Why are you separating the people from their work?" In Pharaoh's economy, the people *are* their work. They have no identity outside of what they produce. In God's economy, the people find their identity in God.

Toward the end of the text, Pharaoh calls the people lazy and retaliates by making their labor even harder. The voice of Pharaoh commands that they work without rest, and when they try to make time and space for God in their lives, they are accused of being lazy.

How does Pharaoh show up in our world today? How might our practices of Sabbath—our choosing to set apart time for God and time for rest—help us resist the idolatry of work, success, and busyness?

Although the king of Egypt died thousands of years ago, the voice of Pharaoh still speaks loudly in our culture, in our lives, and in our own heads. Walter Brueggemann's book *Sabbath as Resistance* and Tricia Hersey's book *Rest Is Resistance* suggest that practices of rest, worship, and Sabbath help us resist the voice of Pharaoh in our day and time. Rest is a way of resisting oppression. Rest allows us to find our identity in God above all else. Rest orients our lives to God and away from other things that try to claim our loyalty and tell us who we are.

Week 3: Jesus as Sabbath
Matthew 11:28–12:14

"Come to me, all you who are weary and are carrying heavy burdens, and I will give you rest. Take my yoke upon you, and learn from me, for I am gentle and humble in heart, and you will find rest for your souls. For my yoke is easy, and my burden is light." (Matthew 11:28–30)

In first-century Judaism, there was an ongoing, robust conversation among religious leaders about the Sabbath. While the Fourth Commandment states clearly that God's people should do no work on the Sabbath day, the rest of the Torah does not make it clear exactly what qualifies as work. In Jesus's day, there would have been some rabbis who agreed with his interpretation of Sabbath practices and others who took a stricter approach like those we see in Matthew 12. Exploring this conflict can help us deepen our understanding of what Sabbath rest means for us and how it is meant to be a gift and not a burden.

In this text, we find Jesus and his disciples walking through a wheat field on the Sabbath day. When some of his disciples pluck grain and eat it, some nearby Pharisees accuse them of breaking Sabbath law.

Jesus responds by retelling a story from their shared history about how King David and his soldiers ate bread that was forbidden by the rules. They broke those rules because they were hungry and were on a mission.

Later that day, Jesus offends these Pharisees again when he heals a man in the synagogue on the Sabbath. It's important to emphasize that the Pharisees and Jesus would all have agreed that, had the man's life been in danger, he should have been healed; but for non-life-threatening situations, these leaders believed that his condition could be cured after sundown.

Jesus uses both situations to teach about the meaning of the Sabbath. It is meant to be a gift to humankind, not a burden. When faced with hungry bellies or illness, we should not hold a set of rules as more important than human flourishing.

Are there ways that we make rules more important than human flourishing? Are there ways that we turn our relationship with God into a checklist of good behavior, into a set of rules to be obeyed? Do we pressure ourselves to do all the right things in order to earn God's favor? How do we become legalistic, making our relationship with God more transactional than transformative?

As we consider what it means to practice Sabbath rest in our daily lives without getting legalistic, the opening verses of this text pack a profound truth: When Jesus says, "Come to me, all you who are weary, . . . and I will give you rest. Take my yoke upon you, and learn from me, . . . and you will find rest for your souls." Could it be that Jesus himself is the Sabbath?

The gift of Sabbath rest cannot be found in a set of rules or stringent practices too burdensome to keep. Rather, the gift of sacred rest can be found in relationship with him. And all our practices of rest simply open space in our lives to abide with him, the Lord of the Sabbath.

The Power of Powerlessness

A six-part series on how Jesus defines power as compassion, not coercion.

BENJAMIN R. CREMER

Series Overview In a time when the misuse and abuse of power is on full display in religious and political circles alike, it is critical for the church to renew its understanding of how Jesus used power and how he called his followers to embody a way of power that is so different from the powers of this world. Where the emperors of this world choose coercion to maintain their empires, Jesus ushers in his kingdom through the power of compassion and self-sacrificial love. At the conclusion of this sermon series, the hope is that hearers come away with a better understanding of how they can embody Jesus's way of making powerful change in the world right where they are.

	Sermon Title	Focus Scripture	Theme
Week 1	From All-Powerful to All-Powerless	Philippians 2:1–11	Jesus came to the world in humility and service.
Week 2	He Said No to the Power of Empire	Matthew 4:1–11	Jesus rejects the power of earthly empires out of fidelity to God.
Week 3	His Way of Power Was Rebuked by His Own	Matthew 16:22–23	Even those closest to Jesus, as Peter was, can still have the power of the world in mind rather than the power of God.
Week 4	See How They Lord Their Power over Them?	Matthew 20:20–28	Jesus critiques both the kind of power used by those in authority during his time and the kind of power his followers are still seeking.

	Sermon Title	Focus Scripture	Theme
Week 5	All Power and Authority Have Been Given unto Him	John 13:1–17	Jesus, aware that all power had been given to him, washed the disciples' feet.
Week 6	Let Everyone Be Subject to the Governing Authorities	Romans 13:1–7	Reading one of the most controversial passages through the lens of Jesus's definition of power.

Tips and Ideas for This Series

Be aware of differences in power within your congregation and acknowledge that in your preaching. Some may have the wealth and privilege that translates to power in our society; some may even be corporate executives or elected officials. Others may have multiple marginalized identities that wield less power. Emphasize how we all have some level of power, even if it is simply the power to choose our actions and have influence on the people closest to us.

John Dickson's presentation on humility is a great resource for preparing this series and also a good option for illustrating elements of your sermon with video clips. The forty-minute video can be found on the Global Leadership Network's website: https://nga.globalleadership.org/videos/leading-yourself/humilitas/.

Week 1: From All-Powerful to All-Powerless
Philippians 2:1–11

Let the same mind be in you that was in Christ Jesus,
  who, though he existed in the form of God,
  did not regard equality with God
  as something to be grasped,
but emptied himself,
  taking the form of a slave,
  assuming human likeness. (Philippians 2:5–7)

This passage is often called the "Christ hymn" because of the beautiful and poetic way it celebrates Jesus Christ's divinity, his descent to humanity, his obedience, and his exaltation. It's a central text in Christian theology, particularly regarding Christology, and is thought to be one of the earliest Christian songs or creeds. One of the most important things to note about this passage is Paul's use of the hymn as pastoral guidance for how the Philippians were to live in community together. Paul points to the very character of

Christ and urges them to mirror that character in the way they conduct themselves with one another.

With poetic precision, the hymn shows how Jesus had the highest possible position in all the cosmos, "equality with God," yet didn't see that equality as something to be exploited for his own gain. Instead, Jesus lowered himself, giving up all cosmic power to take on the role of a servant to all, going even so low as death on a cross. Because of this posture of humility, God lifted up Jesus's name to be above all other names. To be faithful in our worship to God, then, is to embody Jesus's example of humility.

A good contrast to this description of Jesus is his conversation with the rich young ruler found in all the Gospel accounts except for John (Matt. 19:16-30, Mark 10:17-31, and Luke 18:18-30). In many ways, Jesus is a mirror image of the rich, young ruler, accepting the call to give up everything for the sake of the poor and the powerless. Jesus issues the challenge to follow his example of self-sacrifice, and yet the rich, young ruler responds with the opposite behavior and (presumably) keeps his wealth and power instead. The story ends in each case with the rich man walking away disheartened by Jesus's command, leaving readers as well as the man to keep pondering the challenge.

The Christ hymn is rich with how Jesus displays God's power, not by might or coercion but by humility. Unfortunately, we live in a time with far too many examples of those in positions of power who exploit their power for their own gain. As we have seen, this lack of humility can have absolutely devastating consequences, especially for the powerless. A goal for those preaching from this passage might be to give relevant examples of the harm a lack of humility brings to our world. Who suffers when powerful people selfishly think only of their own interests? Urge people, as Paul did his hearers, to "do nothing from selfish ambition or empty conceit, but in humility regard others as better than yourselves. Let each of you look not to your own interests but to the interests of others" (Phil. 2:3-4).

Week 2: He Said No to the Power of Empire
Matthew 4:1-11

Again, the devil took him to a very high mountain and showed him all the kingdoms of the world and their glory, and he said to him, "All these I will give you, if you will fall down and worship me." Then Jesus said to him, "Away with you, Satan! for it is written,

> *'Worship the Lord your God,*
> *and serve only him.'" (Matthew 4:8-10)*

In the third temptation in the wilderness, Jesus was taken up to a high mountain where Satan showed him all the world's kingdoms and promised him power over them if he would just bow down and worship Satan. With power over the Roman Empire, Jesus could free his people from the foreign oppression that kept most of them poor and powerless.

Like all empires, the Roman Empire had developed a rigid social structure and predatory economy where those on top lived the very best life and controlled all the resources for the empire, all while those in the middle and especially the bottom were exploited to maintain the empire. Rome created idols in its own image to justify this kind of controlling power, all of which Satan was tempting Jesus to embody. If he accepted this temptation, Jesus would be worshipped just like Caesar demanded he be worshipped, but this would mean fidelity to the ways of Satan, the ways of the Beast, rather than the ways of God and the ways of the Lamb he came to be. This is why Jesus responded with Deuteronomy 6:13, "worship God alone." Worship equals fidelity.

When we read this through a collective lens in our time as Christians, we see how this passage still has such powerful relevance for us today. If we look at American Christianity as a whole, we are constantly being lulled by these same temptations of selfishness, arrogance, and the worship of power. We are being fed narratives, especially by the politicians in our time, to buy into the myth of scarcity, the impulse to use God as a justification to center ourselves above others in our society, and to control the exploitation of the empire for our own benefit and power.

As we know from the rest of the story, Jesus rejects all these temptations and goes on to live a life of generosity rather than selfishness; humility instead of arrogance; and sharing power with others, especially the most vulnerable, rather than taking power over everyone for himself.

Jesus's rejection of this temptation to exert power over others through the apparatus of the empire is a sharp contrast to the efforts of Christian nationalism, which seeks to enforce a particular brand of morality through governmental means. Instead of seeking the common good of all others, Christian nationalism seeks power and control only for itself.

This sermon gives the preacher the opportunity to show how this temptation is still alive and well in our culture today. It is a temptation to which followers of Jesus are not immune. It gives the preacher an opportunity to invite followers of Jesus to take a step back and ask how they are seeking power for and with others, like Jesus does, rather than over and against others, like the empire does. Every avenue of life, including politics, brings with it the question, "How will I use the power given to me?" Will we give into the temptation to use it for our own gain or for the sake of others?

Week 3: His Way of Power Was Rebuked by His Own
Matthew 16:13–26

And Peter took him aside and began to rebuke him, saying, "God forbid it, Lord! This must never happen to you." But he turned and said to Peter, "Get behind me, Satan! You are a hindrance to me, for you are setting your mind not on divine things but on human things."
(Matthew 16:22–23)

Peter, the one who called Jesus the Anointed One, the Messiah, just a few verses ago, was now taking Jesus aside like a child and scolding him about his prediction of the way things were going to unfold. This is quite the turn of events, wouldn't you say?

In the Old Testament, we see so often how kings would send armies to conquer their enemies and exercise power from their thrones over others. They were often seen as saviors of their nation. Just a little over a hundred years before Jesus, Judas Maccabeus was thought to possibly be the messiah. He led a successful rebellion against Rome and established independence for Jerusalem for forty-seven years before the Romans reclaimed the territory. This was the history that Peter grew up hearing about. This history informed what he expected about the messiah and the kingdom they would bring. The anointed one would mount a violent revolt and reclaim their rightful throne, taking back the nation of Israel for God.

So when Jesus predicted that he was going to suffer and die, this completely conflicted with the way Peter thought victory would come. You just can't overthrow Rome with a dead messiah. This is why Peter then rebuked Jesus for such a prediction. Peter heard him as already admitting defeat rather than describing the way of salvation.

Jesus responds to Peter's rebuke with a rebuke of his own: "Get behind me, Satan!" The rock upon which Jesus was going to build his church was being a stumbling block instead. Peter was defining Jesus's salvific work through the category of imperial power, the way of earthly kingdoms, not the kingdom of heaven. This is why Jesus commanded them not to tell anyone that he was the Messiah, because they were not understanding the kind of messiah he came to be, a messiah who gives up his life for others rather than one who takes up a throne over others.

The way empires define power and the way Jesus defines power could not be more different. Where empires define power through "us vs. them," Jesus defines power through "for and with" our neighbors. While kings of earthly empires send people to die for their kingdom, the kingdom of heaven is ushered in by Jesus laying down his life out of love for the world. Jesus shows us that compassion rather than force and control is the way God has chosen to save the world through him.

As Jesus clarifies a few verses later, "those who want to save their life will lose it, and those who lose their life for my sake will find it. For what will it profit them if they gain the whole world but forfeit their life?" (Matt. 16:25-26).

Preachers can invite their listeners to explore how this power dynamic is at the crux of so many of our issues within American Christianity today. We so often define power the way empires do, determining who the "enemy" is on any particular issue and finding a way to conquer them in order to gain victory. We define victory by way of force rather than by way of compassion and humility.

Week 4: See How They Lord Their Power over Them?
Matthew 20:20–28

"You know that the rulers of the gentiles lord it over them, and their great ones are tyrants over them. It will not be so among you, but whoever wishes to be great among you must be your servant, and whoever wishes to be first among you must be your slave." (Matthew 20:25b–27)

The Greek word we translate into "lord it over" in verse 25 is the verb *katakurieuo*, which means "to exercise authority over, overpower, and master." The Greek word we translate into "exercise authority over," also in verse 25, has the same root word *kata* but is more intense. It is the verb *katexousiazó*, which means "to *exert* authority *downward* (oppressively); to *strongly* dominate or bring *down*."

In contrast to these words, the Greek word for "servant" Jesus uses here in verse 26 is *diakonos*, a word picture of one who kicks up dust (*konis*) by moving in a hurry to minister to the needs of others. Isn't that beautiful? Lastly, the Greek word we translate into "slave" here in verse 27 is *doulos*, someone who belongs to another, without any ownership rights of their own. This term is used over 120 in the New Testament and is given the highest dignity, depicting those who willingly live under Jesus's teachings as his devoted followers. In this context, the word is referring to those who are completely devoted to others, to the disregard of their own interests, an idea Paul would later illustrate in Philippians 2. Jesus then concludes this comparison by clearly stating that he came to be a servant to all rather than someone who came to lord power over others.

These words shape Jesus's response to a very specific question brought by James and John's mother. She requests that Jesus choose her two boys as the ones who would sit on his right and his left when he came into his kingdom. She was asking that they be made second and third in command in the hierarchy of Jesus's kingdom.

Jesus responds that they do not understand what they are asking. Jesus tries to point out that they are assuming he operates in the same way all other world rulers do, but he has a different definition of power than they do. He asks them if they are willing to drink from the same cup as he does, a symbol of God's wrathful response to evil throughout the Bible. This insinuates that he was going to take on the consequences of all evil in the world on himself. They respond that they can, still not understanding Jesus clearly.

As you read through the Gospels, you get a clear picture that many of the disciples are waiting around for Jesus to get a revolution against Rome started. This is why Jesus forecasting his own death and resurrection multiple times continues to not sink in, because Jesus being crucified just doesn't remotely fit into what they thought God's plan was for their nation. Their definition of power would result in their enemies, not their messiah, being crucified. Their definition of power included an earthly kingdom, not one that isn't of this world. Their definition of power had them at the top and in charge of everyone else beneath them, not being the servants of others.

Preachers can use this contrast to invite their congregation to reflect on how Zebedee's sons might have felt about their mother's request—that they sit on Jesus's right and left when he came into power—when they stood at the cross and saw who was hanging on Jesus's right and left. Perhaps it was at that point that they really understood that they didn't know what they were asking for.

Week 5: All Power and Authority Have Been Given unto Him
John 13:1–17

Jesus, knowing that the Father had given all things into his hands and that he had come from God and was going to God, got up from supper, took off his outer robe, and tied a towel around himself. Then he poured water into a basin and began to wash the disciples' feet and to wipe them with the towel that was tied around him. (John 13:3–5)

This text is traditionally read on Maundy Thursday, the day within Holy Week when many Christians around the world reflect on the Last Supper and the events leading up to Jesus's arrest. *Maundy* comes from the Latin word *mandatum*, or "commandment," reflecting Jesus's words, "I give you a new commandment." From John 13:34–35, this new mandate or command was "Love one another. Just as I have loved you, you also should love one another. By this everyone will know that you are my disciples, if you love one another."

Yet just minutes before Jesus gives this command, John 13:3–5 tells us that Jesus reflected on the power he had from God and therefore demonstrated how power is not exempt from loving and serving others but instead leads the way! This is such a profound stream of thought. Jesus knew that God had put all things under his power, *all* things, so he got up and washed the disciples' feet. Knowing that he had all the power of the cosmos and everything was under his authority, what did he do with it? He didn't take over the Roman Empire. He didn't install himself as the rightful ruler of the world. He didn't exploit that power for his own gain. He didn't eliminate his enemies. No, he got up and washed the disciples' feet. Even though he had all cosmic power and even though he was the very Son of God, he used his power and position to compassionately serve others. This is radical.

Unfortunately, there are far too many examples in our world today of powerful people who claim to follow Jesus but who use their power to serve themselves and those like them, rather than to serve others with humility and compassion. We see those in power spending money on things or making rules that make themselves and those like them even more rich and powerful while taking money away from—or even outlawing—things that help people with less. Applied to the Last Supper, we might imagine a powerful person ordering their servant to wash the feet of prominent guests while leaving ordinary people to wipe down their own feet—or denying them water and towels altogether. Instead, Jesus hiked up his own garment and got on the floor, doing the dirty work himself.

The preacher might highlight how Jesus washing his disciples' feet like this could be considered weak or "unmanly." Washing someone's feet was a way of showing they were welcome and honored, helping them feel more clean and comfortable. What actions today help others to feel welcome and comfortable in our home, church, or community? Are powerful people facilitating those things or not? How can we each use what power we have to love people today with the same humility and care that Jesus did? Invite listeners to consider how the radical way Jesus uses all his power in this passage shapes the ways they love one another.

Week 6: Let Everyone Be Subject to the Governing Authorities
Romans 13:1–7

Let every person be subject to the governing authorities, for there is no authority except from God, and those authorities that exist have been instituted by God. Therefore whoever resists authority resists what God has appointed, and those who resist will incur judgment. (Romans 13:1–2)

This series has explored Jesus's definition of and way of using power, asking Christians today how we should use power ourselves and what we should expect of people with the most power in our society. This final sermon, then, looks at one of the Bible's most well-known and straightforward-sounding passages about power in light of Jesus's teachings and example in comparison to other Scriptures, which may seem to contradict it. Start by reviewing the ways Jesus has defined power in the previous passages that were covered. Then invite the congregation to consider how Jesus's definition of power impacts their hearing of Romans 13, commonly quoted as justification for accepting government laws and practices and supporting the individuals in power.

It can be very illuminating to show how Romans 13:1 has been misused by those in positions of power historically, including by Christians who supported the Nazi movement, chattel slavery in the United States, and apartheid in South Africa. The British also used this passage toward the new American colonies. A point of thoughtful humor could be to ask how different the history of our country would be if the founding fathers took a literal approach to Romans 13:1. It is not difficult to find examples of hypocrisy, someone calling for others to be subject to a leader or law they support but refusing to subject themselves to the authority of leaders and laws they disagree with.

Many suggest this verse means that God ordains the specific leaders in authority, which minimizes human involvement in placing people in authority over us, like in 1 Samuel 8 or in democracies like ours. The Greek word we often translate into subject or submit is the word *hupotasso*, which literally means "arrange properly underneath." The original readers would have understood this as social orderliness because God is a God of order, not chaos, so those in authority are a necessary part of maintaining that orderliness, as Paul described. To put it simply, for Paul it was important to always operate in the order established by God, including obeying the governing authorities, who were themselves lower than God's authority.

As is clear by his life, when a law of the land violated the order of God, Paul saw no problem opposing that unjust law in order to maintain the order of God. Paul would even "subject to the governing authorities" by allowing himself to be arrested without fighting back, but his ultimate goal was upholding the order and ethics of God. He'd laid out those ethics just before this, in chapter 12, sounding a lot like Jesus: love one another, show hospitality to strangers, bless your enemies, be humble, and lastly, "do not be overcome by evil, but overcome evil with good" (Rom. 12:21).

Then the very next line is Romans 13:1, "Let every person be subject to the governing authorities." Then verse 8 begins another exhortation to love your neighbor. Romans 13:1–7 is situated between and defined by love of neighbor, which prevents any attempts to use the passage to justify co-opting the state to conquer and control your neighbor in the name of Jesus. At least, it should. Reading Romans 12 and 13 together, Paul is not advocating anarchy, nor is he advocating blind obedience to the governing authorities. Rather, he is advocating an ultimate commitment to the ethics of God, which—as Jesus teaches—reveals a very different kind of power than that of human authorities.

Sensing Faith

A five-part series on deepening our faith by engaging the five senses.

RODGER NISHIOKA

Series Overview Faith is a gift of the Holy Spirit and, by God's grace, comes to us in a variety of ways. Sometimes faith comes to us through hearing: a song, a sermon, a conversation, a story. Sometimes faith comes to us through touch: a fresh breeze on a hot day, a handshake, a high five, a hug. Sometimes faith comes to us through taste: the bread and wine shared at the Lord's Table, a meal brought to a loved one, a dessert that recalls to us a celebration. Sometimes faith comes by seeing: a painting, a sculpture, a beachfront, or a mountaintop. Sometimes faith comes by smelling: incense, the pine scent from the Christmas tree, the baking of fresh bread for Communion. As beings created in the image of God, we have been gifted with a variety of senses. In this sermon series, we will explore how faith is formed and nurtured through our five primary senses.

	Sermon Title	Focus Scripture	Theme
Week 1	Tasting Faith	Matthew 5:13	Living our faith as the salt of the earth.
Week 2	Seeing Faith	Mark 8:22–26	Seeing is believing? Sometimes believing leads to seeing.
Week 3	Smelling Faith	Ephesians 4:25–5:2	Living in imitation of Christ is a pleasing fragrance to God.
Week 4	Touching Faith	Mark 5:25–34	Touch is a powerful healer.
Week 5	Hearing Faith	Matthew 13:1–23	Faith means having ears to hear what God is saying to us.

Tips and Ideas for This Series

Find ways to engage each week's focus sense in worship. For instance, tasting faith would go well on a Communion Sunday. An artist could be invited to create on a canvas during the service on seeing faith. Incense or the scent of fresh bread could be used for smelling faith. A small object like a stone or piece of cloth could be distributed for touching faith. And for hearing faith, emphasize not just the sermon and music, per usual, but also the sounds of the people gathered for worship. Consider using 1 John 1:1–4 as a guiding verse throughout the series: "We declare to you what was from the beginning, what we have heard, what we have seen with our eyes, what we have looked at and touched with our hands, concerning the word of life." (v. 1).

Week 1: Tasting Faith
Matthew 5:13

"You are the salt of the earth, but if salt has lost its taste, how can its saltiness be restored? It is no longer good for anything but is thrown out and trampled under foot." (Matthew 5:13)

It was a World Communion Sunday, and in the church where I was worshipping, that meant the trays of bread passed during Communion looked different. Instead of the usual small squares of white bread, this Sunday the tray also held pieces of tortillas, pita bread, and a dark brown bread, along with a small mound of duk, a Korean rice cake. I was sitting next to Ryan and his family. Ryan was a little guy in second grade. I knew him and his family, and it was already evident to us that Ryan liked things to be consistent. So he seemed a little perturbed when his usual bread tray was different. When he took the tray and passed it directly to his mother, I was disappointed because I thought Ryan was not going to take any bread. I was wrong. Ryan passed the tray to his mom, told her to hold it, then used both of his hands to gather one of each of the different bread offerings. He happily snacked the rest of the service. Later he told me he wished there was more juice. It made me smile.

All of us have taste memories. Some of those memories are great, and some are not. Some might be of a time when you bit into something that was more spicy, or sour, or salty than anticipated. Jesus is intentional, of course, when he tells us that we are salt of the earth. We need to remember that salt was a precious commodity in his day. We get the word *salt* from the Latin *sal*. This is also the basis for the English word *salary*. Often people will say that ancient Romans, especially soldiers, were paid in salt, but that seems to be a myth. What is absolutely true is that salt was valuable in the ancient world for its many uses. Not only was it a flavoring, it was also a preservative and a healing agent. The only way salt can lose its taste is if it is contaminated. Then it becomes useless, like dirt, according to Jesus.

So if we are the salt of the earth, what might contaminate us so that we become useless? There have been too many times when the body of Christ has lost its way. Often that happens when the church turns its attention to its own survival rather than to the proclamation of the gospel.

I was privileged to be leading a group of American seminary students in Prague and visiting with church leaders there. The Czech Republic is one of most secular countries in Europe. When we asked why, local church leaders explained that following World War II, when the Soviet Union took over the government, the communist government promised to leave the church alone if it promised to keep to itself and not cause any trouble. The church leadership agreed and, in so doing, survived but lost its moral authority. The church there lost its saltiness, its ability to flavor and preserve the Czech people with the power of the gospel. We must ask ourselves whether we are at risk of doing the same. The truth may put a bitter taste in our mouths, but consider it we must.

Week 2: Seeing Faith
Mark 8:22–26

They came to Bethsaida. Some people brought a blind man to [Jesus] and begged him to touch him. (Mark 8:22)

Bible scholars have much to say about this healing story of Jesus. Some cite this as one of Jesus's "failed" healing stories; others are not so sure. Some contemporary faith healers cite this story when they, too, cannot perform acts of healing. Some wonder if Jesus was just having an off day. As we explore how we see faith, surely a story about Jesus healing a blind man, apparently not once but twice, is a good place for us to start. And while people debate about Jesus's having to heal the man twice or not, it is good to point out that Jesus really wanted to heal this man, to help him to see. For all of us, Jesus really wants us to see.

Neuroscience tells us that of the five classic senses, seeing or sight is the sense that engages our brain the most. It is no wonder. Sociologists talk about how we have entered the visual age where the image carries more power than the written word. More than any other generation, young people today are accustomed to seeing images. For many of them, if they do not see it, they cannot comprehend it. When children and adolescents and young adults talk about being bored in church, they often mean we are not giving them enough to see.

Several years ago, I recall seeing a news report about a government program to deliver high-speed internet access to rural America. A reporter was interviewing an older gentleman in rural Mississippi. She was asking about his reaction to this new program and explained to him that he would soon be able to talk with his daughter and granddaughter in Chicago through his computer. The man looked skeptical and said, "Well, I'll see it when I believe it." He may have simply misspoken, but I'm intrigued by the idea of believing leading to seeing. I think that's what the story of Jesus healing the blind man shows to us: that seeing comes from believing. Our faith tends to evolve over time; sometimes God and God's vision for us seems blurry, "like trees, walking" around (v. 24), but with more belief, our sight becomes clearer as well. We can see the face of God in everyone we meet, see the way forward in impossible situations, and see the world God wants to build with us.

Week 3: Smelling Faith
Ephesians 4:25–5:2

Therefore be imitators of God, as beloved children, and walk in love, as Christ loved us and gave himself up for us, a fragrant offering and sacrifice to God. (Ephesians 5:1–2)

Sight may engage our brains the most, but neuroscientists tell us that the sense of smell is the strongest trigger for memory. They have determined this because, unlike the other senses, our sense of smell has a direct pathway to the brain's emotional center. The sense of smell, more than any other of our senses, triggers strong emotions and memories, both good and bad. No matter where you are or how old you are, when you get a whiff of certain smells, you are brought back to a certain time and place.

My mother was an amazing cook. I am second of four boys, and growing up, we ate pretty much everything (except lima beans). I know that we thanked her for cooking for us, but as an adult, I am sure we did not thank her enough. When she died, we all gathered at the family home to be with our dad. The day after the funeral service, I made a Japanese stew called *okazu* that Mom would make frequently because it was easy and fed her four sons and husband. When one of my brothers walked into the kitchen, he stopped in his tracks and started to cry. I went over and wrapped him in my arms, and he said, "It smells just like Mom is still here in the kitchen."

Share stories of smells that are pleasing and evoke warm memories: cookies baking in the oven, the smell of the ocean as you approach the beach, a sweater that belongs to a loved one, the perfume of one who has passed. Then share stories of smells that are not as pleasing: the smell of sewage running down an open gutter in an underserved neighborhood, a person with an open wound desperately in need of care, a home burned to the ground. What do you feel when you experience these scents? What might God feel? Explore all of this in light of the letter to the believers in Ephesus to live in a way different from how they were living and in contrast to other communities around them.

The church at Ephesus was a diverse community struggling to come together as a new group and finding it challenging to live with one another. So the letter writer laid out the rules for how they are to treat one another: putting away falsehood, wrath, stealing, and bitterness (Eph. 4:25–31). Instead, "be kind to one another, tenderhearted, forgiving one another, as God in Christ has forgiven you" (v. 32). In doing so, the goal is to imitate God, to be like Christ, who in living his life and giving up his life, became a fragrant offering and sacrifice to God. Explore what it means for us to imitate God and to be like Jesus. Imagine what it means for us, for this community, to be a pleasing fragrance to God, here and now.

Week 4: Touching Faith
Mark 5:25–34

Now there was a woman who had been suffering from a flow of blood for twelve years. . . . She had heard about Jesus and came up behind him in the crowd and touched his cloak, for she said, "If I but touch his cloak, I will be made well." (Mark 5:25, 27–28)

It is called "skin hunger," and it is a real thing. Human beings are created to need the loving, caring touch of others. We need physical contact. God made us that way. When we do not receive the touch we need, the result is skin hunger—when people experience a lack of touch from other living things.

During the COVID-19 pandemic, with so many people isolating for safety, people reported a decline in mental and emotional health. But touch is also about physical health. Science has shown that physical touch reduces stress in the body, lowers blood pressure and heart rate, and enhances the immune system. Further, with record numbers of adults living alone in the United States, especially older adults, the need for touch is increasing. When I greet worshippers after the service, there is one older woman, one of our most faithful, Betty, whom I love. She waits in line to greet me and then, as I wrap my arms around her, she says, "Oh thank you for my weekly hug. I need it." Betty lives alone in one of our retirement communities, and while I know she has friends and sees others regularly, I take our weekly hugs seriously.

Jesus touched people all the time, from the paralyzed man whose friends lowered him through the roof, to the blind and lame and sick and the little children whose parents brought them to Jesus so that he could bless them, and to Jesus washing the disciples' feet. This story of the hemorrhaging woman is an example of her need to reach out and touch even Jesus's cloak, her faith in this desperate situation, and Jesus's knowledge that "power had gone forth from him" (v. 30).

Even in her desperation and weakened state, this faithful woman had the courage and the perseverance to seek out Jesus. There were others who were no doubt touching Jesus. The disciples said as much in response to Jesus's question, "Who touched my cloak?" (v. 30). But it was when this particular woman touched Jesus's cloak that he felt power leave him, an illustration of the relationship between touch and faith.

People are becoming more conscious of things like boundaries and consent, often asking now, "May I touch you?" or "Are you a hugger?" In this spirit, let us be bold about asking others if they need a caring touch—a hand to hold, a shoulder to cry on, or a high five to celebrate. Healthy touch satisfies a deep spiritual need in us, healing wounds that may go unseen.

But the touch of faith is not only for and with other human beings. Our emotional and spiritual well-being is helped through touch with objects and other living creatures from God's creation. Fidget toys and textured stickers can help some of us feel calmer. Petting or cuddling an animal releases positive hormones the same way human touch does. Worshippers in some faith traditions have beads and other objects to touch while praying, and others receive the comfort of knowing they are prayed over through such gifts as a prayer shawl or quilt. Let us never underestimate the healing power of touch.

Week 5: Hearing Faith
Matthew 13:1–23

"If you have ears, hear!" (Matthew 13:9)

Often when I am waiting for the live stream of a worship service to begin, there will be a graphic welcoming me to worship and explaining that worship will begin soon. During that time, I can hear the congregation gathering. It is a lovely sound. I hear bits and pieces of people greeting one another along with laughter. They are the sounds of friends gathering and of a people preparing to worship.

There are sounds to worship, including but also beyond what is included in the order of worship. We assume that people know the ritual and reasoning of our worship, but that is not always true for everyone. So we would do well to discuss the elements of the spoken and sung word in worship, from the call to worship to the confession of sin and the assurance of pardon. I remember being in a worship service where we confessed our sins and there was no assurance of pardon. I felt disoriented for the rest of the service. I found out later the lay liturgist, out of nervousness, simply skipped that part, which was certainly understandable, but then the pastor did not step in and pardon us. I remember being surprised at how much I missed that assurance.

I once shared with my congregation about my process of prayer and study and practicing the sermon before I preach it. People were intrigued, especially when I said that I hoped people were not just listening to me but also praying for me during the sermon. One Sunday, I interviewed our choir director and our organist about how they prepare and what they hope happens when we are singing hymns and when the choir is singing during the prelude and postlude. People were fascinated by what our church musicians shared and by their own deep confessions of faith. Some thought it was just a job for our organist especially, and they were moved to learn it was truly a ministry.

So much of our worship is centered on hearing—some would say too much. Jesus relied on hearing too. He preached and taught a lot. This text in Matthew is a prime example of that. In verse 9, he says, "If you have ears, hear!" Then he goes on later to quote the prophet Isaiah about not seeing and not hearing and then blesses those who actually do hear. In explaining his parable, Jesus says the seed represents the "word of the kingdom" (v. 19) and the various outcomes that come from how that word is heard, received, and understood. There is more to hear from God than the words spoken or sung in worship or read from Scripture. As the United Church of Christ says in its provocative tagline, "God is still speaking." The challenge for believers in every time and place is whether we have ears to hear.

Christian Living

All In

A four-part series on what it means to go all in with our hearts, hands, resources, and future as an act of whole-life stewardship.

JOSEPH YOO

Series Overview

We often hedge our bets with God. We want to trust . . . but only up to a point. We want to give, but only what we're sure we won't miss.

But when God gave, God went all in. God didn't hold back.

This stewardship series explores what it means for us to live with that same kind of bold generosity. What if we stopped compartmentalizing our hearts, our time, our resources, and our futures and instead laid it all on the table?

Over four weeks, we'll examine how to move from caution to commitment, fear to freedom, and passive belief to passionate living. Because when we're all in, we begin to discover just how much God can do through us and with us.

	Sermon Title	Focus Scripture	Theme
Week 1	All In with Our Hearts	Matthew 22:36–40	God wants your whole heart, not just your Sunday best.
Week 2	All In with Our Hands	John 13:1–17	Your time and talents are meant to bless others generously.
Week 3	All In with Our Resources	Mark 10:17–31	We're not entitled to anything; we're entrusted with everything.
Week 4	All In with Our Future	Luke 5:1–11	Trusting Jesus means letting go and stepping into the unknown.

Tips and Ideas for This Series

Use bold imagery like a poker chip with "ALL IN" stamped across it or any imagery that evokes commitment: sky diving, an anchor, roots of plants/trees, a tattoo needle, an image of an empty boat and fishing nets left behind, etc. Consider having a visual response wall where congregants can write what area of their life they're going to go all in on. During the offertory, feature video testimonies of people talking about trust and generosity. You might even consider hosting a one-time "Day of Service" or "Giving Sunday" to help the community put this series into practice in a tangible way.

Week 1: All In with Our Hearts
Matthew 22:36–40

"You shall love the Lord your God with all your heart and with all your soul and with all your mind." (Matthew 22:37)

When Jesus is asked to name the Greatest Commandment, he doesn't blink. He doesn't hesitate. He doesn't get philosophical. He just says it plainly: "Love the Lord your God with all your heart and with all your soul and with all your mind." No disclaimers. No fine print. Just *everything*.

And if we're being honest, maybe it is that *everything* that gets us.

More often than not, we seem to be fine with giving God parts of our lives: the Sunday morning part, the before-meals prayer part, the help-me-I'm-overwhelmed part.

But to give God everything—our desires, our worries, our priorities, our habits, our future, our past—that's a real big ask.

It's also the starting line of stewardship.

Stewardship isn't just about what we put in the offering plate. It's about what—or who—owns our heart. Before we talk about time, talents, or treasures, we have to talk about love. The kind of love that reorients how we live and what we value.

Stewardship begins not in the wallet but in the heart. And not just some or parts of the heart. Jesus says *all*.

If we give everything else but withhold our hearts, we're completely missing the point. Because love—sacrificial love—reshapes what we do with our time, our energy, our priorities, and, yes, even our money.

That's why Jesus doesn't start with rules. Jesus starts with relationship. Not spreadsheets, but surrender.

Perhaps we have been conditioned to compartmentalize everything. There's our "God stuff," our "family stuff," our "work stuff," our "church stuff," our "friends-outside-of-church stuff," and our "financial stuff." When one compartment starts bleeding into the others, we start to panic.

Jesus never offers us a neat and tidy sorting system. Jesus wants it all. Not to guilt us, but he calls us to love because that's where life starts. God wants us all in, not to burden us but to free us. Free us from fear. Free us from chasing false gods. Free us from measuring worth in net gains instead of grace.

The invitation to be all in with our hearts is an invitation to stop living fragmented and disintegrated lives. It's a call to integrity, to integration. When we love God with all our heart, soul, and mind, we stop treating God like a consultant we check in with occasionally. We start living like God is our source, our center, our beginning, and our end.

And that is freeing. This does not mean we'll never struggle. Nor does this mean that all of our doubts will instantly and permanently disappear. But it means we've staked our lives on something—and someone—bigger than our circumstances.

When God has our heart, fear loses its grip. Scarcity loses its voice. And love starts to have an impact on how we live, how we give, and who we become.

This week, the question isn't, "What do you give?" nor is it, "How much are you willing to give?" The question of the week is, "Whom do you love?" And if it's God—truly God—then everything else starts to flow from that source.

A heart all in for God will lead to living a life all in for God too.

Week 2: All In with Our Hands
John 13:1–17

"So if I, your Lord and Teacher, have washed your feet, you also ought to wash one another's feet. For I have set you an example, that you also should do as I have done to you." (John 13:14–15)

On the night Jesus was betrayed, he had every reason to be distracted. The weight of the cross was bearing down. The pain, the abandonment, the injustice he was about to endure—all of it loomed large.

And yet, instead of being consumed by fear or sorrow, Jesus knelt down, took up a towel, and began to wash his disciples' feet.

He stooped on purpose. The One who spoke the cosmos into being got down into the grime. One by one, he moved from disciple to disciple, gently washing dust-covered feet, even Judas. Especially Judas. He knew betrayal was coming. Still, he served him with the same care, love, and tenderness.

This moment wasn't just humility. It was holy. It was the embodiment of love in motion. And then Jesus said, "You also ought to wash one another's feet." This wasn't about hygiene or customs or rituals. It was about the heart. About posture. About what it looks like to live as people who steward what God has given us—starting with our hands.

We often associate stewardship with giving money. But stewardship is much broader. It's about using everything God has entrusted to us—including our bodies, our time, and our energy—for the good of others and the glory of God. Stewardship means showing up with your sleeves rolled up and your heart wide open.

Being all in with our hands means living a life of active service. It means being willing to do what others overlook. It's choosing to send the text, cook the meal, carry the box, babysit the kid, take out the trash, or stay late to clean up—because love isn't just something we feel. It's something we do.

Sometimes we don't serve because we think our offering is too small to matter. But the kingdom of God has never been about flashy gestures. It's about faithfulness. It's about doing the next right thing with whatever we've got. Whether your hands are strong or shaky, clean or calloused, they're capable of holy work.

There's a reason the early church grew. It was not through slick marketing or excellent programming. The early church grew through radical love. People noticed when Christians cared for the sick, fed the hungry, welcomed the outsider, and treated enemies like neighbors. That kind of service flips the world's logic upside down. That kind of love gets under your nails and into your calendar.

This week, we ask: What are our hands doing? Are they serving? Are they healing? Are they creating? Are they giving?

Or have they been idle, fearful, or clenched in self-preservation?

To be all in is to echo Jesus, not only with our words but with our actions—with our lives.

When we go all in with our hands, we start looking less like consumers of grace and more like carriers of it. Because sometimes the clearest sermon we'll ever preach is what we do with our hands.

Week 3: All In with Our Resources
Mark 10:17–31

Jesus, looking at him, loved him and said, "You lack one thing; go, sell what you own, and give the money to the poor . . . then come, follow me." (Mark 10:21)

The rich, young man runs to Jesus with urgency and reverence, falling to his knees and asking, "What must I do to inherit eternal life?"

He's done the right things, followed the rules, and appears genuinely eager. But Jesus, looking at him with love, sees what's missing.

"You lack one thing," Jesus says. "Go, sell what you own, give to the poor, and follow me."

And just like that, the man walks away grieving.

It's one of the most haunting moments in the Gospels—not because Jesus is harsh but because he's honest. He knows this man isn't just wealthy—he's owned by his wealth. And Jesus doesn't want to take his joy; he wants to set him free. He wants him to live abundantly, not anxiously.

That's the core of stewardship: freedom. Not control. Not guilt. Not manipulation. Freedom to trust. Freedom to release. Freedom to live unburdened.

When we talk about being all in with our resources, we're not talking about giving out of obligation. We're talking about a posture of trust. Of loosening our grip. Of recognizing that what we have was never really ours to begin with. Everything we have is a gift. And every gift is an opportunity, not to hoard but to bless.

Stewardship is not about percentages. It's about participation in what God is doing. It's about shifting our mindset from ownership to trusteeship, from scarcity to abundance, from fear to faith, and from mine to God's.

And that's hard in a world where financial anxiety is real. Most of us carry money wounds—whether from seasons of lack or fear of never having enough. We're taught to hold tight. Save more. Secure ourselves. Build bigger barns (see Luke 12:16-21). But Jesus invites us to open our hands. Not recklessly, but faithfully, generously. With eyes fixed not on what we're losing but on what we're gaining and what we're joining.

The rich, young man's problem wasn't his wealth. It was his inability to imagine a life beyond it. Jesus didn't want his money. He wanted his heart. But the two were so tangled up, the man couldn't let go of one without feeling like he'd lose the other.

What about us?

Being all in with our resources means looking at what we've been given—income, time, assets, relationships, influence—and asking: How can I use this to reflect God's heart? What would it mean to treat this paycheck, this home, this account, this moment not as mine but as something I've been entrusted to steward?

When we live with that kind of freedom, generosity becomes less about sacrifice and more about alignment. Our giving aligns with our values. Our spending aligns with God's kingdom. And we stop asking, "How much do I have to give?" and start wondering, "How much more can I be a part of?"

Because when we go all in with our resources, we don't lose. It's actually when we begin to live. That's the invitation: to loosen our grip so that God can use our hands.

Week 4: All In with Our Future
Luke 5:1–11

When they had brought their boats to shore, they left everything and followed him. (Luke 5:11)

The story of the disciples' call begins with failure. They've been fishing all night, and they've caught nothing. They're tired, frustrated, maybe even questioning their ability, their livelihood, and their future. And then Jesus shows up—on the shoreline, in their weariness—with an inconvenient request: try again.

Same nets. Same lake. But this time, with him.

Reluctantly, Peter casts the nets. And then, an abundance. So many fish, the nets begin to break. So much grace, it overwhelms them. Peter drops to his knees, undone. And that's when Jesus makes the call: "Do not be afraid; from now on you will be catching people" (v. 10).

This isn't just a miracle story. It's a surrender story. The disciples walk away from the catch of a lifetime. They leave behind income, stability, and familiarity. They leave their nets, their boats, and even the fish. They go all in.

That's what this week is about: going all in with our lives. Not just with what we have but with who we are and where we're going. It's about stewardship as surrender—not only of money or time but of our future, our identity, and our direction.

Most of us spend our lives trying to secure what's next. We build safety nets. We chase stability. We create five-year plans. We try to control outcomes. We do everything we can to reduce risk and increase certainty. But following Jesus often calls us to let go of the blueprint. It invites us to step into the unknown, not recklessly but faithfully.

Being all in with our lives means moving into our future with open hands. It means trusting that even when the path is unclear, the One who calls us is trustworthy. It means saying yes before we know where it will lead, just because Jesus is the one asking.

It means that while we may not know what the future holds, we know who holds it.

The disciples could've stayed with the fish. They could've justified it. "We'll follow later." "We'll tithe from the profits." "We'll build a ministry fund." But they didn't. They saw the abundance and still walked away because the real miracle wasn't the fish. It was the invitation.

This kind of surrender can feel risky. It may not make sense to others. But it's the same risk God took with us: giving everything out of love, trusting that love could change the world. That's what makes it holy.

So what future are you clinging to? What plan are you unwilling to release? What part of your life is still waiting for a full yes?

Jesus doesn't just call us to believe—he calls us to follow. To go. To step forward even when we're uncertain. Because when we trust him with our future, we find a life that's bigger, bolder, and more beautiful than anything we could've planned ourselves.

This week, ask: What might I need to leave behind to follow more freely? What possibility have I been too afraid to consider? And what might happen if I said yes—not later, not someday, but now?

You Be the Judge . . . or Not

A five-part series about judging other people, how to manage this impulse, and when and how we should (or should not) judge.

COLBY MARTIN

Series Overview The impulse to judge other people is part and parcel of what it means to be human. We don't need to be taught this behavior; it just arises in us naturally. In the creation story, the ability to judge seems to be the one thing God withheld from us. Yet here we are, constantly gorging on the fruit of the knowledge of good and evil. It's not all bad news, though. Jesus and Paul offer guidance on discerning the time and place for proper judgment, but be warned: It's not for the faint of heart.

	Sermon Title	Focus Scripture	Theme
Week 1	The One Thing God Held Back	Genesis 2:15–17; 3:1–7	Exploring God's warning against the fruit of the knowledge of good and evil.
Week 2	When Specks Look like Logs	Matthew 7:1–5	Do not judge others without first dealing with your own stuff.
Week 3	Judge like Jesus	Matthew 23:13–33	Speaking truth to power and calling out religious hypocrisy.
Week 4	Judge like Paul	1 Corinthians 5:1–13	Dealing with Christians in our community who threaten the health of the whole.
Week 5	Holding Space for Different Beliefs	Romans 14	Creating community where we respect diversity of beliefs.

Tips and Ideas for This Series

This series tries to balance a tricky subject, so anything you can do to help hold and illustrate the nuance will be helpful. By nature, judging is about separating into categories—a binary of right and wrong—so using imagery that suggests paradox and spectrums can convey the inadvisability of judgmental postures and attitudes. By the end of the series, hopefully your congregation will have a fuller picture of what judging is and how (rarely) they should utilize it.

Consider surveying your congregation on some nonessential aspects of the Christian faith (for example, the frequency of Communion, infant vs. believer's baptism, styles of music for worship). Then during the later sermons of the series, reveal some of the findings. This will show your community how much diversity of thought exists all around them and hopefully invite them to hold better space for those who think differently.

Week 1: The One Thing God Held Back
Genesis 2:15–17; 3:1–7

And the L<small>ORD</small> *God commanded the man, "You may freely eat of every tree of the garden, but of the tree of the knowledge of good and evil you shall not eat, for in the day you eat of it you shall die." (Genesis 2:16–17)*

The narrative in Genesis 2 explains how God created humans and placed them in a lush garden with every provision needed for flourishing. All things were made available to the first humans, except one thing. One thing God held back. "Don't eat from the tree of the knowledge of good and evil," God told the first humans. But why?

This story can sometimes be misremembered to think that God prohibited humans from eating from "the tree of good and evil," as though God wanted humans to remain perfect. But the fruit God said was off-limits was a fruit that granted the *knowledge* of good and evil—the ability to discern, to separate right from wrong. That's the thing of which God seems to have said, "Hmm, I'd like to keep that for myself, please. No offense, but I'm not sure I trust you with that."

In other words, judgment is the domain of God and God alone.

When you read how the story unfolds from there, how Adam and Eve eat of the fruit and suddenly see themselves and each other in a new light (that is, naked), an even sharper insight emerges about the nature of judgment. There is a difference between judging someone's actions as good or evil and judging someone's identity—their core personhood—as good or evil.

While God had called humanity "very good," they now looked down and across and decided, "We must cover up." Where they had previously felt safety and acceptance, they felt shame and fear.

"Who told you that you were naked?" (3:11). God asked the hiding humans, now intimately aware of their changed condition. The couple's new insight into right and wrong, good and bad, distorted their views of each other.

When it comes to our identity and the identity of every other human, the judgment has already been made: You are God's beloved child, and in you, God is well pleased. There can be a place for judging actions (and we'll talk about that later in the series), but judging the identity of others is absolutely outside our domain—that is for God and God alone.

As we engage with people out in the world (as well as online), let's take with us the story of creation and the divine command to resist judging one another. May we hear God's voice say to us, "Here in this garden you are invited to all sorts of beautiful and lovely things. Eat and drink whatever you'd like. But do not dare start calling my children something other than what I have already declared them to be. That has no place here."

Call it *original sin* or something else, but humans are clearly predisposed to judging the behaviors and actions of ourselves and of others. That kind of judgment makes sense, and we wouldn't survive as a species without it. We'll see in coming weeks, though, that it is a very nuanced, nonintuitive, even sacred thing to make a judgment, and great care must be exercised. Therefore, we begin by establishing the difference between judging identity and behaviors, for only one of those is something we should ever even consider.

Week 2: When Specks Look like Logs
Matthew 7:1–5

"Do not judge, so that you may not be judged. For the judgment you give will be the judgment you get, and the measure you give will be the measure you get." (Matthew 7:1–2)

This week's sermon discusses the complexities and sacredness of judging others. Judging the actions of others (and not their identity, as we established in week 1) should be approached with caution, appreciating the potential boomerang effect of how we will be judged in the way that we judge others. I suggest doing a word study on the Greek word *metron*, which translates as "measure." Jesus suggests that the measure we give will be the measure we get.

While one could theoretically stop after verse 1 ("Do not judge, so that you may not be judged"), such an admonishment is likely not very effective. We are, after all, incredibly judgy creatures, gorging on the fruit of the knowledge of good and evil. Therefore, Jesus offers a kind of framework for how we might proceed in the act of judging if judging we must do.

"First take the log out of your own eye," Jesus said, "and *then* you will see clearly to take the speck out of your neighbor's eye" (v. 5). That both the speck and log are pieces of wood is central to the point. Jesus's example implies that the person doing the judging—the person who has successfully removed the log from their own eye—has experience, insight, and understanding to address the situation at hand. This is key for right judging, for how can we have anything of value to offer another if we've never walked in their shoes? Judgment without understanding is a recipe for bigotry and division.

Not only does the shared substance imply that the judge in question has dealt with wood before, but Jesus also says they must remove their own before saying anything to anyone else. So much hypocrisy in the church (and indeed in the world) comes down to our failure to deal with our own stuff. Instead, we project on to others, or we scapegoat, or we simply lash out at people and their faults, all in an effort to avoid looking in the mirror.

If we haven't done the hard work to deal with the log in our own eye, then we are in no position to have any word of judgment on the specks in others' eyes.

The biggest takeaway here is about the importance of loving, compassionate judgment. The goal must be for the well-being and the flourishing of the other. In fact, sometimes we might avoid proper judgment of others because we don't think it's loving or kind. Which is why I love these words from Francis Spufford in his book *Unapologetic*: "Taking the things people do wrong seriously is part of taking them seriously. It's part of letting them be real enough to be worth loving."[1]

Daring to make a judgment about someone else's actions is tricky, yes. We should be sure that we know what we're talking about (both are made of wood) and that we've dealt with it in our own life first (remove the log). From there, it can actually be quite the act of love to tenderly and with great compassion step into the holy space of helping to point out and remove the splinter that holds back others from a life of flourishing.

---

1. Francis Spufford, *Unapologetic: Why, Despite Everything, Christianity Can Still Make Surprising Emotional Sense* (HarperOne, 2014).

Week 3: Judge like Jesus
Matthew 23:13–33

"Woe to you, scribes and Pharisees, hypocrites! For you clean the outside of the cup and of the plate, but inside they are full of greed and self-indulgence. You blind Pharisee! First clean the inside of the cup and of the plate, so that the outside also may become clean." (Matthew 23:25–26)

When we judge the identity of other people, slinging labels at people, we reduce certain groups of people to a singular word or idea. We eliminate the complexities of a person by dismissing them as *this* or *that*, stripping them of their humanity. Even more so, we obscure the fact that God and God alone gets to judge the identity of all people, and that identity has already been established: a beloved child of God.

So, what are we to make of instances in the Gospels when Jesus does, well, some serious name-calling? We might call Jesus a hypocrite for calling certain people (whom I'm sure Jesus considers beloved children of God) hypocrites. We might give him a pass because he's Jesus, but I'm not sure that does adequate justice to the stories and interactions as they would've been experienced and understood by the first audiences. Jesus is making an important statement about what behaviors are worthy of judgment in God's eyes.

In Matthew 23, Jesus delivers a strong rebuke to the scribes and the Pharisees for how they focus on external appearances but neglect essential aspects of the law, such as justice, mercy, and faith. Consider a word study on the Greek word *hupokrites*, originally used to describe artists who would act out poetry, and then over time it would be used to describe a fraud or imposter.

Rather than being leaders and guides, these religious figures were actively preventing people from experiencing the fullness of the kingdom of God. Jesus denounces them for maintaining an outward appearance of righteousness while being inwardly corrupt. He compares them to cups cleaned only on the outside and to whitewashed tombs that look beautiful but are full of decayed corpses inside.

It was these kinds of actions that would snap Jesus out of his soft and tender side and instead activate his righteous fury. And yet, despite the harsh tone, you can't help but see how Jesus's judgments stem from a place of love. His critiques were aimed at protecting the vulnerable from exploitation. He called out the systemic wrongdoings and the injustices perpetrated by those who were charged with tending to, caring for, and leading the people.

So if we want to judge, may we judge like Jesus did: aimed at those who prevent the vulnerable from experiencing the fullness and flourishing of God's kingdom. Jesus's approach to judgment highlights the importance of addressing hypocrisy, safeguarding the vulnerable, and promoting justice and mercy. His rebukes were not contradictions to his message of love but integral to his mission to lead people toward a more authentic and compassionate life.

In this message, consider what it might look like in your specific context for your congregation to voice their Jesus-styled judgment. For example, is there a particular people group who are experiencing unjust treatment at the hands of hypocritical leaders (political or religious)? Maybe you walk your church through a practice of writing a letter in which they practice holding in their hearts the truth that the leader in question is a beloved child of God, and yet their actions demand prophetic critique.

Looking beyond the shocking rhetoric Jesus used here, we can clearly see the spirit of his teaching that confronting harmful behaviors and systems can be a profound act of love.

Week 4: Judge like Paul
1 Corinthians 5:1–13

But now I am writing to you not to associate with anyone who bears the name of brother or sister who is sexually immoral or greedy or an idolater, reviler, drunkard, or swindler. Do not even eat with such a one. For what have I to do with judging those outside? Are you not judges of those who are inside? God will judge those outside. "Drive out the wicked person from among you." (1 Corinthians 5:11–13)

Last week, we looked at how Jesus modeled a certain approach to right judgment. This week, we'll take a similar approach but this time using the apostle Paul.

One way to think about Paul is not just as church planter but an entrepreneurial experimenter attempting to do something radical: create communities organized around a particular way of life made up of (and this is the kicker) both Jews and Gentiles.

Our modern sensibilities for what diverse churches look like probably don't come close to what Paul was trying to do. We might strive for diversity of ethnicity, sexual orientation, age, and gender in our churches (all of which are great!), but such mixing pales in comparison to first-century Jewish and Gentile Christians. The tenuousness of Paul's vision is most evident in the volatile, diverse church in Corinth, a city well known for its moral corruption.

In 1 Corinthians 5, we read about one specific issue where a man was engaging in sexual relations with his father's wife (his stepmother). Rather than see Paul as a sexual prude, consider how such unchecked immorality could undermine the unity of the church and threaten to unravel Paul's efforts in diverse community building.

The central point for this sermon is how Paul makes a clear distinction between judging people inside the church versus those outside it. Judging the behavior of those like the sexually immoral man is, Paul insists, beneficial for the health of the larger community, whereas judging people who don't belong to the community is outside our jurisdiction and ought to be avoided. Unfortunately, Christians have become synonymous with *judgmental* in the eyes of the world, and we don't do ourselves any favors by judging people outside the family of believers.

This sermon will require a delicate balance as you consider what it might look like to rightly judge people in your own community. While there exists a risk of a passage like this one functioning as a license for people to cast aspersions on one another and claim biblical justification, you can always return to the previous message about the specks and logs. Likewise, revisiting last week's message on what sort of sin Jesus saw fit to judge will help hone the people's ability to judge rightly.

How different would the world look if we focused our energies on rightly judging those within our own community? Are we holding religious leaders accountable when they fail in their commitments? Are we holding our siblings in the faith accountable when they act in ways that betray the teachings of Jesus?

Consider closing this message with an invitation for your community to strive to live in right relations with one another. Communicate the shared values and goals of the church, and challenge your people to be courageous and vulnerable enough to permit others to keep them accountable. While judging other people is often viewed as a negative and destructive posture, we can choose to judge as a form of mutual accountability for the sake of the well-being of the body of Christ.

Week 5: Holding Space for Different Beliefs
Romans 14

Let us therefore no longer pass judgment on one another, but resolve instead never to put a stumbling block or hindrance in the way of a brother or sister. . . . If your brother or sister is distressed by what you eat, you are no longer walking in love. Do not let what you eat cause the ruin of one for whom Christ died. (Romans 14:13, 15)

You've likely heard that something like forty thousand different denominations or iterations of Christianity currently exist, and in each one you will undoubtedly get a unique set of criteria for things such as: What makes a person a Christian? How does one practice Christianity? What beliefs are essential? What rites are necessary?

Likely at your own church you have a statement of belief, some set of shared theological commitments that (at least) your leadership agrees with. However, odds are that within the larger body, you have people who hold differing sets of convictions. While they may agree on the essentials of the faith (according to your unique tradition or denomination), you no doubt shepherd a community of individuals who feel very differently about the nonessentials.

This final sermon in the series is a way to invite your church to practice holding space for people who disagree with them. Using the text of Romans 14, walk your church through the importance of disagreeing well and choosing to put their focus and energy on "righteousness and peace and joy" (v. 17) and not on differences that may cause unnecessary spiritual strife.

It's natural and normal and human to get caught up in nonessentials of the faith. For the Roman church, that looked like eating meat (or not) and celebrating holy days (or not). Consider how that might be illustrated in your own church and context. Then cast a vision for how your people might, as Paul says, "pursue what makes for peace and for mutual upbuilding" (v. 19).

Here are seven key principles for how to hold space for those who think and believe differently:

1. *Welcome Them.* Begin with a posture of inclusion and hospitality.
2. *Remember Who They Are.* Affirm each person's identity as a beloved child of God—yourself included.
3. *Trust Their Journey to God.* We are all on our own spiritual journeys, at our own pace, carried along by the Spirit. It's not up to us to control others.
4. *Keep Things in Perspective.* Don't get caught up in the minutiae of where we disagree; commit to key shared values.
5. *Be Intentional about Making Peace.* Don't just assume peace will happen; it won't. We must intentionally move away from our instincts to judge and toward the goal of unity.
6. *Defer Your Liberties.* The more mature in faith you are, the less uptight you should be.
7. *You Both Might Be Right.* Sometimes two positions that seem at odds with one another might somehow both be right, depending on the person and/or situation.

Screen Time: Troubleshooting Our Relationship with Technology

A four-part series on mindful and faithful use of devices, media, and AI.

MATT MIOFSKY

Series Overview

From phones to tablets, watches to goggles, technology is a bigger part of our lives than it ever has been. Internet-connected devices have changed the way we receive and produce information and continue to impact everything from jobs to raising kids to political discourse. If technology is such a big part of our life, we must think about what our faith has to say about our relationship to it. This series addresses some of the trends and temptations technology presents to us and how our faith challenges us to think and act differently in a tech-driven age. The point is not to beat people up over their use of technology but to emphasize that, when used intentionally, technology can bless us. When used thoughtlessly, technology can harm us.

	Sermon Title	Focus Scripture	Theme
Week 1	Streaming and Self-Control	1 Corinthians 6:12	With limitless options, we must limit ourselves.
Week 2	Social Media and Comparison Culture	Hebrews 12:1–2a	Stay focused on running your own race.
Week 3	Passive Scrolling and Active Connection	Luke 24:13–31	Don't miss opportunities for connection.
Week 4	AI and the Truth	John 8:28–32	Test your sources against the facts and Jesus's example.

Tips and Ideas for This Series

If your worship space utilizes screens, there are many opportunities to illustrate the elements of media technology that each sermon addresses. Contrast a video of an old TV station sign-off with the home page of a streaming service, with all its options. Show a social media post that makes you envious or a comparison between a curated image of your house and a wider shot showing the real-life mess. For the final week, show an AI-manipulated video to emphasize how hard it is to spot a fake.

Statistics on technology usage in teens and adults can be very useful in this series. Find recent studies at Pew Research or www.datareportal.com.

Week 1: Streaming and Self-Control
1 Corinthians 6:12

"All things are permitted for me," but not all things are beneficial. "All things are permitted for me," but I will not be dominated by anything. (1 Corinthians 6:12)

If you're around my age or older, you may recall how TV stations would actually sign off around midnight, purposefully going off air every night, from 12–6 a.m. There were, therefore, some external limits on how much TV you could watch. Little by little, those limits disappeared. Cable increased the number of options for programming and made it more likely you could find something interesting any time you turned on the TV. Then the VCR came along and allowed you to record a show to watch later. Finally, streaming made it possible to access nearly unlimited content at any time, night or day. Whatever limits used to exist are now gone, leaving us able to consume content whenever we want, whatever we want, for as long as we want.

A lack of limits may seem like ultimate freedom, but without some parameters, we may find our mental health and relationships suffer. As the apostle Paul wrote, "'All things are permitted for me,' but not all things are beneficial. 'All things are permitted for me,' but I will not be dominated by anything" (1 Cor. 6:12). He was writing about food and sex, two things that are not intrinsically good or bad but can be good or bad depending on how you use them. Technology, I believe, also falls into this category.

We have to stay in control of these things we can freely use, lest they control us. We need to practice self-control, which means setting up systems and habits that help regulate our behavior.

God established one system to help us regulate how we spend our time: the practice of Sabbath keeping. Six days for work, one day for rest. The biblical rhythm of Sabbath can help us regulate our use of technology. Maybe that means literally setting aside one day per week to go totally tech-free—no phones, no TV, no computers. Some Orthodox Jews observe Sabbath this way, forgoing all technology on the Sabbath because it uses electricity. Avoiding electricity is a modern application of the Bible's commandment not to light a fire on the Sabbath (Exod. 35:3).

I don't think that we are going to probably do that, but it is worth thinking about whether we carve out intentional time for rest from tech on a daily and weekly basis: at meal time, first hour of the day, last hour before we go to bed, Sunday afternoons. Do we intentionally build into each day and week space for rest or pause from tech, knowing that if we don't, it easily can take over every minute of every day?

We can choose to place these limits on ourselves but also know that self-control doesn't mean going it alone. We can help hold each other accountable. Accountability means putting people and systems in place to help us monitor what we do. Parents can set limits for their kids. Adults can use screen-time-monitoring apps to see exactly how much time is being spent on various apps. Check in with and listen to the people closest to you; your loved ones can likely tell you ways your tech use distracts you from your relationships. This week my challenge to you is to start tracking, audit your time, ask the people around you, and then set some goals for how you would like to begin to intentionally control the time you spend with screens.

Week 2: Social Media and Comparison Culture
Hebrews 12:1–2a

Therefore, since we are surrounded by so great a cloud of witnesses, let us also lay aside every weight and the sin that clings so closely, and let us run with perseverance the race that is set before us, looking to Jesus, the pioneer and perfecter of faith. (Hebrews 12:1–2a)

It is estimated that over five billion people worldwide are active on social media. And there is a reason that these apps are so popular. They are helpful in many ways! Social media is not bad. But when we aren't careful, it can have some negative side effects like depression, anxiety, loneliness, poor body image, and low self-esteem. One of the primary drivers is what many social scientists call comparison culture, the pervasive phenomenon in which individuals compare themselves to others and often feel inadequate or inferior.

The Bible addresses the fundamental human temptation to look around and compare ourselves to others. So what do we do to combat this temptation to fall into comparison culture?

The key is to focus on our own race. The story of a 1954 race between Roger Bannister and John Landy makes a great sermon illustration here; Landy turned his head to see where Bannister was and lost the race by less than one second. (See www.miraclemile1954.com for more details of this story.) Athletic metaphors were popular in the Roman world, and the author of Hebrews makes use of that to encourage disciples, saying, "lay aside every weight and the sin that clings so closely, and let us run with perseverance the race that is set before us" (v. 1).

This passage follows what is called the faith hall of fame, where the author of Hebrews recounts all these famous Old Testament heroes and what they did. People like Noah and Abraham, Sarah and Rahab, Moses, and David. But as soon as the chapter ends, we get this. Why? Because what others did can inspire us, but we have our own race to run—the race "set before *us*"—and it is different than theirs. The more you are focused on the race of others, the more likely you are to miss the race laid out for you.

I have three tips that can function like blinders on a racehorse, keeping your eyes focused on the road ahead of you. First, stay grateful. Comparison culture has us looking around and noticing what is going on in the lives of others, drawing our attention to what they have and we don't, what they are getting to do and we are unable to do, what they can afford and what we cannot afford, what they are accomplishing and what we are failing to accomplish. Comparison focuses on what we lack; gratitude focuses on what we have.

Second, stay real. Remember that no one is perfect, and no one has a perfect life. Social media shows us a highly curated version of life. We're comparing others' best (and possibly edited) photos to our own outtakes. Pictures and posts *never* tell the whole story, and sometimes these pictures and posts actually cover up the real story.

Third, stay centered. Remember who you are. Who you are is not accidental. Everyone has flaws, but you are not a mistake. You don't need to be curated. God loves the imperfect you. And God wants to use the imperfect you in a unique way. When it comes to connecting online, try to minimize the people who aren't helping you be you. Focus on your race and the people who help you run it best.

Week 3: Passive Scrolling and Active Connection
Luke 24:13–31

While they were talking and discussing, Jesus himself came near and went with them, but their eyes were kept from recognizing him. (Luke 24:15-16)

Technology has made us both the most connected people in all human history and simultaneously those people who can feel the most isolated and alone. The key is whether or not passive connection brings us to actively see and engage with the human beings who are right in front of us.

Technology can be an incredible tool of active connectedness. We can celebrate one another or offer help in hard times. But more often, we're just scrolling, receiving, liking posts, and never following up in a way that actively seeks out further connection. We can get caught in a loop of scrolling through, clicking "like" or "share," then continuing on in an endless loop. Passive engagement can actually lead us away from connecting with other people.

We see a version of this in today's Scripture. Jesus's followers had heard reports that Jesus's tomb was empty, and people were on edge, wondering if anyone who'd followed Jesus might be next on the Roman authority's hit list. So, two disciples skipped town and were walking toward Emmaus when a stranger started walking alongside them. The two disciples didn't realize the man walking with them was Jesus. Something was interfering with their ability to see who was with them. Jesus even asked what they had been talking about as they walked, and the men said, essentially, "Haven't you heard the news?!" They proceeded to tell the man everything about Jesus—not realizing it was Jesus right there with them.

Maybe it was the weight of their grief and loss that kept them blind to who was with them. It's like they were on their phones, flipping from one story about the tragedy to the next, sharing videos and memes back and forth with one another until they were numb. The shocking news story was all they could see, and they couldn't stop doomscrolling about it. It became a walking echo chamber of grief, loss, and horror, each of them *passively* caught up in a loop of pain, and because of that, they missed the connection that was *actively* being offered by the person right in front of them.

Are we using our technology to help connect us to one another, not just out there, on social media and around the world, but right here, face-to-face? Is it helping us to truly see one another and build trust with one another, in the present moment? Is it empowering us into real, vulnerable relationships with people right in front of us, or is it making it harder?

We've all seen how, online, it can become far too easy to reduce people to an idea that we need to battle or an ideology that we need to tear apart or destroy. We forget that every person we engage with online is a real person, and we may be tempted to say things that deny others' humanity. The anonymity afforded by technology can lead us to be terrible to other people and can all too easily spill over into real life, affecting how we treat other real people in the laws we pass and the decisions we make.

The disciples on the road finally recognized Jesus, but only when they stopped walking and sat down for a meal. Likewise, let's remember to slow down and really see one another, to actively connect with one another, whether online or in person.

Week 4: AI and the Truth
John 8:28–32

Then Jesus said to the Jews who had believed in him, "If you continue in my word, you are truly my disciples, and you will know the truth, and the truth will make you free." (John 8:31–32)

It's ironic how, when I was a kid, it might have taken a lot of time to get information through encyclopedias and other books, but the information was fairly reliable. Now, with the internet and especially artificial intelligence (AI), information is easy to get but more unreliable than ever. Because AI and technology can feed us information, it is possible to also now feed people misinformation, false information, or manipulated information. From videos showing political events that never happened to AI-generated robocalls from famous people, seeing is no longer believing.

In addition, we now also have thousands of highly tailored news sources created for certain segments of people and presenting the news (with varying levels of veracity) from a very particular angle. We receive entirely different versions of what is happening, what is real, and what is true, depending on who we are listening to! With an unprecedented amount of information and narratives being shared, we have to test the sources of our information. Sometimes those sources are not easy to find or track. But the source matters.

Once Jesus was speaking to a group of people wondering whether he was really from God. They wanted to know how to tell the difference between something they should listen to and something they should ignore, who was speaking truth and who was not. Jesus said, "If you continue in my word, you are truly my disciples, and you will know the truth, and the truth will make you free" (John 8:31–32).

The truth matters, and we have to work to figure out what is true, both in terms of accuracy and faithfulness. Does a story, image, or video accurately convey what factually happened? And is the source urging an attitude or response that reflects or contradicts the teachings of Jesus?

If something helps us to be more of the people Christ teaches us to be, then it is true.

I think about people I know who listen to news and facts that only make them angry and violent. That is not the truth.

I think about religious people who become more judgmental and self-righteous. That is not the truth.

I see efforts to demonize certain groups of people in order to make others fearful. That is not the truth.

I see people who want to do things that will hurt those they love. That is not the truth.

I see a lot of information crafted to sell something, promote something, or benefit only one person. That is not the truth.

I think about teenagers who take in media that is causing them to question and hurt themselves. That is not the truth.

The truth should make us humble, loving, generous, at peace, servants who are gentle, kind, and just. That is truth.

Think about information as you would think about the food you put into your body. Do an audit of your mental diet. Who are you listening to? What are you listening to? And do those voices and information help you to be more like Jesus?

Ready for It

A four-part series on biblical resilience in the face of personal challenges and unsettling world headlines.

BETHANY PEERBOLTE

Series Overview

World headlines can make us feel insecure about how to live day-to-day, much less make a significant impact. Daily challenges and conflicts drain our energy, making it hard to be the best versions of ourselves. This is not what God wants for us. In Scripture, we read about people, even Jesus, facing challenging situations in faithful and courageous ways. This series explores some of these examples and what we can learn from them about resiliency and readiness. By centering our worth in God, being prepared to seize opportunities and respond in moments of crisis, and knowing how to recover after setbacks, we can be ready to face whatever life throws at us.

	Sermon Title	Focus Scripture	Theme
Week 1	Worth Rooted in God	1 Samuel 1:1–20; Luke 1:26–38	God says we are worthy of love and respect.
Week 2	If You Stay Ready, You Don't Have to Get Ready	Luke 19:1–10	Setting achievable goals and being ready to say yes can change your life.
Week 3	Clarify Your Values	Luke 10:25–37	Think about how you want to show up before the unexpected happens.
Week 4	Even Jesus Had Rough Starts	Isaiah 61:1–11; Luke 4:21–30	When times get rough, give chances, believe people's actions, and set boundaries.

Tips and Ideas for This Series

Graphics for this series might feature common stressors, such as traffic, spilled coffee, or a family fight, juxtaposed with calming scenes like a geometric breathing visualization, gentle waves on the beach, or smiling faces. In worship, take time to teach mindful and spiritual practices like breathing techniques, prayer labyrinths, and meditative coloring. These can easily replace the call to worship or benediction.

Consider offering classes and activities to support the themes of the series outside worship. These might include support groups around specific stressors (for example, work, family, or world news) or a book club reading of *Micro-Resilience* by Bonnie St. John. Bring in experts; for example, a therapist could teach about the effects of stress on the body and specific techniques to help relieve stress. A financial adviser or life planning lawyer could walk people through stressful things we often put off.

Week 1: Worth Rooted in God
1 Samuel 1:1–20; Luke 1:26–38

"Do not regard your servant as a worthless woman, for I have been speaking out of my great anxiety and vexation all this time." Then Eli answered, "Go in peace; the God of Israel grant the petition you have made to him." And she said, "Let your servant find favor in your sight." Then the woman went her way and ate and drank with her husband, and her countenance was sad no longer. (1 Samuel 1:16-18)

I regularly have conversations about the church that raise the question of its unique value compared to other organizations. While aspects like community, worship, and mission are often highlighted, these are not exclusive to the church. Various social settings, such as sports teams or concerts, can foster community and evoke worshipful experiences, leading to the question: What truly makes the church unique?

I believe that there is a distinct quality within faith communities, a gem that cannot be found elsewhere and that is central to people's inner peace and strength. This gem is the affirmation of worth, a constant reminder that individuals are inherently valuable regardless of societal standards. In a world where worth is often measured by superficial criteria—such as appearance, wealth, or social media presence—the reminder the church can give becomes crucial. The church offers a perspective that worth is defined by God, not by external expectations, worldly success, actions taken, or mistakes made.

The stories of Hannah and Mary illustrate this concept. Both women face cultural pressures that diminish their perceived worth. Hannah struggles with her identity and value due to her inability to bear children, a situation that brings her immense distress. Despite her husband's attempts to affirm her worth, Hannah feels the weight of societal expectations. In her desperation, she prays silently in the temple, fearing judgment from others. A faith leader, Eli, initially misjudges her and questions her behavior, further compounding her feelings of worthlessness. However, when he acknowledges her worth and offers her peace, Hannah experiences a transformation, realizing her value in God's eyes.

Mary's story contrasts with Hannah's experience. When the angel Gabriel visits her, he begins by declaring that she is favored before presenting her with the challenge ahead. This affirmation of worth empowers Mary to accept the news of her unexpected pregnancy, despite the social stigma she will face. Her confidence stems from knowing that her worth is rooted in God's favor, allowing her to respond with acceptance and willingness to serve.

Whether we are currently facing trials like Hannah's infertility, a cancer diagnosis, financial stress, or other hardships—or just want to be ready for whatever comes our way—we can find invaluable inner strength in the assurance that we are beloved children of God, valued and worthy of good things.

The church's role is to consistently remind its members of their intrinsic worth, helping them regain stability and confidence. This practice is exemplified in the tradition of passing peace during gatherings, serving as a reminder of individual worth and mutual support within the community. In today's world, where mental health issues and feelings of loneliness are rampant, the church has a critical responsibility. The stigma surrounding mental health often forces individuals into silence, mirroring Hannah's initial struggle. Many Christians' attitudes toward poverty, unwed motherhood, and nontraditional family structures—all pressures Mary would face—make people distrust the church in general. Feelings of worthlessness can lead to dangerous behaviors, particularly among the youth.

The world needs faith communities that foster people's sense of worth. By reflecting this intrinsic value back to individuals, the church can help them understand their place in God's eyes, ensuring that everyone feels deserving of peace and wholeness. This mission is essential for revitalizing the church and addressing the deeper issues faced by society today, as the declaration of worth has the power to transform lives and communities.

Week 2: If You Stay Ready, You Don't Have to Get Ready
Luke 19:1–10

So he ran ahead and climbed a sycamore tree to see him, because he was going to pass that way. When Jesus came to the place, he looked up and said to him, "Zacchaeus, hurry and come down, for I must stay at your house today." So he hurried down and was happy to welcome him. (Luke 19:4–6)

The story of Zacchaeus is often limited to kids; think of the classic Bible song about the "wee little man." However, it carries deeper meanings that resonate more profoundly with adults. Zacchaeus, a tax collector, is despised by his neighbors for his role as an agent of the Roman imperial system. Being short in stature may have caused him additional ridicule. Despite these factors, he climbs a tree just to catch a glimpse of Jesus. This act reflects his determination and desire to overcome societal barriers. The effort he puts into climbing that tree demonstrates his longing to connect with something greater than himself.

Zacchaeus's decision to climb the tree illustrates the importance of setting achievable goals. His initial aim was simply to see Jesus, a goal that, while challenging, was within reach. He climbed the tree and achieved a good view of Jesus—and Jesus also had a view of him! Zacchaeus probably never intended to make personal contact with the famous man coming through town, but Jesus called him by name and invited himself to stay at Zacchaeus's house. Imagine his shock! Unexpected circumstances can paralyze us with fear, convincing us that we are unworthy or unprepared for the blessings that come our way. But Zacchaeus disregards his doubts and the mutterings of the crowd, choosing instead to focus on Jesus's invitation.

This theme brings to mind the insights of investor Kevin O'Leary, known as Mr. Wonderful on the TV show *Shark Tank*. As Mr. Wonderful met with the leadership teams of the businesses he invested in, he noticed that the practice that set successful teams apart was setting achievable goals. This led to higher morale and better performance. (That these teams were often led by women may or may not be beside the point.) In contrast, companies with far-reaching aspirations often faced burnout and failure. The lesson here is that setting achievable goals fosters a sense of accomplishment and encourages continued progress. Just as Zacchaeus aimed for a glimpse of Jesus, adults can learn to set manageable goals that pave the way for future successes.

Another compelling example from *Shark Tank* involves an entrepreneur who pitched a natural deodorant. Initially, all the Sharks rejected her offer. However, it was discovered that she had not even been scheduled to give her pitch that day. That morning, someone else backed out, and she received a call while in the middle of a mountain hike, asking that she come into the studio immediately. Her willingness to seize an opportunity despite being unprepared—wearing hiking attire instead of business attire—impressed the sharks, and she made the deal. Her ability to say yes to an unexpected invitation demonstrated resilience and determination.

The lessons from Zacchaeus are clear: Set achievable goals and be ready to embrace opportunities without letting fear dictate your worth. Climbing the figurative tree to seek out God's glory can lead to blessings beyond our imagination. God honors those who strive for a glimpse of his glory, offering even more in return. By embodying Zacchaeus's spirit, we can navigate our paths with confidence and openness to the incredible opportunities that God places before us.

Week 3: Clarify Your Values
Luke 10:25–37

But a Samaritan while traveling came upon him, and when he saw him he was moved with compassion. He went to him and bandaged his wounds, treating them with oil and wine. Then he put him on his own animal, brought him to an inn, and took care of him. The next day he took out two denarii, gave them to the innkeeper, and said, 'Take care of him, and when I come back I will repay you whatever more you spend." (Luke 10:33–35)

We all experience moments when unexpected situations arise, leaving us feeling frozen or unsure of how to respond. Whether it's a sudden argument where we struggle to articulate our thoughts or a hasty decision that leads us to second-guess ourselves later, these experiences can lead to regret. Reflecting on our choices and examining what drove us to make them is a valuable practice; it helps us learn and be better prepared to respond as we want to in the future.

The question posed to Jesus—"And who is my neighbor?" (Luke 10:29)—illustrates this struggle. The lawyer likely grappled with his past actions and boundaries, pondering who he was obligated to care for and when it was acceptable to ignore someone in need. Jesus responded with a parable that shifts the narrative by changing who it is who helps the person in need. His hearers would have expected the helper in the story to be an Israelite and the one who ignores a person in distress to be a Samaritan. By reversing this, Jesus challenges their preexisting value of helping only people who are like us by showing that unexpected individuals can be neighbors to us, so we should be neighbors to the unexpected.

The story prompts introspection as people consider how they would respond in such a situation: "Would I cross over to the other side of the road? Would I help a Samaritan the way this Samaritan helped the man who was robbed?" Considering and clarifying what our values are—what we stand for and whom we care about—is essential to our ability to face unexpected situations with confidence. This forethought prepares us for unexpected encounters, ensuring we respond compassionately when faced with an opportunity to assist someone in need.

This concept of preparation is mirrored in the failed DARE program from the 1990s, which focused solely on encouraging children to "just say no" to drugs. Researchers found that simply telling kids what to do without providing a personal why led to increased drug use. In contrast, European antidrug programs emphasized real-life stories from individuals impacted by drug use, allowing children to develop their own motivations for saying no based on their values. This approach instilled a deeper understanding and commitment to not doing drugs that transcended mere instructions.

Anticipating difficult situations can help us respond more effectively when they arise. In moments of crisis, our bodies react instinctively, often overriding our rational thoughts. By deciding in advance how we want to behave during challenging moments, we can better align our actions with our values. We can envision our best selves and commit to responding in ways that reflect our true character, even when faced with unpredictable circumstances.

Ultimately, life will present us with unexpected moments, but by preparing ourselves mentally for how we want to react, we can navigate these situations with grace and integrity. Establishing a clear sense of self before we meet the unexpected will enable us to embody our best selves when it matters most. Decide who you want to be in those chaotic moments, and when the time comes, you'll be ready to respond in a way that reflects your values and beliefs.

Week 4: Even Jesus Had Rough Starts
Isaiah 61:1–11; Luke 4:21–30

When they heard this, all in the synagogue were filled with rage. They got up, drove him out of the town, and led him to the brow of the hill on which their town was built, so that they might hurl him off the cliff. But he passed through the midst of them and went on his way. (Luke 4:28–30)

The beginning of Jesus's ministry presents a contrast between the initial excitement of his hometown and the rapid shift to hostility. The crowd, initially thrilled to hear Jesus speak, quickly turns against him, leading to a dramatic attempt to throw him off a cliff. This swift change in sentiment highlights both the community's expectations of the messiah and Jesus's understanding of their mindset.

The people of Nazareth have known Jesus since his childhood. However, recent rumors about his miraculous abilities and profound teachings have piqued their interest. They gather to see if he truly embodies the messiah they have long awaited, a savior who would liberate them from oppression. On the flip side, Jesus is acutely aware of the expectations his community has of the messiah. He knows they yearn for a political and military messiah who will restore their nation and defeat their enemies.

Instead of confirming their hopes for a triumphant messiah, Jesus recounts stories from their shared history that reveal God's grace extended beyond Israel, including to foreigners. He mentions the widow of Zarephath and Naaman the Syrian, both of whom received favor from God despite their outsider status. This revelation ignites anger among the townspeople, who feel threatened by the implication that their messiah may not prioritize their needs over those of others. The once-joyful crowd transforms into an angry mob.

Jesus's experience serves as a lesson for all of us when we face our own rough starts. His approach provides a framework for navigating difficult moments in our lives. First, Jesus gives people a chance, acknowledging their potential for understanding and growth, even when he anticipates a negative reaction.

The second key lesson is to believe people when they show us who they are. Jesus does not plead with the crowd or attempt to soften his message when they react violently. Instead, he respects their response and chooses to move on. Recognizing when to step back and protect oneself is vital, especially in situations where hostility arises.

Establishing boundaries is the third principle exemplified by Jesus. After experiencing rejection and hostility from his own community, he refrains from returning to Nazareth. This boundary serves to protect him from further harm. Jesus's later interactions with his family (Matt. 12:46–50) illustrate the importance of boundaries; he acknowledges their lack of support and creates space for healing. By doing so, he allows them the opportunity to reflect on their behavior and demonstrate that they are recommitted to him later on.

Moreover, boundaries are not merely punitive but also provide feedback about how we interact with others. If someone establishes distance from us, it may be an indication that our actions or words have not been well received. This feedback can prompt personal reflection and growth, allowing us to better align with the needs of those around us.

Ultimately, rough starts are a part of life, and Jesus's example offers guidance on how to navigate these challenges. Resiliency is all about getting back up again when circumstances knock us down. This framework allows us to view rough starts not as definitive failures but as beginnings from which we can learn and grow.

Imagine the Impossible

A six-part series on imagination and the future of our faith and the church.

ADRIENE THORNE

Series Overview

With this latest global pandemic mostly in our rearview mirror, the world and the church have shifted dramatically. Deep division and distrust flavor our social, religious, and political interactions. Church attendance (now a hybrid experience) is growing in multiracial and multicultural churches but on the decline almost everywhere else. What is next for the church, and where can God's people look for direction and reassurance?

In season and out, God's holy word holds holy power, comfort, and possibility for ways out of the knots that entangle us. Spiritual ancestors beckon us, through their lives and stories, to leave the familiar and strike out to places and perspectives unknown.

As we live into an unknown future, what awaits our faith communities and us when we let go and embrace new ways of being the breath and heartbeat of God in the world? This sermon series seeks to invite those who follow Jesus to imagine this impossible future.

	Sermon Title	Focus Scripture	Theme
Week 1	Imagine Fearless Faith	Genesis 15:1–6	A star-filled sky speaks to possibilities for creation and the church.
Week 2	Imagine Pausing to Eat	Exodus 12:1–13; 13:1–8	Pausing to eat in hard times speaks to the importance of community connection.
Week 3	Imagine Living on the Edge of Trust	1 Kings 17:1–24	God provides. Do we believe it?

	Sermon Title	Focus Scripture	Theme
Week 4	Imagine the Economy of Right Relationship	Luke 16:19–31	We have what is needed to live as God expects.
Week 5	Imagine the Ones Who Get It	Luke 19:29–40	Some people did not need the crucifixion to get who Jesus was.
Week 6	Imagine Trust Falling on a Wilderness Road	Acts 8:26–39	Trust falling into the mystery of Christ is the only requirement.

Tips and Ideas for This Series

This series is an opportunity to explore a move from certainty to mystery, learning from our ancestors and growing in faith as we go. Ask church participants what they imagine for the church. Record individual stories of how people have journeyed through the unknown and share them in worship as your inspiring invitations for others to give and serve. John Lennon's song "Imagine" makes an excellent theme song for the series.

Week 1: Imagine Fearless Faith
Genesis 15:1–6

He brought him outside and said, "Look toward heaven and count the stars, if you are able to count them." Then [God] said to him, "So shall your descendants be." And he believed the Lord, *and the* Lord *reckoned it to him as righteousness. (Genesis 15:5–6)*

Abram makes a courageous move in these early chapters of the first book of the Bible. At age seventy-five, Abram is called by God to leave the place that he knows, the place where he grew up, and travel to a new place. Abram is like every human who has ever been born. He is like every human who has ever entered a new space, changed schools, gotten married, welcomed a baby, started a new project, or imagined a new life for themselves. It's scary to make a change, to do new things, to start going and not be 100 percent sure where the trip is going to take you.

Everything and anything is possible for Abram, but we get our first inkling in this text that Abram is afraid. He is beginning to question whether he made the right choice listening to this God of imagination and new possibilities.

In the opening verse, God speaks what many believe are the most powerful words in our holy book. God speaks to Abram and to *everyone* who cannot imagine a future. For the first time in the biblical account,

God says, "Do not be afraid." Don't let your questions and your doubts shortchange your dreams and hopes and imagination. God says with deep tenderness and love, "Do not be afraid, Abram, I am your shield; your reward shall be very great" (v. 1). And we are reminded here that after the flood, God finds this particular person, this specific child of God, to work with and work through. The enormity of being chosen is often lost on Abram but never on God, who says to this beloved child, "I am your shield." I got you. Through trust and fear, I got you. When you see the promise and when you can't, I still got you. When life feels possible and when it does not, I got you. When you can't do it yourself, which is going to be . . . always, I got you!

Here's the thing: Following God is often like driving in the dark. Our headlights illuminate two hundred feet ahead of our faith, and fear is in the passenger seat. As we move forward into God's future, sometimes fear is riding shotgun. We see the next two hundred feet and the next two hundred feet until, like Abram, we are seventy-five years old leaving the familiar place for the next place. We *want* to see from here to the end of God's path, but we just need to decide that we will make the next move. Decide that we *want* to step into the story God promises is in front of us and trust that the next movement, and the next movement, and the one after that, and the one after that . . . each will emerge as we go together. Do we know where we're going? We know the next two hundred feet. We know that we've got each other. And we know that we want to make this road trip together, remembering, as Abram remembers, that God is our shield. Imagine that!

Week 2: Imagine Pausing to Eat
Exodus 12:1–13; 13:1–8

They shall eat the lamb that same night; they shall eat it roasted over the fire with unleavened bread and bitter herbs. . . . Moses said to the people, "Remember this day on which you came out of Egypt, out of the house of slavery, because the LORD *brought you out from there by the strength of hand." (Exodus 12:8; 13:3)*

You may have heard the joke that the story of most Jewish holidays is this: "They tried to kill us. We survived. Let's eat." This tongue-in-cheek summary appropriately captures the Passover remembrance that is born out of this Scripture reading. The Egyptians, and most notably, Pharaoh, tried to kill the Jews, and just before their flight from Egypt, their flight from tyranny, their flight from fascism, the community gathers to eat. They tried to kill us. We survived. Let's eat.

In the face of extermination, imagine pausing to eat. In the face of all that is wretched in the world, imagine that God *instructed* our spiritual ancestors, and now us, to pause and eat. In the face of the angel of death making his rounds right now, in our present reality, how shall our community of faith engage?

Among other definitions, the word *torah* means instruction, and we hear in this reading from the book of Exodus some exceedingly precise instruction for how to plan this first Passover meal, instructions on how to gather and how to share. We know what the side dishes will be and how everyone should dress for the occasion. God has cooked up many good things in the life of our faith community. We are historic and history making. We are, like this text, speaking to the past *and* being called out of the place we are now, to the preferred future God has for us. The instructions for how to get where we are going are precise. The people pause to fortify themselves for a future time. They pause to be in community. They pause to remember who God is and who they are in God.

Pausing to eat is preparation for a forward moving time. This meal is the beginning of a future as yet unknown, and there will be many beginnings, many opportunities to pause and eat. How fantastic is that?! Our faith centers around a table, reminding us to pause, to nourish ourselves and one another, to regroup, to check the plan, to check on one another, to make sure we understand God's precise instructions, to gather our wits and our will before striking out into the places God has for us.

The angel of death is always and everywhere passing over the places we inhabit, and I offer you a new invitation. Pause to eat. The One who bids you tell your children the marvelous things God has done, the holy God who has delivered you from dangers seen and unseen, the great God almighty who has brought you to this day, invites you to the table. Don't just come today. Keep coming back. Pause for strength and power. Pause for connection and community. Pause to remember and imagine, and then forge forward together.

They tried to kill us. We survived. Let's eat.

Week 3: Imagine Living on the Edge of Trust
1 Kings 17:1–24

"You shall drink from the wadi, and I have commanded the ravens to feed you there. . . . Go now to Zarephath, which belongs to Sidon, and live there, for I have commanded a widow there to feed you." (1 Kings 17:4, 9)

This text is about life and death. It's about daily bread and basic sustenance. This text is about scarcity and trust. It's about living on the edge and finding faith *way* out there, where you feel too close to the abyss. I hope this story of life on the line, in this book that we love, gives wings to your faith and brings you into deeper connection with the One who meets us *way* out there on the edge where there is drought and famine and death. I hope you will come to know a God who comes through with what you are thirsty for, hungry for. I hope you will grow to trust this God to bring dead things, like the widow's son, back to life. This is Elijah's story, and we are invited to imagine ourselves living on the edge of trust with him.

When Elijah encounters the widow, she is gathering a couple of sticks to make a fire. This is the desperate situation in Sudan. This is the Congo. The widow is gathering a couple of sticks for a final supper for herself and her child. She has a handful of meal and a few drops of oil. Maybe she makes a small cornbread loaf to split with her child before they starve to death. And you have to pay attention in the text when desperate times get worse. It's not enough that the widow is down to her last bit of food; the next movement of the story tells us that the near-starving widow's child dies! Her hope, her love, her everything dies. Pay attention in the text, and in your lives, when desperate times get worse.

Desperate times often signal a surprise, a miracle, an unexpected plot twist. Sometimes God does bring our loved ones literally back from death. And other times God brings back our dead faith, our dead hope, our dead joy, our dead imagination, our dead calling, our dead trust.

Through the horrors of enslavement; through the suffrage movement in this country; through apartheid and genocide around the world; through folks fleeing persecution, lynchings, and pogroms, the faithful have always lived on the edge, trusting God for water, for bread, for life. On the edge are opportunities to grow in faith. On the edge are opportunities to witness God's goodness. Most importantly, on the edge are opportunities to fall more deeply in love with the God you claim and the God who claims you. May you go into this week, but also all the weeks of your life, knowing that on the edge of trust is where you need to be. It's where God is. So head out there to the edge. And know that the God of Elijah, the God of the widow, will meet you. May it be so. May it always be so.

Week 4: Imagine the Economy of Right Relationship
Luke 16:19–31

"He called out, 'Father Abraham, have mercy on me, and send Lazarus to dip the tip of his finger in water and cool my tongue, for I am in agony in these flames.' But Abraham said,

'Child, remember that during your lifetime you received your good things and Lazarus in like manner evil things, but now he is comforted here, and you are in agony.'" (Luke 16:24–25)

It's too easy to read ourselves out of this parable in ways that let us off the hook, *and* it is too easy to read ourselves into this parable in ways that leave us paralyzed. One reading of the text asks the question, "How rich are we talking?!" I live in New York City, where the rents are insane. If you look at my bank account, no way am I rich. Jesus surely isn't talking about me, so I'm off the hook. Another reading admits that many of us live in the wealthiest nation in the world. Compared to most people on the planet, we have more than our share of resources: clean drinking water; a choice of shoes and clothing; and not too much worry, many of us, about our next meal. Many of us have disposable income that makes certain comforts possible: cars, vacations, dining out, mobile phones, higher education, gourmet coffee. Many of us figure, yep, Jesus is probably talking about me, and we become paralyzed, thinking to ourselves "What do I do?! I can't help where I'm born or the job that pays me more than I truly need or the house I inherited from my family or the stock that tripled in value. It's not my fault." This text typically produces a don't-you-worry-you're-not-that-bad sermon or a get-your-act-together sermon. This leaves the listener either off the hook or paralyzed.

I'm not convinced that either approach is helpful for faithful living or faithfully following Jesus. Rather, this parable strikes me as one of those case studies that professors love to give for the final exam. Those exams where we see who was really paying attention all semester; who came to class and stayed until the end? Those exams where there is more than one right answer. This kind of exam demands you bring to bear all that has been poured into you this past academic year, revealing who did the reading and who glanced at the AI summary. The exam that doesn't care if you're a scholarship student, first generation in your family to attend school, or a legacy kid whose family name is on the building where the exam is being held. In other words, the exam doesn't care if you're a Lazarus or a rich man or somewhere in between. It cares if you did your homework. It cares if you can make a case and support it with what you know to be true about the One who shows us the way. What does Professor Jesus say through this marvelous parable? He says students have Moses and the prophets; they should listen to them.

It's not the money. It's the listening. It's our imagination. When we listen, we can't do anything but act from a Jesus-centered place. We know what the world's troubles are. This parable, this case study, these final exams, this is Jesus inviting us to imagine what could be. What could be if we listened and followed the way of Jesus?

Week 5: Imagine the Ones Who Get It
Luke 19:29–40

Now as he was approaching the path down from the Mount of Olives, the whole multitude of the disciples began to praise God joyfully with a loud voice for all the deeds of power that they had seen. (Luke 19:37)

I've been intrigued for nearly twenty years with the notion that Jesus met people during his earthly life who got it. They saw him. They understood that in his presence they were experiencing someone divine. They didn't need Jesus on the cross in order to get it.

What might it have felt like for those in the crowd and for Jesus to experience him riding into Jerusalem? What did it feel like for Jesus to lock eyes with the ones who got it? Who were these multitudes who had seen Jesus's deeds of power? We've met many of them. Through the Gospels, we have met many of the faces that might be in this crowd. We know the ones who have followed Jesus from town to town, who have witnessed or experienced miracles, who have hung on his every word. We know the ones whom Pharisees want Jesus to silence. We know the ones taking off their cloaks and throwing them on the ground, and they're all shouting:

> "Blessed is the king
>   who comes in the name of the Lord!
> Peace in heaven,
>   and glory in the highest heaven!"
>   (v. 38)

The king?! The King?! These are treasonous words, words punishable by death. Words that will get Jesus crucified. There is only one king in the minds of the empire, and Jesus is not it. The Pharisees begin to engage in word control. "Teacher, order your disciples to stop" (v. 39). In other words, the crowd can't use words like *king*. Words have power, and this crowd . . . this crowd gets it. With word control, the empire attempts to erase and silence the people/the rocks that would cry out.

What a crowd! What an extraordinary group of nobodies—nobody the empire would care about, not alone . . . but together? Together their voices rattled the empire, agitated the empire. Upset the empire enough that they ordered Jesus to shut them up, but they won't be silent! They saw Jesus. They got Jesus. They didn't need the cross to know who he was or what he had done.

Very few of the individuals in the crowd are household names. Very few of them changed anything all by themselves. The only reason we are talking about them is because they formed a crowd, a crowd who got it. They gave each other strength, and I have to believe they gave Jesus the strength to do what was next for him: to lay down his life for the ones who got it and the ones who missed it.

We often read this text during Holy Week and focus on how quickly the story turns from joy and exultation to brutality and betrayal. Even in the very next verses of Luke 19, Jesus weeps over the ones who *don't get it*, who do not know the ways of peace and justice. But this is still a good-news story, a crowd story. Imagine what can be done with a crowd of people who get it, who hear and understand Jesus's words, who know that they can't do it alone. Get yourself a crowd and together witness loudly to God's great deeds of power.

Week 6: Imagine Trust Falling on a Wilderness Road
Acts 8:26–39

As they were going along the road, they came to some water, and the eunuch said, "Look, here is water! What is to prevent me from being baptized?" (Acts 8:36)

We are now in the book of Acts, which contains stories of the early church, stories of identity, stories of who gets to belong and who gets to decide. God, of course, says everyone belongs, but not everyone agrees with God's expansive love.

Violence has broken out against the church in Jerusalem when an angel of God tells Philip to head south for an encounter with a man. Philip finds himself running on a wilderness road stretching from Jerusalem to Gaza—a rich, powerful, and opulent city that was of great significance in the Roman geopolitics of the time.

What you might miss in the description of the Ethiopian man in the chariot is his connection to luxury and power. This court official, reading a scroll, in a chariot, oversaw the queen's entire treasury. Few people owned chariots or horses or scrolls to read, and so this queen and, by association, this court official in her chariot, were wealthy, educated people in a time when few people were wealthy or educated.

According to the Center for Biblical Equality, the Candace ruled the Kingdom of Kush, which the Romans called the Kingdom of Nubia. She was wealthy, powerful, and dark skinned—a minor celebrity in her day and, as you might imagine, a threat to the Roman Empire and later a threat to the narrative of the church. Early church fathers, including Origen and Philo, made harmful inferences about race and skin color. In her story are the beginnings of the misogyny and anti-Blackness that plague humanity to this day.

The Ethiopian man, of course, sees nothing preventing his baptism or his belonging—not his ethnic background, not his skin color, not his geographic location, not his sexual status. Though the text identifies the man only by his sexual status, as a eunuch, he does not see this as a barrier to belonging. Biblical scholar Wil Gafney gives the man a name, Abdimalkah, to honor his humanity.[1]

Philip agrees with Abdimalkah that there is nothing preventing his baptism or his belonging. After asking Abdimalkah if he understands what he is reading and leading a brief Bible study in a moving chariot, sharing who Jesus is and how a love like his is good news for us, Philip prepares for a baptism.

All Abdimalkah needs for baptism is trust, not his rational mind, not his intellect, not his education. But can you, Abdimalkah, trust fall into the mystery of the Christ who was crucified and resurrected to prove God's belief that you are to die for? God believes that you are so worth it. God believes that you are beloved.

Abdimalkah stops the chariot, and the writer describes both men getting down into the water for baptism. There is no preponderance of questions; there is no examination of conscience; there is no profession of faith. Only trust falling on a wilderness road into the mystery of Christ, who is good news for all who believe.

---

1. Wilda Gafney, "Black, Jewish and Queer: The Ethiopian Eunuch," *Womanists Wading in the Word* (blog), May 4, 2012, https://www.wilgafney.com/2012/05/04/black-jewish-and-queer-the-ethiopian-eunuch/.

Justice and Inclusion

Fight like Jesus

A six-part series on nonviolence as a way of life, exploring Martin Luther King Jr.'s six principles of nonviolent resistance.

MARK FELDMEIR

Series Overview

Jesus was a devoted peacemaker, but he was far from a pushover. He constantly challenged the powers-that-be but never once took up arms against them. He denounced injustice whenever he encountered it, but he never condemned its perpetrators.

In today's polarizing environment in which nations, communities, friends, and even families are deeply divided over religion, politics, tribal identities, and ideological loyalties, it often feels as if every disagreement or conflict inevitably turns into a zero-sum game in which someone, or some group, is invariably scapegoated as the enemy or the other. Jesus proposed a faithful alternative that history has proven to be transformative.

This series explores the six principles of nonviolence developed by the Rev. Dr. Martin Luther King Jr. Interpreted through a uniquely biblical lens, we discover key insights about how to apply these principles to our daily lives as we seek, like Jesus, to be peacemakers and bridge builders in an increasingly divided world.

	Sermon Title	Focus Scripture	Theme
Week 1	Nonviolence as a Way of Life for Courageous People	Matthew 5:38–41	We save the world not by *inaction* in the name of peace and unity but by courageous *action* for the sake of God's loving aims.
Week 2	Winning Friendship and Understanding	Romans 12:14–21	Transformation happens when we prioritize relationships over being right.

	Sermon Title	Focus Scripture	Theme
Week 3	Defeating Injustice, Not People	Matthew 26:47–52	Nonviolence is a powerful and just weapon that cuts without wounding.
Week 4	Believing That Suffering Can Be Redemptive	Luke 23:33–49; Romans 5:4–5	Sometimes the only way to conquer violence is to absorb it.
Week 5	Choosing Love instead of Hate	Matthew 5:43–48	Agape love is a way of seeing that frees us from hating the enemy, even as we might hate what the enemy has done.
Week 6	Believing the Universe Is on the Side of Justice	Isaiah 11:6–9; Hebrews 11:1	We are collaborators with God in bending the universe toward justice and shalom.

Tips and Ideas for This Series

The graphic our church used for this series portrayed an image of Jesus holding a dove in his right hand while his left hand is clenched in a fist and wrapped in tape. This provocative design was intended to capture the genuine tension we often feel between our longing to be peacemakers and our violent impulses.

Congregations might consider an all-church read of Martin Luther King Jr.'s *Stride toward Freedom* or a small-group study on King's "Ten Commandments for Nonviolence."

Week 1: Nonviolence as a Way of Life for Courageous People
Matthew 5:38–41

"You have heard that it was said, 'An eye for an eye and a tooth for a tooth.' But I say to you: Do not resist an evildoer. But if anyone strikes you on the right cheek, turn the other also." (Matthew 5:38–39)

In one of Jesus's most misunderstood and misused teachings, we discover that the nonviolent way of life is not passive but requires courage and active resistance. Jesus illustrates how his people, while enduring daily injustices under Roman military occupation, can preserve their dignity and transform their oppressors without resorting to violence.

Jesus points to three nonviolent, subversive actions grounded in courageous self-love and the daring conviction that the possibility for our enemy's transformation lies in their capacity to recognize our humanity and dignity. For a more insightful exegesis of this biblical text, see Walter Wink's *Jesus and Nonviolence*:

1. "Turn the other cheek." Rather than advocating passivity, this was a tactical response to a backhanded slap (a gesture of humiliation). By turning the other cheek, the victim forces their oppressor to see them as an equal, making the usual method of humiliation impossible.
2. "Give your coat as well." This references the legal practice of using clothing as loan collateral. Jesus suggested that when sued for their undershirt, people should give their outer garment too, thereby exposing themselves as a means of protesting the legal system's dehumanizing nature.
3. "Go the second mile." Under Roman law, soldiers were permitted to force civilians to carry their heavy packs for them for one mile. By voluntarily carrying it further, the occupied people demonstrated agency and humanity, forcing soldiers to see them as equals.

King likewise taught that nonviolence is not passive but requires courage and active resistance. It is aggressive spiritually, mentally, and emotionally, and it requires that we love ourselves enough to claim our dignity and belovedness. It assumes that enemies can be transformed through love.

The teaching and example of both Jesus and King offer an alternative to the myth of redemptive violence, which is the timeless and dominant cultural narrative that suggests that good must violently triumph over evil to save the world. The idea that "good guys" are justified in their acts of violence, as seen in popular media from *Popeye* to Marvel movies and in public discourse, is not the perspective of Jesus. Jesus taught that violence only perpetuates violence, while only love can transform enemies. The goal of our actions should not be to do harm to our enemy but to make the enemy see the humanity of the other, leading to genuine change.

Week 2: Winning Friendship and Understanding
Romans 12:14–21

"Do not repay anyone evil for evil, but take thought for what is noble in the sight of all. If it is possible, so far as it depends on you, live peaceably with all." (Romans 12:17–18)

In another often-misunderstood teaching, Paul prescribes the Christians in Rome a challenging directive to feed their enemies and repay good for evil and, in so doing, "heap burning coals on their heads" (v. 20).

This message was originally addressed to Roman Christians facing social persecution and rejection from family and friends due to their conversion. Paul isn't prescribing responses to extreme cases of violence, such as acts of terrorism or a home invasion, in which violence may be justified in self-defense; rather, he's addressing how to handle personal enemies (*echthros* in Greek)—hostile people we might encounter in daily life, like difficult neighbors, aggressive drivers, bullies, or adversarial coworkers.

Peacemaking is a challenging task, so we can give thanks that Paul noted "so far as it depends on you." As they say in recovery communities, "Keep your own side of the street clean." In other words, you can control only yourself. No making excuses about how someone else started it and you were just responding to them. Paul and King emphasize being responsible for our own actions.

Paul's teaching calls us to three key commitments:

1. Break the cycle of violence by not repaying evil with evil, stymying our natural inclination toward retaliation and recognizing that there is good in everyone, even our enemies.
2. Leave room for God's judgment rather than taking vengeance ourselves. This connects to King's and Gandhi's principles that all life is one and that humans are more than their worst actions.
3. Feed our enemies and "heap burning coals on their heads." This phrase is often misinterpreted as a vindictive or punitive act, infuriating your enemies by refusing to play their game. "Killing them with kindness," in other words. In historical context, however, this phrase refers to the generous act of filling a neighbor's empty brazier with hot coals for cooking and warmth, symbolizing life-giving generosity toward enemies.

This sermon should emphasize how breaking the cycle of violence requires refusing to repay evil with evil and instead showing kindness and compassion to those with whom we have conflict. True transformation comes from rekindling light in those whose inner fire has gone out. For King, the goal of nonviolence is not simply winning for "our side" but creating the Beloved Community in which all people are reconciled.

Week 3: Defeating Injustice, Not People
Matthew 26:47–52

Suddenly one of those with Jesus put his hand on his sword, drew it, and struck the slave of the high priest, cutting off his ear. Then Jesus said to him, "Put your sword back into its place, for all who take the sword will die by the sword." (Matthew 26:51–52)

Nonviolence is more than an ideal—it's a courageous way of life. It requires a conversion from our default worldview of self-protection, retributive justice, and vengeance.

Even King, after studying Gandhi's nonviolent philosophy, was initially reluctant to fully embrace it until his friend and fellow activist Bayard Rustin intervened in 1955. When King was arming himself for protection, Rustin convinced him that nonviolence meant completely rejecting weapons. This became a turning point in King's commitment to nonviolent resistance.

Our default worldview says: If your enemy strikes you, strike him back. If he sues you, sue him back. Curse your adversary. Repay his evil with some evil of your own. Take revenge until he cries uncle. If he's hungry, let him starve to death. If he's thirsty, do not give him even a drop of water.

But Jesus says, famously, "All who take the sword will die by the sword." We may respond to violence with violence, believing we'll feel justified, or valued, or redeemed—or at least a little safer in the end. But the truth is such actions leave us only feeling exhausted, bruised, ashamed, and estranged. We feel less human for having done them. They drain us of emotional, mental, physical, and spiritual energy—because not only does nothing good come of them, but in doing them, it feels as if something vital within us has died. Jesus was right: Those who take the sword die by the sword.

In the Greek, the word *take* can also imply to "live by." It can literally mean "to take" or "to draw" a sword, as if from its sheath; but it can also mean, metaphorically, "to take or receive into oneself" or "to give assent to" an idea of what the sword represents. In other words, the sword is not just an actual weapon to be taken up in battle. The sword is a philosophy we take up in life—a philosophy about how to deal with conflict; a myth that claims that only violence can defeat violence. The sword is a symbol for the violent cultural narrative by which we live our lives.

This is why King's approach to nonviolence was deeply spiritual. He called people to reorient their lives around a radically different narrative of nonviolence shaped by spiritual disciplines. He required participants in the movement to commit to such actions as:

1. Meditating daily on the teachings and life of Jesus.
2. Walking and talking in the manner of love.
3. Praying daily to be used by God in order that all might be free.
4. Sacrificing personal wishes in order that all might be free.
5. Observing with both friend and foe the ordinary rules of courtesy.
6. Seeking to perform regular service for others and for the world.
7. Refraining from the violence of fist, tongue, or heart.
8. Striving to be in good spiritual and bodily health.

Such disciplines make it possible to live courageously in the face of evil; to defeat destructive ideas without demonizing people; to understand that the real battle is against systemic injustice, not individuals; and to see nonviolence as a transformative power that can change systems and hearts by affirming the image of God in everyone, even those considered enemies.

This spiritual foundation served King personally throughout his nonviolent struggle. On one occasion, when he was feeling overwhelmed by death threats, he heard an inner voice saying, "Stand up for justice, stand up for truth; and God will be at your side forever."[1]

Week 4: Believing That Suffering Can Be Redemptive
Luke 23:33–49; Romans 5:4–5

When the centurion saw what had taken place, he praised God and said, "Certainly this man was innocent." And when all the crowds who had gathered there for this spectacle saw what had taken place, they returned home, beating their breasts. (Luke 23:47–48)

All of us will inevitably suffer *from* something in life—heartbreak, heartburn, illness, grief, tragedy, disappointment, disillusionment. Suffering from something is unavoidable. But sometimes it happens that people will voluntarily choose to suffer *for* something in life, believing that, in the end, their suffering will produce some greater good beyond themselves.

Note that redemptive suffering is different from redemptive violence—a myth we addressed in week 1. Redemptive suffering is suffering in the hope that individuals and society will be transformed. King's philosophy of nonviolence emphasizes that redemptive suffering is not about tolerating abuse but about willingly enduring hardship for a meaningful cause without resorting to violence.

Historical examples illustrate this principle of redemptive suffering:

- Rosa Parks refusing to give up her seat on a bus.
- Nelson Mandela enduring twenty-seven years in a South African prison.
- Gandhi leading millions to fast for India's independence.
- Tank Man standing before a column of Chinese tanks in Tiananmen Square.

---

1. Martin Luther King Jr., "Our God Is Able," sermon, Montgomery, Alabama, January 1, 1956, https://kinginstitute.stanford.edu/king-papers/documents/our-god-able.

- John Lewis marching across the Edmund Pettus Bridge into a crowd of dogs and hoses.

Jesus's crucifixion is the ultimate example of redemptive suffering. Instead of fighting back to save himself, Jesus absorbed the world's violence, responding with love and forgiveness. This act of voluntary suffering ultimately exposed the truth about the world's violent ways. Disarmed of their weapons and laid bare by this love, Jesus's executioners could finally see the truth of what they had done and who they had become. And when the crowds who had gathered for this spectacle saw what had taken place, the Gospel reading says they returned home "beating their breasts"—an act of contrition and repentance.

King drew inspiration from this narrative, believing that nonviolent resistance could wear down oppressors by appealing to their conscience. His approach was revolutionary. As he wrote in a 1957 letter to Chester Bowles, oppressed people must say to their oppressors, "We will meet your physical force with soul force. Do to us what you will, and we will still love you."[2]

In the face of violence, our natural instincts of fight or flight dominate our conscious response, but there are moments when absorbing suffering can be more powerful than fighting back or running away. Sometimes the only way to conquer violence is to take it into oneself and transform it through love.

Embracing this principle in everyday life invites us to:

- absorb conflict instead of escalating it;
- stand up for what's right despite potential consequences;
- transform moments of tension through love.

What are we willing to suffer for? As a character in South African writer Alan Paton's novel *Ah, but Your Land Is Beautiful*, says, "When I go up there, . . . the Big Judge will say to me, Where are your wounds? and if I say I haven't any, he will say, Was there nothing to fight for?"[3] Voluntary suffering—choosing to endure hardship for something meaningful—is not about being a victim but about actively choosing a path of love and justice, even when it's difficult.

---

2. Martin Luther King Jr. to Chester Bowles, letter, 23 October, 1957, box 142, group 628, Chester Bowles Collection, Beinecke Rare Book and Manuscript Library, Yale University.
3. Alan Paton, *Ah, but Your Land Is Beautiful* (Scribner, 1981), 66-67.

Week 5: Choosing Love instead of Hate
Matthew 5:43–48

"You have heard that it was said, 'You shall love your neighbor and hate your enemy.' But I say to you: Love your enemies and pray for those who persecute you, so that you may be children of your Father in heaven, for he makes his sun rise on the evil and on the good and sends rain on the righteous and on the unrighteous." (Matthew 5:43–45)

Living in the way of nonviolence, it should be clear by now, is not a practice in passivity but an extraordinary action to take against injustice. Etymologically, *mediocre* derives from the Latin meaning "middle of the mountain," which symbolizes a state of being neither here nor there, stuck in an unremarkable existence.

Jesus's Sermon on the Mount challenges this mediocrity, calling followers to transcend self-imposed limitations. He declares, "You are the salt of the earth . . . and the light of the world," metaphors for distinctiveness and purpose (vv. 13, 14). Salt adds flavor, enhancing what is good in the world; light provides clarity, illuminating that which is true and beautiful. We are called to be salt and light, witnesses to a different way of living.

The most radical witness to this way of living is love for one's enemies. This isn't about liking everyone but about a profound spiritual understanding of the other that transforms our human relationships. King appreciated how the Greek language allows for three types of love:

1. *Eros*: Aesthetic, passionate love focused on beauty and emotional attraction.
2. *Philia*: Reciprocal love between friends, based on mutual enjoyment and connection.
3. *Agape*: A transcendent, unconditional love that seeks nothing in return—the divine love of God.

Agape love is the highest form of love. It means loving others not because they are likeable but because they are fundamentally valuable. King argued that within the best of us exists some evil, and within the worst of us, some good. This perspective allows us to see even our enemies as fundamentally redeemable. This love is challenging. It requires seeing people through a divine lens and recognizing that every person carries an inherent worth that transcends their actions. When Jesus says, "Love your enemies," he's not suggesting an emotional response but a transformative way of perceiving humanity.

King's fifth principle of nonviolence, choosing love over hate, emerges from this understanding. When presented with an opportunity to defeat an enemy, the truly extraordinary response is to recognize the enemy's inherent human dignity—the image of God.

This approach is particularly difficult for those who have experienced trauma or suffered violence. (We must pastorally clarify that loving one's enemy and seeing them as a child of God does not mean accepting abuse.) Yet Jesus presents agape love not as an option but as the essential characteristic of those who would be salt and light in the world.

The core message here is both simple and profound: We are capable of far more than mediocrity. We can choose an extraordinary path that sees beyond surface-level differences, that loves unconditionally, and that recognizes the potential for redemption in every human being.

Week 6: Believing the Universe Is on the Side of Justice
Isaiah 11:6–9; Hebrews 11:1

They will not hurt or destroy
  on all my holy mountain,
for the earth will be full of the knowledge of the LORD
  as the waters cover the sea. (Isaiah 11:9)

The nonviolent way of life makes sense only if we believe that history is heading somewhere good and hopeful. In the face of injustice or evil, nonviolent resistance would be inconceivable apart from the belief that the universe, and every living thing in it, is all moving—sometimes reluctantly—toward some higher purpose, some ultimate good. Without this belief, we would be left to conclude that we are completely on our own and that justice is entirely up to us.

But the universe really is moving toward the good. This movement is not happening randomly but as a response to the loving, persuasive call of God to pursue it. In today's text, Isaiah calls this ultimate good *shalom*. It means something like peace. But whereas we often think of peace as simply the absence of war or conflict, throughout the Bible, this kind of peace implies wholeness or well-being—a state in which goodness, justice, and order abide in completeness.

Yet Isaiah suggests that shalom is far more radical than well-being. In all its fullness, shalom is that state in which enemies and opposites will finally be reconciled: "The wolf shall live with the lamb; the leopard shall lie down with the kid; the calf and the lion will feed together . . . the cow and the bear shall graze" (11:6–7).

God is constantly calling the created world toward this shalom. But the world doesn't always cooperate. Often it resists. Progress toward shalom is slow, and it moves across such a prolonged timeline that it can be difficult to measure. And while it may seem that, on the whole, there is more goodness, justice, and order in the universe today than in previous generations, there is still so much evil, injustice, and disorder that we can easily grow hopeless and assume that things will never get any better than they are.

It's out of this hopeless place that we often turn to violence as our last and only resort. If we do not believe in the active presence of a loving God who is relentlessly calling the created world toward shalom, we'll likely seek the only other kind of peace humans have ever really known: peace through violence—a false peace that always seeks to settle the score but never creates genuine shalom.

King once paraphrased a line from the abolitionist Theodore Parker, who believed that the universe was headed toward the shalom we all long for. He said, "The arc of the moral universe is long, but it bends toward justice."[4]

Parker and King both named what we all hope but often struggle to name: that the universe is heading somewhere good. History marches and sometimes stumbles toward some higher, ultimate good. Because they believed this essential truth, they could reject violence to achieve their ends. Instead, they saw themselves as collaborators with God in the faithful work of bending the universe toward justice, or shalom, through nonviolent action.

King's sixth principle of nonviolent action, believing the universe is on the side of justice, gives us perspective, allowing us to see the bigger picture and reminding us that when we work for what is good and just in the world, we are not alone. Not only is God ever before us, calling us to it out of great love, but even the universe is on our side.

---

4. Martin Luther King Jr., "Our God Is Marching On," sermon, Montgomery, Alabama, March 25, 1965, https://kinginstitute.stanford.edu/our-god-marching,

Take Up Your Mat

A four-part series focused on the healing justice ministry of Jesus in the Gospel of John.

AMOS DISASA

Series Overview   Conventional readings of the Gospels often separate the healing and justice ministries of Jesus. However, that distinction breaks down when we consider that the absence of justice breaks bodies by creating tension, anxiety, and internal conflict—manifested in the harmful choices we make to avoid placing our bodies in physically uncomfortable settings.

Four powerful stories from John's Gospel can help us rediscover how Jesus uses the healing of bodies to reorder social hierarchies. Along the way, we note that healing justice is different from plain justice because healing justice begins with the restoration of the body from broken to whole, from dead to alive, from wounded to well. In John, Jesus consistently senses in his own body that the bodies around him are broken and traumatized. These are bodies in need of more than advice on where to go for help, more than a book recommendation or the telephone number of their elected representative.

Healing justice in John does not flow from the top down. It flows from side to side, in an ad hoc, unplanned, and deprogrammed manner, shaped and nurtured in the course of daily life.

	Sermon Title	Focus Scripture	Theme
Week 1	Healing Justice Can't Wait	John 4:46–54	Generosity is how you tell healing justice from justice that makes you wait.
Week 2	Healing Justice Is between the Brackets	John 7:53–8:11	Grace is healing for the part between the brackets, in the unauthorized parts of our story.

	Sermon Title	Focus Scripture	Theme
Week 3	Healing Justice Is a Complete Sentence	John 9:1–16	We have a lot of questions, but when Jesus brings healing, we have the answer we need.
Week 4	Healing Justice Wears a Tunic	John 13:1–17	Jesus embodies healing justice by taking the clothing and role of a servant.

Tips and Ideas for This Series

While the titular phrase "take up your mat" (John 5:8, WEB) does not appear in the four texts from which the sermons are drawn, it does serve as a shorthand image for Jesus's healing ministry. You might consider introducing the series by touching on the story in Matthew 5:1–9, which immediately follows the text for week 1's sermon. To feature an image or object for each week, use a mat for week 1, a stone for week 2, a bowl or handful of mud for week 3, and a towel for week 4.

Week 1: Healing Justice Can't Wait
John 4:46–54

When he heard that Jesus had come from Judea to Galilee, he went and begged him to come down and heal his son, for he was at the point of death. (John 4:47)

Capernaum is a real place. The Jewish historian Josephus mentions it, along with other ancient sources. Capernaum is *as real as* the fact that kids with high fevers that don't come down will eventually die; there's nothing we can do about it. It's *as real as* the fact that royal officials representing corrupt kings should get what they deserve; there's nothing they can do about it. Capernaum is *as real as* the facts we've come to believe about America: that access to quality healthcare is not a basic human right but a privilege to be earned; that second chances are for those who can afford them; that divisions between people are a fact of life; and that generosity is the opposite of justice.

Capernaum is real, but as far as we know, Cana is not. The Gospel writer of John is responsible for all three recorded mentions of it, ever. You can't find evidence that it existed anywhere else, which fits the story told by John. The royal official should have stayed put instead of packing a bag to go to Jesus. Cana should have been a figment of his imagination, a fictional place you go when reality is more than you can bear.

But the royal official with a deathly ill son went anyway. Two days gone from his son, he is unaware of the boy's condition when he arrives at Jesus's feet with no leverage, no negotiating strategy, nothing but himself and fresh memories of his son's suffering.

You may be tempted to ask what Cana, a feverish son, his desperate father, and Jesus have to do with the subject of this sermon series. This sounds like an ordinary healing story. But to generalize this healing as just another in a long line of miracles ignores *who* was healed and *how* it happened.

The father begs Jesus to return with him to Capernaum, but Jesus chooses not to go. Instead, Jesus heals the son from a distance. Why is this worth noting? Well, it takes two days to get back to Capernaum from Cana, and the father has already been gone for two himself. The extra two days of travel may have been more than the son could afford. If the boy had died while they were on the road, Jesus could not have been faulted.

But in Cana, the constraints of reality aren't just suspended, they are subverted. Jesus would have been just merely trying. But instead, he chose to be *generous* with his healing. He gave the royal official—from the court of a king everybody hated—*immediate* release from the pain of grief, loss, and helplessness he carried in his body.

Generosity is what distinguishes healing justice from justice that makes you wait. The son was sick, but the trauma of facing death was shared up and down the family tree. By announcing the miracle immediately, Jesus ensured that not another minute of pain would pass from the son to the father. He could go home in peace.

Justice that makes you wait is different. Justice that makes you wait says the time isn't right to talk about our willful ignorance of the pain that racism imprints on the bodies of Black and Brown people.

Justice that makes you wait says a couple more generations must pass before systemic injustice is undone.

Justice that makes you wait says keep your place, don't ask too many questions, enjoy your freedom, be thankful for what you have.

Healing justice is generous in the time it returns to the people who've acted out of faithful irrationality to demand that those in a position to heal do it immediately.

Week 2: Healing Justice Happens between the Brackets
John 7:53–8:11

The scribes and the Pharisees brought a woman who had been caught in adultery, and, making her stand before all of them, they said to him, "Teacher, this woman was caught in the very act of committing adultery." (John 8:3–4)

In the Bible translation I use, this story is set apart from the surrounding text with brackets, and a footnote is appended. None of the most ancient manuscripts include this famous story about a woman caught in adultery, the men prepared to condemn her to death, and the trap set for Jesus.

The brackets at the beginning and end of our reading, along with the footnote reminding us that the official, authoritative versions of John's Gospel do not include this story, are more than a fun fact to remember the next time you find yourself in a game of Bible bingo.

The brackets remind us of the parts of our own lives that do not make it into the official, authoritative version of the testimony we share with others about ourselves. The parts of ourselves that need healing but would rather point out the sickness of others. It is there, between the brackets, where the remedy for the affliction of injustice can be found.

She was a nameless, faceless woman. As far as Jewish law was concerned, her sin was not adultery; it was her gender. Even though adultery necessitates the involvement of two people, you would not know it from the sections of Jewish law in Leviticus and Deuteronomy that mandate death for women caught in an affair. There is no mention of what should be done to the man. The law permits him to place his complicity between the brackets and move on with life as if nothing ever happened.

We enjoy the same privilege. Between the brackets, in the unauthorized parts of our story, are accounts of letting our families down. Between our brackets are the names we call people who do not meet our standards, who don't fit within our circles of friends, and who clearly do not come from around here. Between our brackets are regrettable moments when we failed to use our power to rescue the powerless and moments when we used the powerless to accumulate more power. In between the brackets are records of rock throwing that we initiated.

The men with their hands clasped around the arms of the nameless, faceless woman are quick to reference their familiarity with the law but do not even bother to explain who is missing from the portrait of lawlessness they present.

After Jesus says, "Let anyone among you who is without sin be the first to throw a stone at her" (v. 7), he is silent. He knows the story is incomplete. He knows that if the woman's prosecutors were to name what is between their own brackets, the eyes of the crowd gathered at his feet would not be focused on the woman and her unrighteousness. Jesus knows that if the men determined to catch him in a public spectacle of careless disregard for the kind of law and order that keeps the powerless in their place were to disclose what is between their brackets, the woman would not be the only sinner the crowd was whispering about. So instead of speaking, Jesus doodles in the dirt and waits.

Week 3: Healing Justice Is a Complete Sentence
John 9:1–16

But they kept asking him, "Then how were your eyes opened?" He answered, "The man called Jesus made mud, spread it on my eyes, and said to me, 'Go to Siloam and wash.' Then I went and washed and received my sight." (John 9:10–11)

The people were full of questions. Everybody wants to know what happened and who is at fault. The disciples begin the cross-examination of the blind man by asking whose sin, his own or his parents', led to the blindness. After the man is healed, the neighbors question his identity, asking, "Is this not the man who used to sit and beg?" (v. 8). Once the man confirms who he is, the neighbors press him: "Then how were your eyes opened?" (v. 10). When he credits Jesus, they demand to know where Jesus is. After the neighbors are done with their part of the story, the religious authorities take over the interrogation. Eventually, they call in his parents to confirm he was blind from birth. Then the man born blind is summoned again for another round of questioning: "What did he do to you? How did he open your eyes?" (v. 26).

Unsurprisingly, their loaded, leading questions result in unsatisfactory answers. The disciples are sure someone's unconfessed sin caused the blindness. The neighbors are sure the man made up the part about Jesus. The parents are sure they do not want trouble from the synagogue leaders. And the religious leaders are sure it is better for a man to remain blind than to be healed by an uncredentialed rabbi.

It is as if the mud Jesus spread over the blind man's eyes got stuck in the eyes of everyone else, and the blind man was the only one who knew to wash it out. They are all in the dark—cynical about good news, resistant to the story of healing, and certain they smell a scandal. Out of all the people we encounter in this story, somehow it is the man born blind who is most adept at knowing where to find light.

He was born blind so that the light of the world might be revealed in him. We do not want to apply this logic to every disability or illness we see today, but we should not be afraid to claim the hopeful scandal of this particular healing story.

This is the lesson of the man born blind. For all the years he was a blind beggar, nobody noticed him enough to ask for his name. They simply knew him as the man who sits and begs. Blind and nameless, his daily struggle for survival kept him too busy to think about the politics of leveraging power, the utility of pandering to others, or the lie we often live by—the lie that if you are not moving up in this world, something is wrong with you, not with us.

It is no surprise, then, that he credits the name of Jesus, not his own, for the transformation. "The man called Jesus made mud, spread it on my eyes, and said to me, 'Go to Siloam and wash'" (9:11). He doesn't engage all their other prying questions. His simple answer is "Jesus." The healing justice Jesus brings is enough. Jesus is a complete sentence.

Week 4: Healing Justice Wears a Tunic
John 13:1–17

He came to Simon Peter, who said to him, "Lord, are you going to wash my feet?" Jesus answered, "You do not know now what I am doing, but later you will understand." (John 13:6–7)

Jewish men did not leave the house with fewer than three layers of clothing. Their outermost layer was a heavy cloak, which was removed when entering someone's home. Beneath the heavy cloak was an outer tunic or robe, and under the robe was an inner tunic. The use of clothing to define ourselves relative to our context is not a modern phenomenon. As in the ancient world, our clothing communicates our expectations for intimacy, our level of comfort with those around us, and the manner in which we expect to be treated.

Jesus would probably have removed his outer cloak as soon as he entered the home where they were eating. But then, during the meal, he stood up from his seat and surprised everyone by undressing in the middle of the room. He removed his robe, revealing his inner tunic, and tied a towel around his waist.

You can almost hear the record player screech to a halt and the chatter quickly die down. The strict social norms have been upended, and not because Jesus is dressed inappropriately, now standing in his underwear in a crowded room on the sacred occasion of the annual Passover meal. The scandal is that he is now dressed like the help, wearing the uniform of a servant. There are others dressed like him in the kitchen, the cellar, and the fields. A tunic and a towel are what you wear in rooms where you have no agency, no seat at the table, no protection from abuses of power, and no recourse when you are wronged. Jesus came to heal these injustices, but could he not do it from his seat at the head of the table?

Jesus is wearing the costume of the underclass and the attire of the economically afflicted. Dressed in a tunic and a towel, the leader suddenly looks out of place. His seat at the head of the table is now empty.

I am acutely aware of what it is like to be mistaken for the help at a party. When I officiate weddings, I put my clergy robe on as early as possible, especially if the ceremony is in the same location as the reception. I have learned from experience that a Black man wearing a dark suit in a fancy venue is likely to be handed an empty glass with a genial thank-you or told that the band is getting dressed in the room upstairs. To be mistaken for the help is a common occurrence for Black people who occupy White spaces in America. Our color became our clothing at the moment Black bodies were stolen and herded like farm animals across the Atlantic. Our reward for surviving the Middle Passage was a towel and a tunic that, four hundred years later, no matter how good we try to be, we have not been able to completely exchange for another outfit.

That night in the upper room, Jesus put on the uniform of the towel-and-tunic people and gave up his seat. But instead of asking whether any of the other towel-and-tunic people scrambling around the table to keep glasses full wanted to take his seat, he offered to take theirs, healing injustice by showing us all the way of servanthood. The brash disciple, Peter, voiced everyone's shock, saying, "Lord, are you going to wash my feet?" (v. 6). Jesus answered, "Unless I wash you, you have no share with me" (v. 8).

Faith That Frees

A four-part series celebrating Black history and the role of faith in the stride toward freedom for African Americans.

DIANE GIVENS MOFFETT

Series Overview Ideal for Black History Month, this series explores the role of faith in the rich tapestry of spiritual resilience, social justice, prophetic leadership, and cultural expression that shapes and sustains many African American communities. Faith can be a powerful catalyst, enabling us to confront historical truths, acknowledge divine guidance, and commit to constructing a more just and peaceful world that reflects God's reign and character. The focus on faith can help believers of all backgrounds understand that celebrating Black history isn't about assigning guilt but rather about equipping followers of Christ to recognize historically evil and unjust events and prevent their recurrence. Congregations can draw inspiration and glean lessons for what faithful discipleship requires as disciples of Jesus are challenged to deal with current issues confronting our world.

	Sermon Title	**Focus Scripture**	**Theme**
Week 1	An Overcoming Faith	Hebrews 11:1	Those who have come before inspire us to overcome the injustices that persist.
Week 2	A Resilient Faith	Mark 5:21–43	Resilience allows us to resist over the long haul, refusing to participate in our own oppression.
Week 3	A Courageous Faith	Micah 5:6–8	To do what the Lord requires, we must meet defining moments with courage.
Week 4	A Singing Faith	Psalm 137:1–4	Our exiled ancestors sang the Lord's song in a foreign land, and we continue their song.

Tips and Ideas for This Series

Include the singing of "Lift Every Voice and Sing"[1] as well as spirituals each week in worship.

Schedule a visit to a museum featuring Black history exhibitions. Plan a neighborhood walk and inquire about the presence, or lack of presence, of African Americans in your community and what action your church may take to address any findings.

Visit the website, www.asalh.org, of the Association for the Study of African American Life and History (ASALH) for graphics, posters, kits, and information about Black History Month.

Week 1: An Overcoming Faith
Hebrews 11:1

Now faith is the assurance of things hoped for, the conviction of things not seen. (Hebrews 11:1)

This week's Scripture introduces a list of people selected in what some call "the hall of faith." It highlights Hebrew ancestors' acts of faith and the results of their trust in God's promises, even when the promises were not fulfilled in their lifetime. While some people wonder why we should take the time to celebrate Black History Month in church, the role of faith in the struggle for liberation from chattel slavery similarly demonstrates what faith in God can do. And because the struggle for justice continues, the role of faith remains relevant for what took place in the past and is still taking place in various forms today.

Free labor on plantations is now replaced by the prison industrial complex. The role of slave catchers is replaced by corrupt police officers patrolling inner-city neighborhoods, hunting down and murdering a disproportionate number of Black people like Breonna Taylor and George Floyd. Research from Stanford University and UCLA shows that public schools are just as segregated today as they were in 1954 when Brown v. the Board of Education was passed. Yet there has been some significant progress made. In the words of the hymn writer Albert A. Goodson, "We've come this far by faith."[2] Faith inspires. Faith renews. Faith causes one to trust God, when we cannot trace God; to follow God when we are not feeling God; to walk with God when we wonder if we will ever get to our destination. Faith makes the difference!

---

1. James Weldon Johnson, "Lift Every Voice and Sing," in *Glory to God: The Presbyterian Hymnal* (Westminster John Knox Press, 2013), #339.
2. Albert A. Goodson, "We've Come This Far by Faith," in *Glory to God: The Presbyterian Hymnal* (Westminster John Knox Press, 2013), #656.

In his book *What Makes You So Strong?* the Jeremiah A. Wright Jr., pastor emeritus of the Trinity United Church in Chicago, speaks of how enslaved Africans applied their faith to overcome seemingly insurmountable odds. Wright makes the point that "no other race was brought to this country in chains. No other race had laws passed making it a crime to teach them how to read No other race had skin color as the determining factor of their servitude and their employability. No other races were physically mutilated to identify them as property, not people."[3] Yet, despite the hard times, Black people were able to rise against the forces that would define and diminish us, through faith.

To be sure, there are obstacles confronting this nation today. There is a toxic air, a spirit of division, a tumultuous energy at work. Some state lawmakers have created new standards for instruction that seek to whitewash slavery, downplaying the brutality and dehumanization of the system. Others are banning books but not assault weapons. International students and immigrants are being swept off the street and taken away without due process.

People of faith would do well to take a page from the history of enslaved Africans in this nation who believed in God's love and justice even when they could not see it. They kept fighting for liberation. Because burning in their soul and hidden in their heart was a faith that kept beating, against the counterpoint of death, providing a sense of purpose and meaning. And it is this sense of purpose that can be a powerful motivator and source of strength to overcome obstacles of every kind that people of every race and hue face.

Week 2: A Resilient Faith
Mark 5:21–43

But the woman, knowing what had happened to her, came in fear and trembling, fell down before him, and told him the whole truth. He said to her, "Daughter, your faith has made you well; go in peace, and be healed of your disease." (Mark 5:33–34)

As we celebrate Black History Month, I am reminded that we are surrounded by a great cloud of witnesses, people who bear witness to the rising power of Jesus—mothers, fathers, big mamas, grandfathers, god-mamas, siblings, aunts, daughters, sons, cousins, and friends—who by their lives and legacies demonstrate resilient faith, a faith that heals and subdues the oppressive forces that threaten our lives.

---

3. Jeremiah A. Wright Jr., *What Makes You So Strong? Sermons of Joy and Strength from Jeremiah A. Wright, Jr.*, ed. Jini Kilgore Ross (Judson, 1993), 144.

Psychologists define resilience as the quality that allows people to be knocked down and get back up again when hit by the adversities of life. Resilient faith is faith that believes despite despair and distress. It is faith that knows that facts are not always final. It is faith that can "take a licking but keep on ticking." Like the woman in our Scripture today, people with resilient faith resist being circumscribed by their circumstance. When trauma and trouble punch and push them up against the boxing ropes of life, people with resilient faith come back swinging. They rise.

I learned about resilient faith from Diane Nash, a historic freedom fighter in the civil rights movement. My husband, Mondre, and I were attending a banquet given by the Greensboro International Civil Rights Museum in February of 2017. Nash was being honored that night. As she was sharing stories of her involvement in civil rights, she gave an example about the role of resistance. She said as long as Black people would pay our bus fare and walk to the back of the bus, we were cooperating and participating in our own oppression—thus perpetuating the unjust law. It is when we refused to ride the bus because of the treatment we experienced and we were willing to pay the sacrifice to walk, carpool, and do whatever we could to get where we needed to go, that the law was changed. This refusal to ride the bus, this resistance to the laws operating, it cost the protestors something—even the very lives of those who were part of the movement.

Then Nash took it further. She took it home, if you will—because oppressive relationships happen everywhere. She told the story of how one day her friend called her, and her friend was complaining about how her husband expects her to cook all the time. She went on and on, telling Nash, "I think he should have dinner prepared for me sometimes. I work too. I tend the children. Clean the house. Do the laundry, you know—all the things women do." Nash listened and finally said to her friend, "May I ask you a question?" Her friend said, "Sure." And Nash said, "Does he make you prepare the food? Does he stand over you and force you to cook?" Her friend refused to answer. Then she said, in her quiet manner, "You don't have to participate in your own oppression."

Week 3: A Courageous Faith
Micah 6:5–8

He has told you, O mortal, what is good,
 and what does the Lord *require of you*

*but to do justice and to love kindness
  and to walk humbly with your God? (Micah 6:8)*

My maternal grandfather, William Jennings Pope, was the parent of ten children. While my aunts and uncles were growing up, the family lived in North Little Rock, Arkansas. It was during a time when voting was a risk for a Black man. You could be beaten up, tarred, and feathered, or strung up and burned for exercising your right to vote. My mother told me how my grandmother would cry every time my grandfather went to the polls. Grandmother would say to granddaddy, "What will happen to the children if they kill you?" He would say to her, "What kind of life will my children have if I live but do not vote?" It was a defining moment for my grandfather. Defining moments happen when our faith is tested, when it takes courage to make decisions that align with the beliefs we profess.

There is a story told of Charles Blondin, a mid-nineteenth-century tightrope walker who wanted to perform his most daring feat. So he went to Niagara Falls where he stretched a two-inch steel cable from one side of the falls to the other. As he climbed the ladder to reach the top, he had a sandbag the weight of a human on his shoulders. He asked the crowd, "How many of you believe I can walk across this rope with the weight of a one hundred eighty pound human on my shoulders?" They all shouted, "We believe!" And with that, Blondin carefully set out to cross the rope, finally landing on the other side. The crowd clapped with excitement and relief. He then said, "How many of you believe I can actually carry a person across?" They cried out "We believe." Then he said, "Which one of you is willing to let me carry you?" And there was silence. Everyone believed Blondin could carry a person across the falls, but nobody wanted to be the person he carried. It takes courage to make decisions that align with the beliefs we profess.

The words of the prophet ring with prophetic eloquence. "[God] has told you, O mortal, what is good, and what does the LORD require of you but to do justice and to love kindness and to walk humbly with your God?" While these words are easy to say, there are defining moments in our lives that require courage to act. It takes courage to stand up for justice, to practice mercy, to stay humble while defending your humanity. Courage is not the absence of fear but acting in the face of fear because we deem what we do to be more valuable than the fear we face. For generations yet born, granddaddy took a courageous walk of faith to the polls. With faith in the future, African Americans, along with White allies and sympathizers, risk their lives to make freedom a reality for Black people. With faith in our future, Jesus had the courage to die so that we might live. What we do in defining moments matters not only for us but for generations beyond us.

Week 4: A Singing Faith
Psalm 137:1–4

*How could we sing the L*ORD*'s song
in a foreign land? (Psalm 137:4)*

Our sermon series for Black History Month would not be complete without addressing the role of music and faith in the Black church tradition. While in a strange place, subject to the whim and fancies of their White captors, enslaved Africans answered the exiled Judeans' question, "How could we sing the LORD's song in a foreign land?" With creativity and innovation, they used music to soothe their sorrow and comfort their cries. They used music to critique their condition and encourage emancipation. They used music to signal revolt and stage escapes. They used music to tame their traumas and fortify their faith. They sang through their heartaches and hallelujahs, through the horrors and hope in God's presence and power to deliver them. Faith was stirred up and belief held down through the music in the church.

In his book *Slave Religion: The "Invisible Institution" in the Antebellum South*, Albert J. Raboteau writes about how the power of music to inspire, reenergize, and reinvigorate those who were enslaved was so intimidating that their White captors prohibited drumming and singing on some plantations. Indeed the songs sung held dual messages. Spirituals like "Swing Lo, Sweet Chariot" or "Steal Away to Jesus" on the surface seemed to express the singers longing for heaven, but in reality it was a code to those planning to escape, signaling it was time to make a move to travel to the place of safety provided by those risking their lives to hide them. When they sang "Wade in the Water," it may appear to be speaking of baptism and the cleansings of sin, but many times it was the advice given to escapees to get into the streams and rivers to throw off the scent of the bloodhounds being used to track them down. Music stirred up faith in the spiritual and practical dimension.

Faith was fortified through participation in musical expression. The sound of music—the ring shouts, the moaning, the melodies, and the biblical stories set to song—was transformative. Even today in the Black church tradition, one does not come to worship to listen passively to the choir but to participate in singing as call and response to both personal and corporate faith. It is common to hear voices rising and shouts emerging and to see bodies swaying, feet tapping a beat, and hands being lifted in praise and surrender to the God at work in our lives. The music of worship is meant to lift the spirit and inspire faith.

In answer to the critics who wondered what all the singing, stumping, shouting, and lifting up of holy hands in worship was about, Gospel artist Kirk Franklin wrote the song "Why We Sing."[4] Franklin riffs on the old hymn "His Eye Is on the Sparrow,"[5] substituting the last line in the refrain, "His eye is on the sparrow, and I know he watches me," with "His eye is on the sparrow, That's the reason why I sing."

While we may not be living in Babylon, in some aspects we are in a strange land—the land to which many of our ancestors were forcibly exiled. This Scripture invites us to consider how and why we sing, sustaining the faith that has brought us this far and ourselves for the journey that continues.

---

4. Kirk Franklin, "Why We Sing," in *Kirk Franklin and the Family* (Gospocentric, 1993).
5. Civilla D. Martin, "His Eye Is on the Sparrow," in *Glory to God: The Presbyterian Hymnal* (Westminster John Knox Press, 2013), #661.

I Wish You Love

A four-part series for LGBTQ+ Pride month, weaving Scripture with the life and music of Dolly Parton.

SAM LUNDQUIST

Series Overview

Across her decades-long career, Dolly Parton has emerged as a beloved icon for the LGBTQ+ community. Her larger-than-life persona, ongoing philanthropy, and musical song telling has continued to be a beacon of hope, belonging, and acceptance. This series honors and celebrates our queer siblings by pairing Dolly's honest, inclusive music with the stories of Scripture to proclaim God's boundless love for all people—no matter who they are or how they express themselves. Open and affirming churches will find all congregants inspired and energized by the joy and camaraderie of a Pride month series and the warm invitation it provides to visitors who may have been harmed or put off by the church's treatment of LGBTQ+ people.

	Sermon Title	Focus Scripture	Theme
Week 1	Dreaming in Exile	Genesis 45:4–14	Featured song: "Coat of Many Colors." Embracing the ways that queer people love and care for one another will transform the church.
Week 2	I Am Who I Am	Exodus 3:1–15	Featured song: "Backwoods Barbie." God calls us to live uniquely and fully—just as we are.
Week 3	We Don't Have to Walk Alone	Acts 2	Featured song: "Travelin' Thru." We all need sanctuary when the world gets hard.
Week 4	I Will Always Love You	1 John 4:7–21	Featured song: "I Will Always Love You." Our task is to always love.

Tips and Ideas for This Series

The "I Wish You Love" worship series is all about music. Make sure your musicians are able to bring Dolly's songs to life so that your congregation can connect with the song and story. Consider hiring musicians to recreate the original track as closely as possible. To keep everyone in the Dolly spirit, put together a Spotify or Apple Music playlist so that your congregation can listen together during Pride month.

This series begs for a Dolly Parton aesthetic: butterflies (Dolly's symbol of love), glitter, rhinestones, and rainbows all have a home here. Your sanctuary, choir, bulletin, even the congregation can get all "Dolly'ed" up. To connect with your community, consider a special offering for an LGBTQ+ organization with a performance by a local drag performer or queer choral or dance group.

Week 1: Dreaming in Exile
Genesis 45:4–14

Then Joseph said to his brothers, "Come closer to me." And they came closer. He said, "I am your brother, Joseph, whom you sold into Egypt. And now do not be distressed or angry with yourselves because you sold me here, for God sent me before you to preserve life." (Genesis 45:4–5)

Exile often forms the queer experience. Family, community, even society as a whole continues to push people out and tell queer people that they don't belong. Churches in particular have historically been places that have proclaimed unconditional love but told queer people that they are undeserving of that love.

And yet, even in exile, God's love will arise.

The story of Joseph in Genesis is the story of a man exiled because of who he is and how he sees the world. His unique dreams are a threat to his family, who kick him out and leave him for dead. Eventually, Joseph is rescued, and he discovers that his gift—the thing that makes him different—is precisely what saves him and his new community from famine. When his family comes needing food, it is Joseph—the tossed-out, the forgotten, the exiled—who cares for them and shows them a new home.

Like Joseph, queer people have spent generations in exile discovering that the things that make them different are the very things that bring life and love. They have found chosen families who are bound together not by blood but by acceptance and belonging. They have developed communities—like cycling clubs and choruses—with new rituals that connect themselves to God and to each other. They have created the artform of drag, in which performers stretch the boundaries of identity and expression to invite an audience into freedom from the shackles of expectation.

And like Joseph's family, a church in famine has much to learn from the bounty of the queer community that has learned that worth and love come from God. Dolly Parton's song "Coat of Many Colors" illustrates this perfectly. The lyrics tell the story of a girl who joyfully goes to school wearing a new coat, handmade from colorful rags, only to be met by bullies and laughter. In the face of contempt, the girl knows that her value comes from God and can never be taken away.

As you consider this text and the story within these lyrics, consider the church's relationship with queer people. How has your faith community treated LGBTQ+ people in its history? What have been the challenging moments? What have been moments of progress and new life? What has the queer community taught your church? What elements of queer life, spirituality, and culture might make your community more open, real, and loving?

Week 2: I Am Who I Am
Exodus 3:1–15

But Moses said to God, "If I come to the Israelites and say to them, 'The God of your ancestors has sent me to you,' and they ask me, 'What is his name?' what shall I say to them?" God said to Moses, "I AM WHO I AM." He said further, "Thus you shall say to the Israelites, 'I AM has sent me to you.'" (Exodus 3:13–14)

Why does Dolly look like Dolly? As she tells it, when Dolly was growing up, she would go into town and be captivated by a flamboyant woman who wore short skirts, high heels, red lipstick, and red fingernails. Dolly thought the woman was just beautiful, and when people would tell her, "She ain't nothing but trash," Dolly would always reply, "Well, that's what I'm gonna be when I grow up: trash!"[1] In her song "Backwoods Barbie," Dolly reflects on the challenges of holding to that personal identity and expression against the expectations and judgments of the public as she sings, "I might look artificial, but where it counts, I'm real."

In Exodus, Moses grapples with similar questions of identity when God calls out to him from the burning bush, summoning him onto a new journey of life and inviting him to become who he was meant to be. But all Moses sees are the things that separate him from his old life and home—his past, his identity, even what he thinks about himself. Consider summarizing Moses's objections in Exodus

1. Emine Saner, "Dolly Parton on Style, Stardom and Sexists: 'I Know How to Push Men Off and Get the Hell Away'" *The Guardian*, October 9, 2023.

3:13–15 and 4:1–17. Moses is afraid and asks, "Who am I to go? What will people think of me?"

In reply, God reveals the divine name—an expression of God's unique identity. "I AM WHO I AM." God's identity is meant to assure Moses in his own abilities as he obeys God's call.

Moses's shame-filled, fearful questions of identity echo the experience of queer people who face internal and external obstacles to being who they are: internalized homophobia, book bans, violent hate speech, and threats to legal protections. This fear can suffocate the spirit so much that it becomes nearly impossible to take the next steps forward. But queer people have also heard the voice of God calling "I AM WHO I AM" and have created joy-filled, life-giving culture as an antidote to that fear.

That life and joy is a model for all of us to embrace our unique identity and expression. That is part of why some people demonize drag performances. Drag is brave art that crosses the boundaries of gender, appearance, and social expectation. Just like in a Dolly Parton show, drag performances are a protest that proclaims that there is more to this life than what we see—more than the expectations of the world, the difficulties of life, even the pain that we feel. Drag shows us that the very name of our creative, artistic, dancing God is written on our hearts and constantly calling out to all of us.

As you consider this text and the story within these lyrics, think about the church's relationship with queer identity and expression. What are the unspoken expectations of your community? How can your church offer more freedom in your gatherings? What might your community learn from a drag performance?

Week 3: We Don't Have to Walk Alone
Acts 2

Now there were devout Jews from every people under heaven living in Jerusalem. And at this sound the crowd gathered and was bewildered, because each one heard them speaking in the native language of each. . . . Awe came upon everyone because many wonders and signs were being done through the apostles. All who believed were together and had all things in common. (Acts 2:5–6, 43–44)

Dolly wrote the song "Travelin' Thru" for the film *Transamerica*, the story of a trans woman reconciling with her past and present during a roadtrip across the country with her long-lost son. The lyrics tell of a woman's difficult journey to find a sense of home while realizing that "holdin' to each other, we don't have to walk alone."[2] This song speaks to life's puzzling paths, our need to travel together, and our yearning for sanctuary.

Acts 2 is the familiar story of Pentecost and the so-called birthday of the church. With the aftermath of the resurrection and the threat of empire lingering outside the door, the apostles are huddled together along with followers who have traveled from all over the region. Suddenly, the spirit of God fills the space, and the apostles can miraculously speak in the native languages of all who are gathered. It is a room where everyone can gaze around and say, "I understand, and I am understood." What arises is a community of love, sharing, joy, and unity—an anchor in the midst of the great challenges just beyond the room.

For queer people, "sometimes the road is rugged and it's hard to travel on," as Dolly sings. With legislation like book bans and educational restrictions, many are trying to silence and erase the stories of queer people. Bans on gender-affirming care aim to make transgender people invisible. Entire groups of people are being asked to disappear, creating a culture of contempt in which certain identities are deemed more worthy, valuable, and acceptable than others. The antidote is sanctuary: communities and places that offer safety and understanding when the world can't or won't.

Dolly herself has created one of those sanctuaries. In a region where many are challenged by legal and cultural threats, Dollywood has become a magnet for queer people. People travel from all over the region to gather in a place where they can feel safe and understood and to hear, as Dolly sings, "God made me for a reason and nothin' is in vain."

As you consider this text and the story within these lyrics, reflect on how the church can provide a safe and welcoming sanctuary for queer people. Through both words and actions, how have churches closed their doors to queer people? Is your church a safe place and a community in which all people can thrive? What messages do queer people hear about themselves from your community? How can your sanctuary be a better sanctuary where everyone feels understood and accepted?

---

2. Dolly Parton, "Travelin' Thru," track 21 on *Transamerica*, Nettwerk, 2006.

Week 4: I Will Always Love You
1 John 4:7–21

So we have known and believe the love that God has for us. God is love, and those who abide in love abide in God, and God abides in them. . . . The commandment we have from him is this: those who love God must love their brothers and sisters also. (1 John 4:16, 21)

Perhaps Dolly Parton's most well-known hit, "I Will Always Love You," is a song of unconditional love. It is both a love song and a farewell song written when Dolly made the decision to leave her longtime business partner, Porter Wagoner, and launch her own solo career. Unable to find the right words, she wrote this song and performed it for him so that he would remember an "I love you" in spite of a painful past and a bittersweet goodbye.

The writer of 1 John reminds us of God's boundless, eternal love—a love that transcends every difficult moment—and paints a beautiful picture of the flow of love. Love begins beyond us: It is unending, it is divine, it simply is. That same love is within us because we were all created and birthed by that love. We bring that love to life as we love others with our words and our lives. Life's task is to live in that flow of love, attuned to the love beyond us and within us, and to extend that love around us.

For many queer people, this fundamental flow has been severed. They've been told by families, churches, and culture that they can't love or they don't love in the right way or they aren't loved or they're unlovable or they're cut off from God's love. Many are left with wounds to that deepest part of their spirit that desires to love and be loved. Celebrating Pride is a balm to those scars, a protest against the contempt of the world, and a proclamation that there is an "I love you" that belongs to everyone.

The words of 1 John remind us of the simplicity and necessity of saying "I love you" with our whole selves. Our task is to live a life of love with all the gifts, identities, journeys, and expressions that God has given to us. The more we share it, the more we live it, the more we become it.

First John 4:20 is a warning against the hypocrisy of claiming to love God while showing disdain for or doing harm to others. Many Christians justify this hypocrisy by twisting the meaning of love, but we know what love looks like. Love is not about fear or punishment but about the abiding grace of God, demonstrated by the Son of God and sustained through the Spirit.

As you consider this text and the story within these lyrics, think about the church's relationship with queer love. How has your community loved queer people? What have been the challenges in doing that? How can you offer a bigger "I love you" to the queer community? What aspects of queer love might make your church stronger?

Seasonal

Holy Darkness, Holy Light

A five-part Advent and Epiphany series.

SHAWNA BOWMAN

Series Overview This Advent series that includes Epiphany Sunday is meant to disrupt the light and dark binary that turns up in our liturgy, music, and interpretations of the Advent texts and season. Rather than paint the dark as something to avoid and the light as the only expression of good (a form of binary thinking that can perpetuate White supremacy), this series embraces the holy darkness and the holy light. This series invites the congregation into an Advent season in which they will be both challenged and nourished by seeing the gifts to be found in the darkness as well as in the light, and in the mysterious space in between

	Sermon Title	Focus Scripture	Theme
Advent 1	Waking Up to Injustice	Mark 13:24–37	Many of us go to sleep when it's dark. But Jesus invites the disciples to wake up to the dark.
Advent 2	Seeking Peace in the Darkness	Mark 1:1–8	John speaks into the darkness, preparing the way of the Lord.
Advent 3	Reparative Light	John 1:6–8, 19–28	John's Gospel invites us to explore how God came into the world made of flesh and light.
Advent 4	Between Light and Dark	Luke 1:26–45	Mary's life changed in the in-between space of dusk on an ordinary night.

	Sermon Title	Focus Scripture	Theme
Epiphany	Delight	Matthew 2:1–12	The magi's journey reminds us not to miss the opportunity to run toward God with utter delight.

Tips and Ideas for This Series

Play with the elements of darkness and light in your worship space. At Friendship Presbyterian Church, we did this by literally dimming the lights so that our Advent worship services began in the dark and became increasingly lighter over the hour. Rather than lighting Advent candles, we reimagined this liturgy and ritual and created Advent lamps that were turned on at the beginning of worship each week, building on liturgy that honored both the darkness and the light. An additional lamp was added each week until we lit five lights on Christmas Eve; the fifth light was a paper star lamp meant to be the Christ light.

Advent 1: Waking Up to Injustice
Mark 13:24–37

"But in those days, after that suffering,

> *the sun will be darkened,*
> *and the moon will not give its light,*
> *and the stars will be falling from heaven,*
> *and the powers in the heavens will be shaken." (Mark 13:24–25)*

Like many Advent texts, we begin with what often feels like desolate darkness. Some scholars call this portion of Mark's Gospel the "little apocalypse." When we read apocalyptic texts, we often read them as if the world is coming to an end, thinking of judgment and fire, of total annihilation. But really, the word *apocalypse* simply means to reveal, to uncover, or to face reality.

Much of Jesus's ministry is about uncovering: uncovering greed that hides behind temple taxes, uncovering the misuse of power that parades as authority, uncovering the hypocrisy that hides behind elitist morality. Jesus is asking his students to do one of the hardest things: to let go of their illusions of grandeur, to peer into the darkness and face the reality of the world as it is, because the only way forward, the only way to truly seek the kind of justice God wants for us, is to tell the truth about the current state of things—not so that we can wallow in how bad it is but so that we can be relieved of any pretense and notice not only the hard things but the absolutely beautiful things as well. When we're really paying attention, we begin to notice not only what's dying but also what is *emerging*, what is *possible*, what is even *thriving*.

We might associate darkness with going to sleep, but in today's text, it is in the darkness that the Messiah is revealed. When things feel like desolate darkness, that is the time to wake up and see what is going on around us. We can wake up to the inequity that keeps our neighbors from thriving and so glimpse the joy of creating community with one another. We can wake up to the devastation of war and poverty and so realize what it means to be cared for, to be checked on, to care for one another.

Name something that your congregation has been collectively waking up to in recent months or years. I think a lot about our journey at Friendship Presbyterian Church waking up to the deep issues that lead to homelessness and food insecurity. Our journey has taken us from a place of charity to one of advocacy and activism, where we've invested our resources in becoming a space of solidarity with our unhoused and newly housed neighbors. I think of how much we've had to wake up to or uncover over the years, gaining knowledge and new awareness that has brought us here to this very intentional and specific ministry now unfolding in our space.

When I read through this Gospel story, I am caught short by Jesus's instruction to "stay awake" because it's one of the key phrases in the movement for racial justice. Groups like #blacklivesmatter began using the phrase #staywoke as a tagline over ten years ago because all too often a crisis happens and folks are surprised. A crisis wakes people up to the reality of how many marginalized people live day in and day out, but if it doesn't impact us directly, we tend to fall back asleep. It's essential that we hear and understand #staywoke as more than a pithy saying or a signal about our political leanings. Understood correctly, it is a discipline, a practice, a way of life. It conveys a commitment that we are in this with one another—that we won't fall asleep, or give up, or stop learning more, that we won't stop telling and hearing stories, that we won't stop asking questions.

Advent 2: Seeking Peace in the Darkness
Mark 1:1–8

The beginning of the good news of Jesus Christ.
As it is written in the prophet Isaiah,

> *"See, I am sending my messenger ahead of you,*
> *who will prepare your way,*

the voice of one crying out in the wilderness:
  'Prepare the way of the Lord,
  make his paths straight.'" (Mark 1:1–3)

Could the darkness we often experience in the world actually be good news? Mark's Gospel promises it is. Like the Isaiah text quoted in verses 2–3 suggests, God's messenger knows people are in the midst of despair and yet promises something new, a new beginning that will be born of their struggle and their willingness to live into the possibility of peace.

I used the letters of the word *peace* to frame how John the Baptist embodies a radical and transformative relationship with God that makes his vision for peace possible even in the midst of darkness and shows this path to those who have come to him seeking redemption.

Prepare. Preparing the way of the Lord is to lay the groundwork for Jesus's work of peace. This is not a passive peace but an active one, bringing peace through justice. They belong together; they can't be separated from one another. "Know justice, know peace," or "No justice, no peace," is one of the common chants of activists at rallies and protests, and I like to think of this chant as the liturgy of resistance and transformation. The darkness challenges us to see more clearly, owning up to the truth of human injustice and the pain we have caused. John is a prophet dressed like Elijah, and like those prophets of old, he is not a fortune teller but a truth teller. One way to prepare for peace is by telling the truth.

Every Day. John the Baptist knows that real and sustaining peace gets made day in and day out. It's hard to keep praying for peace in the midst of such ongoing destruction, but just as morning follows night, God calls us to do more than turn up once at the riverside or the protest or the city center. God's invitation is about the long haul; it requires endurance and resilience. John's call to repentance isn't accomplished by that ritual dunking we call baptism by itself. The ritual he offers is a sign of a new way of being in the world, a new way of being he calls folks to live out every day.

Agitated. Peacemaking isn't about calm and quiet. John is a lot of things, but quiet isn't one of them. He's not afraid of the dark; he's yelling into the dark, dressed like a wild animal and demanding folks upend their lives. Sometimes we call Jesus the Prince of Peace, but that doesn't mean he was calm and gentle all the time. Jesus was angry and opinionated, and he was unyielding when it came to things like greed, hypocrisy, and folks with no imagination. Jesus was agitated *and* an agitator.

Contagious. Both violence and peace have the potential to spread like a disease. John understands this and is using his voice and power to spread hope as an antidote to the violence of the empire. He interrupts, almost theatrically so, the status quo. He speaks truth to the folks who come to see him, no matter who they are. And as word gets out about John's promise of redemption, the people come in droves. Why? Because they want so badly to believe there is another way, a better way, a way forward out of the wilderness, and they want to be part of it.

Embodied. Advent is leading to the incarnation, the embodiment of God in Christ. John is pointing to an incarnational, embodied peace. The path of peace requires our own capacity to embody, enliven, or animate peace through our own actions and to point to the One who would show us how to do this with his very life. In becoming human, in choosing to walk with us even in dark places, the incarnate God will demonstrate what it means to choose peace, not as an outcome but as a living, breathing way of life.

Advent 3: Reparative Light
John 1:6–8, 19–28

There was a man sent from God whose name was John. He came as a witness to testify to the light, so that all might believe through him. He himself was not the light, but he came to testify to the light. The true light, which enlightens everyone, was coming into the world. (John 1:6–9)

We've spent the first two weeks of Advent exploring the gifts of the darkness. This week's text invites us to explore the gifts of light, just after John's Gospel opens with a song about God coming into the world made of flesh and light, a light that nothing can extinguish, and then it goes on to introduce us to John the Baptist, the one prepared to speak, preach, teach, and usher in the light. John is clear: He is not the light. But he will make his life's purpose pointing to it and its potential to repair the world.

Consider what we know about light and how it works:

- The potential for light to perform work is called light energy.
- Light energy is the only form of energy that we can actually see directly.
- Light is a type of electromagnetic energy.
- Light travels fast, at a speed of about 300,000 km/s.
- The speed of light changes when traveling through different objects.
- Light energy is always moving, and therefore, it cannot be stored; it can only be absorbed.

- On the electromagnetic spectrum, humans can see only a very small amount of light—this is what we call visible light. There's a whole lot more energy we cannot see.
- Light exists in relation to other things. Space is dark because light is visible only when it has an object to bounce off of.
- Light energy has healing properties. It can help regulate our systems and even promote wound healing. It is essential for life through the process of photosynthesis.

Like light . . .

- Christ's energy moves quickly. It is fully present, not held up or held back.
- Jesus's movement would change as he encountered obstacles, such as real humans in need, and as he confronted the powers and principalities of his own day.
- Jesus's energy, love, and compassion cannot be stored up or hoarded; it can only be absorbed.
- We can see just a small amount of Christ's visible light, a sliver of what God is up to in the world. *God with us* is a mystery, worthy of our curiosity and wonder.
- Christ is revealed in our relationships with one another; we need one another in order to glimpse Christ's light. We will never find it groping around in the dark by ourselves.

Most significantly, Christ embodies the kind of light that leads to repair. Just as light energy has healing and reparative properties, so does Christ, in whom we live and move and have our being. Just as plants use sunlight to power growth and renewal, repairing the natural world with its leaves and seeds, we receive the light of Christ to power us in the work he calls us to do repairing the world.

What might this repair look like? At our church, we turned to stories of Truth and Reconciliation Commissions around the world and played a short video that tells the story of the truth and reconciliation process unfolding in Canada. This video, called "Namwayut: We Are All One," is available on YouTube.[1] How will the light of Christ empower you to repair the world?

---

1. CBC, "Namwayut: We Are All One. Truth and Reconciliation in Canada," December 18, 2017, YouTube video, https://www.youtube.com/watch?v=2zuRQmwaREY.

Advent 4: Between Light and Dark
Luke 1:26–45

In the sixth month the angel Gabriel was sent by God to a town in Galilee called Nazareth, to a virgin engaged to a man whose name was Joseph, of the house of David. The virgin's name was Mary. And he came to her and said, "Greetings, favored one! The Lord is with you." But she was much perplexed by his words and pondered what sort of greeting this might be. The angel said to her, "Do not be afraid, Mary, for you have found favor with God. And now, you will conceive in your womb and bear a son, and you will name him Jesus." (Luke 1:26–31)

Sometimes there are liminal moments in our lives. Instead of blazing light or blinding dark, they are open spaces, soft hues of purple fading into orange, like dawn or dusk. They are not day or night but the space between them—the gap in certain categorization. Is it day yet? Or still night? These are moments we might miss, but if we stop, if we watch, if we notice, if we dare to step across the threshold, our lives will forever be changed.

Mary knows this moment. The moment her life changed—not with blinding light, not because she found her way through the dark. But in the quiet dusk of an average night, she received a messenger, a voice, a new reality, an invitation: "You will conceive and give birth to a son, and you will name him Jesus."

And the most amazing thing happened. Mary said yes.

Mary handed her heart over to God, interrupting the certain life she thought she was going to have, and entered a life she couldn't yet imagine. She couldn't imagine the journey she would take, the beauty of the child she would birth, the heartbreak of mothering this being. She could not imagine the way it would end. She couldn't imagine it, but she trusted it and she understood that the world as it is could be turned upside down by this kind of yes.

Mary says yes at dusk, and at dawn, she is on the road. She doesn't just walk; she runs to her kinswoman—seeking solidarity, seeking answers, seeking another story not so unlike her own. And Elizabeth comes out to meet her, to enfold her, to bless her (Luke 1:41–45).

And that is all Mary needed: to be met, to be seen, to be believed, and to be blessed.

Mary sings, "My soul magnifies the Lord" (v. 46).

Mary sings a song about a world transformed, a song of her own expanded understanding of a God whose love keeps enlarging. She sings a song of power and resistance about a God who undoes the most powerful and fills the hungry with good things to eat. Mary sings a song written on her heart by her ancestor Hannah and set loose by her cousin Elizabeth. This is Mary making a claim about her own child, but she's also making a claim about herself—a commitment to step into the uncertainty of what is and what will be.

There is a gap between Mary's song and the reality of the world. There is a gap between what we know to be God's dream for the world and the world we live in. Compassion and solidarity is how we step into the gap, how we begin to build a collective vision and collective power for a new way of life together.

Solidarity is incarnation. God sees the suffering of the world and decides to live and love together with us. God decides to enter this world and our human experience, to suffer with us in the gaps between darkness and light, the gap between poor and rich, the gap between powerless and powerful, the gap between brokenness and reconciliation.

Just as Mary answered the call to stand in the gap with her whole body and soul, to magnify the Lord, to proclaim good news to the poor, to raise a child who will have the power to close the gap, so can we.

Epiphany: Delight
Matthew 2:1–12

In the time of King Herod, after Jesus was born in Bethlehem of Judea, magi from the east came to Jerusalem, asking, "Where is the child who has been born king of the Jews? For we observed his star in the east and have come to pay him homage." When King Herod heard this, he was frightened, and all Jerusalem with him. (Matthew 2:1–3)

The incarnation has happened. God has arrived, born in the night and wrapped in human skin. *God with us.* It's terrifying and amazing news. The Gospel accounts of this news always open with the words "don't be afraid" and "do not fear." Indeed, the news should stop us in our tracks. But the word *fear* in our biblical text can also be translated as *awe* (with the same root as *awful*)—it's a visceral reaction in our bellies, isn't it?" God has arrived. Whether this fills us with awe or an awe-ful dread, apathy is certainly not an option.

Matthew's Gospel tells the story of two ways human beings respond to this news of the incarnation—the possibility that God has arrived here, in our midst:

There's Herod, a powerful ruler, beholden to Rome but wielding his power with a vengeance in Jerusalem. He's filled with dread. And there are the magi, who respond to the light in the sky by venturing out to find, celebrate, venerate, and bear witness to that which will fill them with awe or delight!

Herod runs away from God.

The magi ran toward God.

For Herod, the magi come looking for a king and he's not it. What if this sign in the heavens means losing his foothold on Jerusalem? What if it does mean losing his standing with Rome? The magi's search doesn't come with reassurance or hope for Herod, and he responds to his fear by bolstering his power. Herod isn't about to join the magi's quest, and instead Herod chooses death. Not his own, but he condemns to death a whole generation of babies. Herod chooses death to protect himself. Herod's story is a story about terror, about violence born of fear. And this violence and terror are not limited to an outrageous or sociopathic few; the text tells us that the whole city gets caught up in such fear. We are no strangers to how those in power induce fear and goad violence. January 6 is the official day of Epiphany, but now it's also a day in which a modern-day, would-be tyrant unleashed their power, echoed and amplified by a collective attack on the United States Capitol. A frightened leader wielding power induced the fear of the whole community.

But there is another way. The magi's story is the story of those who respond to fear by taking stock of what they see and what they know, leaning into hope that defies imagination—and running toward God with utter *delight*. Seeing signs in the stars, they choose to go on a journey of discovery, to relinquish their power and belongings in order to pay homage to something completely unexpected. The magi choose openness, curiosity. They are dreamers and seekers and are filled with wisdom.

What does it mean to choose delight in response to life-altering news? What does it mean to choose reverence in the face of fear? On this Epiphany Sunday, what does it mean for us to choose delight as an orientation to our lives in this new year?

In Plain Sight

A seven-part series for Advent, Christmas, and Epiphany using the ordinary stuff of life.

JILL J. DUFFIELD

Series Overview At Christmas, God came into our ordinary world in the form of a child, and still today, God is at work through the ordinary stuff of life, if we train our eyes to see. Scripture bears witness to the fact that our God chooses to work through all creation, through worldly, unnoteworthy things and people. Moses hears God's voice in a burning bush. Balaam's donkey speaks. Jesus says that if people keep silence, the rocks will cry out. A star guides the magi, and on-duty shepherds are the first to get word of the Messiah's birth. The appeal of this series is its simplicity and relatability, using seven ordinary objects that appear in the biblical narratives of messianic prophesy and incarnation—objects we encounter in our own lives. Through things such as gates, trees, cloth, light, and water, we can find new meaning in the biblical account of Jesus's coming.

	Sermon Title	Focus Scripture	Theme
Advent 1	Gates	Genesis 28:1–5, 10–22; Matthew 24:29–35	Like Jacob's "gate of heaven," Advent is a liminal space.
Advent 2	Tears	Psalm 126; Revelation 7:13–17	Grief and sorrow don't take a break for the holidays, but God is there with us in the pain.
Advent 3	Belts	Jeremiah 13:11; Mark 6:7–9	God wants to be as close as the garment around our waist.
Advent 4	Trees	Job 14:1–17; Matthew 13:31–32	Abundant life grows in unexpected places.

	Sermon Title	Focus Scripture	Theme
Christmas Eve	Cloth	Luke 2:1–7	As we greet the swaddled baby Jesus, we also prepare for whom he will become.
Sunday after Christmas	Hearts	Psalm 51:1–12; Luke 2:8–20	Whether our hearts are full of sorrow or joy, God is there with us.
Epiphany	Gold	Exodus 32:1–6; Matthew 2:1–12	Will our treasure become an idol or a gift?

Tips and Ideas for This Series

Make use of the objects described in your altar decor and bulletin/screen imagery, and encourage congregants to carry the symbolism of these ordinary items into their daily lives. Congregants might use the daily devotions and small-group study materials in the book *Advent in Plain Sight*, from which this series is drawn.[1] Downloadable slides and other materials are available at www.wjkbooks.com/AdventInPlainSight.

Advent 1: Gates
Genesis 28:1–5, 10–22; Matthew 24:29–35

And he was afraid and said, "How awesome is this place! This is none other than the house of God, and this is the gate of heaven." (Genesis 28:17)

Advent is a liminal space, positioned on the threshold between what is and what will be, as we look forward both to Jesus's birth and the ultimate appearing of Christ at the apocalypse—a scary word that really just means "revealing"—of all things. Gates are a perfect symbol of that spiritual threshold, holding the potential for both entry and exit. We arrive at the Lord's gate, approaching the incarnation, but Christ is simultaneously "near, at the very gates" (Matt. 24:33), preparing to return.

In our Old Testament text for this week, we find Jacob rooted on earth, sleeping with a rock for a pillow but experiencing the divine presence of God and many angels—a sight so mind-blowing, he declares it must be the "gate of heaven." Those thin spaces, when heaven and earth touch, are the moments that change lives and assure us of God's presence among us. This convergence is the glory and the

---

1. Jill J. Duffield, *Advent in Plain Sight: A Devotion through Ten Objects* (Westminster John Knox Press, 2021).

paradox of Advent, as we simultaneously await Jesus's earthly and cosmic arrivals, looking expectantly for a glimpse of the Divine.

We may be surprised when we read traditional Advent texts like this one from Matthew about Christ's return, the sun and moon going dark, and the need to make ready not only for sweet baby Jesus but also for justice-bringing, sheep-and-goat-sorting, and the risen and returning Christ. The latter is a tougher sell in this season of twinkling lights and "Here Comes Santa Claus." All the more important, then, that disciples prepare not only for the birth of Jesus but for Christ's return as well.

What would it mean for our daily living, the choices we make, the lens through which we see the world, if we considered the fig tree and wondered if, in fact, Jesus Christ is as near as the gates through which we pass daily? Our front door? The city limits of our town? The border of our country? What if the risen Christ returned and showed up at one of the many barriers we erect to keep those we consider insiders safe and those we consider outsiders at bay?

The ultimate opening of the gates of heaven, of God come to earth, the incarnation, continues God's promise of blessedness and blessing. As we prepare for the birth of Jesus and the return of Christ, all around us God opens the gates of heaven, breaches whatever barriers we erect, puts in place not just ladders between the Divine and the dailiness of our lives, but comes and sits beside us, blessing us and making of us a blessing, not to just a company of peoples, but to all the families of the earth.

When we think of a gate as a boundary, who do you picture waiting near the gate to be let in? Who is waiting along the edge of our communities needing an invitation or voice of welcome? Who is being shut out?

Advent 2: Tears
Psalm 126; Revelation 7:13–17

"They will hunger no more and thirst no more;
   the sun will not strike them,
   nor any scorching heat,
for the Lamb at the center of the throne will be their shepherd,
   and he will guide them to springs of the water of life,
and God will wipe away every tear from their eyes." (Revelation 7:16–17)

Despair doesn't disappear with Jesus's birth, nor does it disappear at the holidays. On the contrary, the festive atmosphere exacerbates many people's grief and depression. So many psalms voice the laments and fears of those who mourn and struggle even today, offering a sound reminder that tears are not antithetical to faith, but part of the human journey we honor throughout Advent and year-round.

Jesus always seems to seek out those who know what it means to sow long seasons of tears. He goes to the demoniac tethered to the grave, the lepers excommunicated from society, the woman chronically ill for eighteen years, the tax collectors despised by their own people, the woman about to be stoned for adultery. Those humbled by circumstances, some out of their control and some of their own making, provide soil fertilized by tears and subsequently ripe for receiving the seeds of the gospel that brings forth shouts of relieved, resurrected joy.

A consistent theme in Scripture, however, is that *one day*—one day that is very far off but that we continually long for and work for—our sorrowful tears will come to an end. As Psalm 126 says, "Those who go out weeping . . . shall come home with shouts of joy" (v. 6), and as so beautifully depicted in Revelation, "God will wipe away every tear from their eyes" (7:17).

Knowing that ultimately God's justice and love prevail gives us hope in the here and now. This knowledge gives us the courage for the living of these days. No matter the challenges and travails, we followers of Jesus Christ persist in doing justice, loving kindness, and walking humbly with the God whose home is among mortals, the God who becomes mortal, the God who will wipe every tear from the eyes of those who have known great suffering. The description of heavenly worship in Revelation 7 paints a picture that inspires us to strive for God's kingdom, so near and yet so far away on earth.

Nonetheless, while offering this hopeful word, the preacher must be careful not to minimize painful feelings or too quickly make the move Psalm 126 describes, turning tears to joy and weeping to shouting, but offer the assurance that God is faithful throughout our pain. Our comfort is that God sees our tears and mourns with us. Scripture offers us hope that, while real and valid, our tears will not last forever but will be wiped away by the very hand of God when all is made well in God's kingdom.

Advent 3: Belts
Jeremiah 13:11; Mark 6:7–9

He called the twelve and began to send them out two by two and gave them authority over the unclean spirits. He ordered them to take nothing for their journey except a staff: no bread, no bag, no money in their belts, but to wear sandals and not to put on two tunics. (Mark 6:7–9)

This week's object may be the most unusual of the series. What's so spiritual about a belt? But examining what such an essential item of clothing signified in ancient times can reveal intriguing insights. The terms we translate as *belt* refer to a variety of garments a man would wear around his waist, serving purposes of protection, modesty, and/or utility.

The prophet Jeremiah proclaims that God desires intimacy with us, to be as close to us as a loin cloth (or whatever we wear closest to our skin!) and to help us recognize our dependence on God. The people Jeremiah was speaking to had refused the gift of that close communion with the Divine, he said, and instead tossed God aside, leaving their relationship to decompose and disintegrate. They forgot who and whose they were, and subsequently they lost their purpose of praising and glorifying God. In short, they would not listen to the God who created, loved, and called them; when that relationship gets neglected, all others get misordered. True intimacy does not come easily. Often, we reject the opportunity to know and be known honestly and fully. We want to hide behind layers of clothing that cover our flaws and present our best features to the world. We would rather not let others know our vulnerabilities lest they exploit or belittle them. We even attempt to keep parts of ourselves off-limits to God, refusing to listen to God's commandments and promises because we do not want to cede control and therefore enter into a relationship with God that requires us to open our hearts fully to all God loves. God wants to be as close as a belt wrapped around our waist, but we fear that nearness will be constricting rather than comforting.

As we anticipate the appearance of Emmanuel—God with us—we should consider what it means to be with God, in relationship with God. We must open up to God and learn to trust as Jesus's disciples do when he sends them out without money or other supplies in their belts. Jesus told them to go. Proclaim. Teach. Heal. Cast out demons. Do not do this alone. Do not be weighed down by baggage, by the need to protect your possessions, your investment in worldly security. Radical trust in the One who sends you is needed because you are not to stuff your belt with all the things you think will keep you safe and keep you apart from the pain of those you encounter along the way.

Jesus came in the most vulnerable and dependent form—a human infant. May we approach God with that same vulnerability this Advent.

Advent 4: Trees
Job 14:1–17; Matthew 13:31–32

"For there is hope for a tree,
  if it is cut down, that it will sprout again
  and that its shoots will not cease.
Though its root grows old in the earth
  and its stump dies in the ground,
yet at the scent of water it will bud
  and put forth branches like a young plant.
But mortals die and are laid low;
  humans expire, and where are they?" (Job 14:7–10)

Are you a real tree family or an artificial tree family? There are some benefits to fake Christmas trees, but one thing you miss out on (besides the pleasant piney smell) is the lesson in life and death that comes from having a formerly lush plant slowly withering in your home. Some Christmas trees seem to thrive into January even apart from their natural nourishment, while others dry up and lose their needles despite constant watering.

Life is precious and unpredictable. This week's focus Scriptures emphasize abundant life emerging in unexpected places—a coppiced stump and a tiny mustard seed. What once thrived might thrive again despite setbacks, and what is small may hold more wonder than we can imagine.

Job, in the midst of all his trials, is lamenting human finitude, death, and the real limits of our power and longevity. There is a big difference between our finite lives and trees that can sprout new branches out of a stump and its remaining roots, right? Or can we find hope in the things that outlive us—the branches that will bloom from the legacy we leave behind? Job's statement reminds us of the "shoot . . . from the stump of Jesse" named in Isaiah 11:1, a prophetic confidence that despite Judah's defeat and exile, a savior would come from the lineage of Jesse's son, the great King David. Salvation may emerge even from places of death, like trees that grow out of the compost of a forest floor.

Similarly, Jesus spoke of God's salvific kingdom, the kingdom of heaven, being like a mustard seed: tiny, easily overlooked, yet capable in the right conditions of producing a sizable tree that provides shelter for the birds of the air. God's realm entails utilizing the common and the insignificant in life-giving ways that defy expectation and human imagination. What if we really believed that the kingdom of heaven, present even now on earth, is like a tiny mustard seed that explodes in growth and spreads exponentially, invading the landscapes all around us in order to create places of relief and protection and care and joy?

We've seen it happen before—in a tiny baby, born in an unexpected place under less-than-ideal circumstances, who starts a movement and gives life everlasting.

The Savior of the world, who entered this world as an infant in a powerless family, proclaims that God operates through ordinary things and everyday events. During Advent, with its cold and short days (in the northern hemisphere, that is), let us seek the unexpectedly evergreen life that God brings, and seek to pass it on.

Christmas Eve: Cloth
Luke 2:1–7

While they were there, the time came for her to deliver her child. And she gave birth to her firstborn son and wrapped him in bands of cloth and laid him in a manger, because there was no place in the guest room. (Luke 2:6–7)

Those of us who have cared for newborns know the skill required to swaddle them effectively. I remember attempting to swaddle my firstborn a few hours after his birth. The nurse unwrapped the sleeping bundle, so snug and content, quickly gave me a demonstration, and invited me to give it a try. It looked so easy. It proved to be more complicated in practice. What she had made look neat and secure, I managed to make look like a lumpy mess from which my son's head was barely visible. His little legs kicked, he flailed his arms inside the spacious sack, and he started to cry. The experienced nurse swooped over, unrolled the flannel blanket, and within seconds had him looking once again like a fuzzy, pale blue burrito in a knit cap. Instantly, his crying ceased. She handed me my baby and assured me I would master the swaddling technique soon enough.

I picture Mary, exhausted from her trip and from childbirth, taking each strip of cloth and tenderly wrapping it around her firstborn son. I wonder if she did so haltingly, unsure if she was getting it right. Did she feel as stunned as I did that her child, long growing in the hidden place of her womb, was finally out, staring at her with bright eyes and dependent on her to care for him? Did she feel prepared for all that would come with mothering a child—especially a child she knew would one day turn the world upside down?

We have been preparing ourselves for the incarnation, the baby Jesus, but do we also hold in our minds the reality that this child wrapped in bands of cloth will one day grow into the man who made a whip and drove money changers out of the temple? Who called people to expand their notions of love and mercy, of insider and outsider? It is easy to sentimentalize the baby Jesus. We can almost hear that familiar hymn about the little Lord Jesus, no crying he makes, picture the pristine images of a serene Holy Family and a tidy stable. Our Savior gets domesticated and therefore controllable and safe. We tend to eliminate the messy realities of childbirth and caregiving. Infants control our waking and sleeping and change our comfort level around handling bodily fluids. Though small, their influence and disruption impacts every aspect of the household they enter. So it should be for the infant Jesus in our lives, challenging us to rethink what we think we know about God and life and love.

On Christmas Eve, the full humanness of Jesus stuns me no less than when I looked at my own firstborn. Mary wraps him in bands of cloth, for warmth, security, comfort, and so much more. Mary swaddles the baby in whom we will be clothed, all of us enveloped by the unrelenting compassion and grace of our God. Even as we stumble and bumble, learn and fail, nothing can undo the mantle of love in which we are covered. We see the baby Jesus wrapped by his mother in bands of cloth and know the One she holds has the whole world in his hands; therefore, we can rest secure.

Sunday after Christmas: Hearts
Psalm 51:1–12; Luke 2:8–20

And Mary treasured all these words and pondered them in her heart. (Luke 2:19)

The week after Christmas is often calm, a good time for rest and reflection after the weeks of busyness, preparation, and events. While church attendance is often low on this first Sunday after Christmas Day, encourage those who make worship a priority this week to take time to attend to their own hearts. What are we carrying into worship as we close out the year and holiday season? Some may have regrets, things they hope to do better next year. Some may still be feeling the cozy glow of a happy Christmas, vaguely aware of pressures and responsibilities that will soon be felt again. Our Scriptures for today make room for both.

Psalm 51 honors the breathtaking reality that God sees and knows our hearts. "Create in me a clean heart, O God, and put a new and right spirit within me" (v. 10). We think of this psalm more with Ash Wednesday than with the season of Christmas, but reflecting on our sin against God in the wake of the incarnation invites us to a level of honesty commensurate with the revelation that Jesus came to save sinners. We can lay bare all our heart and hold nothing back from the mercy of God evident in the coming of the Messiah. We can acknowledge our need for God to act, to cleanse our hearts, and to set us right, and see unequivocally that through Jesus Christ, God does act to put a right spirit within us, that nothing will or can separate us from the love of God. This frees us to pour out our heart and soul without fear to the God who loves us.

On the other hand, Mary in our Gospel reading is not purging her heart of transgression but taking in the wonder of her son's reception into the world, treasuring the shepherds' words and holding them in her heart. No doubt, as Jesus grew, Mary would return to the shepherds' proclamation and that of Gabriel's before them. God's calling and all that call entails remains a mystery, no matter how long one lives into it. When raising the Son of God got complicated and painful, when Jesus went missing as an adolescent or when he began to get in trouble with the authorities, Mary must have pondered in her heart all the more, mulling over treasured words to reassure her of her son's well-being, despite all the danger his mission engendered.

As we reflect on the year behind and ahead, let us decide what we need to treasure and what needs to be cleansed.

Epiphany: Gold
Exodus 32:1–6; Matthew 2:1–12

On entering the house, they saw the child with Mary his mother, and they knelt down and paid him homage. Then, opening their treasure chests, they offered him gifts of gold, frankincense, and myrrh. (Matthew 2:11)

The second Sunday of the Christmas liturgical season falls in the first several days of each new year, and congregations often use this date to celebrate Epiphany, since January 6 might be any day of the week. This sermon is useful for observing both the secular new year and the visit of the magi.

New Year's resolutions often reveal what we truly treasure and value. These articulated vows and goals can point to an idol, such as a beach bod or a big raise—or they can be a gift to use for the good of others, such as making more time for family or devoting a certain time each week to serving those in need. The Hebrews in the wilderness, under stress, revealed that they valued a god they could see and touch, and so Aaron made them one out of gold. The magi, on the other hand, gave generously of their gold and other treasures to honor an unlikely king.

When anxiety swells and uncertainty persists, as it did for the Israelites in the desert, human beings will do a lot to mitigate their stress, even temporarily. While we may not form farm animals out of our jewelry, we do find less than helpful ways to ease our apprehensions. We self-medicate. We scapegoat and blame. We distract ourselves with things or distance ourselves from those who might tell us truths we do not want to hear. This story is, of course, about idolatry, but it is also a story about trauma and pain. The narrative of the golden calf reminds us to pay attention to what we do when we, and the systems, institutions, and communities we inhabit, are under duress. Recognize where that idolatrous urge comes from and, rather than give in to it, address the root cause. Instead of using energy and resources for a false god, recognize the grief and know God sees the hurt of God's people and will respond with compassion.

While the magi's gifts of frankincense and myrrh symbolized Jesus's divinity, his sacredness, his saving death to come, gold represents his humanity, the truth that this Messiah will know the trials and tribulations of work, earthly economics, and all the vicissitudes of human finitude. Like it or not, gold, or lack thereof, greatly impacts people's well-being. I wonder if Mary and Joseph saw the gift of gold and let out a sigh of relief. Perhaps they thought they could tuck it away, like a savings bond or the seeds of a college fund, a small bit of security to be used if times got really tough. This magi's gift of gold reminds us that the Holy Family was a real family, not unlike real families we know, attempting to raise children while working, imparting values, cooking meals, shaping character, and getting tired. When we share what we have, we, too, can provide a real, material help to our neighbors in need.

So, will our "gold"—not just our material wealth but our time, energy, and attention—be used to make an idol or a gift? Consider leading the congregation in a practice using the tradition of "star words" to replace typical new year's resolutions with a guiding word or phrase that will enrich others, not ourselves.

Women in the Wilderness

A seven-part Lenten series on fugitivity, feminism, and the fierce grace of survival.

ROBERTO CHE ESPINOZA

Series Overview

This Lenten season, we follow the sacred footsteps of women who dared to survive in the wilderness. Some were cast out. Some walked away. All of them—biblical, historical, and mythic—carried within them a truth the world was not ready to hear. From Hagar's flight into exile to María Sabina's whispered healing in the forest, from Ruth's migration and chosen kinship to Mary Magdalene's witness of resurrection, we will walk with women who have shaped liberation histories across time and terrain. These are women who were often misunderstood, silenced, or erased. And yet, their stories endure.

In this series, we weave transnational feminism, fugitivity, mystery, and an ethic of care into our Lenten reflections. Together, we will explore what it means to be seen by God, to speak truth, to carry sacred grief, and to birth resurrection in a broken world. This is not just a journey toward Easter. It is a remembering of sacred ancestors and call to repair what empire has exiled.

	Sermon Title	Focus Scripture	Theme
Lent 1	Hagar—The Wilderness of Seeing and Being Seen	Genesis 16:1–14	The fugitive mother who names God.
Lent 2	Sojourner Truth—The Wilderness of Truth-Telling	Exodus 3:1–12	Prophetic fire and embodied voice.
Lent 3	The Samaritan Woman—The Wilderness of Thirst and Taboos	John 4:1–30	Sacred conversation in forbidden places.

	Sermon Title	Focus Scripture	Theme
Lent 4	María Sabina—The Wilderness of Healing and Plant Wisdom	Mark 1:35–39	Mysticism and Indigenous healing.
Lent 5	Ruth and Naomi—The Wilderness of Migration and Chosen Kin	Ruth 1:1–19	Kinship, loyalty, and survival migration.
Lent 6	Deborah—The Wilderness of Protest	Judges 4:1–10; 5:1–9	Woman as prophet, protest, and judge in the wilderness of violence and empire.
Lent 7	Mary Magdalene—The Wilderness of Witness	John 20:1–18	First witness to the resurrection.

Tips and Ideas for This Series

Use desert landscapes, cracked earth, and blooming wildflowers as visual motifs—symbols of resilience and emergence. Create a wilderness altar with sand, stones, and fabric in earth tones. Invite women to share personal wilderness stories through art or testimony. Host a midweek class on biblical women and survival. Offer a journaling workshop or guided labyrinth walk for reflection. Include music from women composers and poets. Consider hosting a wilderness potluck featuring ancestral or comfort foods. On Easter, place wildflowers on each pew, echoing Mary Magdalene's witness that even tombs can blossom.

Compile a companion reader of poetry for your congregation to reflect on contemporary poetry alongside the ancient Scriptures:

- Lent 1: "won't you celebrate with me" by Lucille Clifton
- Lent 2: "A Litany for Survival" by Audre Lorde
- Lent 3: Choose an excerpt from *salt.* by Nayyirah Waheed
- Lent 4: "For Calling the Spirit Back from Wandering the Earth in Its Human Feet" by Joy Harjo
- Lent 5: "Home" by Warsan Shire
- Lent 6: "Jesus in the Wilderness" by Malika Booker
- Lent 7: "Where You Thought You Had Left Her" by Jan Richardson

Lent 1: Hagar—The Wilderness of Seeing and Being Seen
Genesis 16:1–14

So she named the LORD who spoke to her, "You are El-roi," for she said, "Have I really seen God and remained alive after seeing him?" (Genesis 16:13)

> To do theology from the perspective of Hagar means to allow the wilderness to speak—not just as metaphor, but as real geography of survival.
>
> —Delores S. Williams, *Sisters in the Wilderness*

What does it mean to be seen by God when the world turns away?

Hagar's story is not one of comfort but of collision. She is displaced, enslaved, and discarded—a woman fleeing into the wilderness pregnant and alone. She is doubly marginalized: an Egyptian in a Hebrew household, a servant used and then expelled. And yet, she becomes the first in all Scripture to name God—*El-roi*, which means "the One who sees."

To name God is to claim theological agency. This act is radical—especially coming from a woman who is not part of the covenant lineage. Hagar is not Israelite, not free, and not considered central to the story. Yet she is granted a theophany in the desert, a divine encounter where she is not only seen but *spoken to*. Her survival becomes sacred. Her suffering becomes part of the sacred narrative.

Hagar's story disrupts the theological frameworks of supersessionism, patriarchy, and empire theology. It challenges the idea that God's blessing is limited to the chosen or the powerful. Instead, the wilderness becomes the site of revelation. Not the temple, not the tabernacle, not even a mountain, but a barren stretch of land where a pregnant, exiled woman stops to catch her breath: that is where God shows up.

This narrative invites preachers to interrogate systems of domination—enslavement, forced surrogacy, displacement—that still persist in our world. Hagar's plight echoes in the lives of migrant mothers at the border, Black women in the U.S. medical system, and the ongoing exploitation of domestic workers across the globe. These are Hagar's descendants, still crying out in the wilderness, still being told they are expendable. But Scripture says otherwise: They are *seen*.

Fred Moten's notion of "the undercommons" (in his book by the same name) helps us frame Hagar's wilderness not as absence but as subversive presence. The undercommons is the space where the discarded gather—not in silence but in song. It is where fugitivity becomes a form of theological resistance. Hagar is not simply a victim—she is a theologian of the wilderness. She names God. She reclaims narrative. She lives.

For sermon preparation, linger in Genesis 16:7–13. Who initiates the encounter? What does the angel say? Notice that God does not erase her pain. There is no gaslighting here. There is acknowledgment, presence, and promise. And the naming of her son—*Ishmael*, "God hears"—is itself a sermon. God hears the cries of the outcast.

Preachers might invite the congregation to ask: Where do we place the center of our theological imagination? Do we assume God is most present in stability, power, and lineage? Or are we willing to find the holy in the hidden places—in stories that refuse closure, in voices that unsettle the dominant narrative? Let us question who we exile, who we see, and what it means to be known by a God who chooses the margins as holy ground.

This Lent, we walk with Hagar and other women who have walked in the wilderness, both literally and figuratively. We unlearn theologies of domination and learn to honor stories born in exile. Let us enter the wilderness not to find answers but to be found. To be seen. To know again that God's vision reaches even the places the world forgets.

Lent 2: Sojourner Truth—The Wilderness of Truth-Telling
Exodus 3:1–12

There the angel of the LORD *appeared to him in a flame of fire out of a bush; he looked, and the bush was blazing, yet it was not consumed. Then Moses said, "I must turn aside and look at this great sight and see why the bush is not burned up." When the* LORD *saw that he had turned aside to see, God called to him out of the bush, "Moses, Moses!" And he said, "Here I am." (Exodus 3:2–4)*

> The function of art is to do more than tell it like it is—it's to imagine what is possible.
>
> —bell hooks, *Talking Black*

Sojourner Truth stood barefoot and tall in the wilderness of White supremacy and patriarchy, and she did not flinch. Like Moses before the bush, she was summoned—not by comfort, but by compulsion. Her truth was inconvenient. Her body was politicized. Her speech was divinely disruptive.

Born into slavery in New York in 1797, Truth was given the name Isabella Baumfree. She was sold, beaten, and violated—like Hagar, a Black woman made fugitive by the systems that claimed dominion over her body. But like Hagar, she survived. And in her survival, she encountered the Divine. After escaping enslavement with her infant daughter, she underwent a spiritual transformation and changed her name to Sojourner Truth. She became a traveling preacher, abolitionist, and women's rights advocate—a prophet whose voice would not be contained by church walls or political platforms.

Her most famous speech, delivered in 1851 at the Women's Rights Convention in Akron, Ohio, pierced the mythologies of White womanhood and false religion with a single, burning question:

"Ain't I a woman?" In that question is a theology of interruption—a dismantling of theological frameworks that center whiteness, purity culture, and patriarchal readings of Scripture.

Sojourner stood in a time and place where both the church and the state conspired to deny her humanity. And yet, she claimed sacred space. She spoke as one who had seen the wilderness and lived to name God in it. Like Moses, she did not speak with eloquence or polish. She spoke with fire.

For preachers, this is a week to dwell with the image of the burning bush in Exodus 3:1–12. Who gets summoned to speak? What is God's name in this passage—and what does it mean to hear the call from within the flames? Use this text not as a metaphor for power but as a mirror for presence. God does not call Moses from the throne but from the blaze. God does not call Sojourner Truth from a seminary but from the deep groan of a people in bondage. This is a theology of combustion: that which burns but is not consumed.

Let this Sunday's liturgies carry the tone of reverent defiance. Invite the congregation to locate themselves not in the halls of Pharaoh's palace but at the edge of the bush, sandals removed. Let prayers sound like protest songs and confessions echo with the truths we've long silenced. The fire is not to destroy us but to purify us—to burn away the gods of dominance, erasure, and false peace.

Ask your community: What must we name in this wilderness? What truths are we afraid to speak? Who do we silence in order to feel safe in our sanctuaries?

Sojourner Truth teaches us that to speak from the margins is to speak from the heart of God. Let her voice ring in our pulpits and her question echo in our prayers. Not just "Ain't I a woman?" but "Ain't this also the gospel?"

Lent 3: The Samaritan Woman—The Wilderness of Thirst and Taboos
John 4:1–30

The woman said to him, "Sir, you have no bucket, and the well is deep. Where do you get that living water? Are you greater than our ancestor Jacob, who gave us the well and with his sons and his flocks drank from it?" (John 4:11–12)

> *Lo cotidiano* is the space where oppression is most felt and where liberation must be forged.
> —Ada María Isasi-Díaz, *Mujerista Theology*

At the heat of the day, she came—alone, unclean in their eyes, thirsty for more than water. The Samaritan woman at the well is no meek figure. She is a threshold walker, bearing within her body a history of exile and survival. Her encounter with Jesus is a collision of taboo and truth, of thirst and theology, and it takes place not in a temple or a synagogue but at a well—on contested ground, at an inconvenient hour, in a forbidden conversation.

This woman is not named, but she is known. Jesus sees her, not just her reputation or her ethnicity, but her *being*. Their exchange is the longest recorded conversation Jesus has with anyone in the Gospels. Let that settle in: A Samaritan woman, considered impure by Jewish standards, becomes a partner in theological dialogue with the Messiah. And not a passive recipient—she *asks questions*. She challenges. She wonders aloud. This is not submission; this is sacred curiosity.

She is a liminal figure: Samaritan and woman, sexually suspect and spiritually thirsty. Her marginalization is manifold, and yet, it becomes the very ground on which Jesus chooses to reveal his identity. "I am he" (v. 26), he says—words spoken not to the temple elite, not to the learned Pharisee, but to a woman whose entire presence was considered inappropriate. The wilderness she occupies is not geographic but social: the wilderness of taboos, of being unwanted, of thirsting in public when others come to the well in cool shadows.

This week in Lent, we enter the wilderness of desire—the terrain where longing itself becomes holy. What are we thirsty for? Whose desires are deemed dirty, inappropriate, or too much? Desire, here, is not just sexual. It is existential. It is the ache to be known, to be met in the heat of the day with dignity, not dismissal.

Preachers might reflect on how this passage upends purity culture and theological gatekeeping. Jesus refuses to shame her. He doesn't correct her theology so much as expand it. Their conversation moves from the politics of worship location to the presence of living water—a flowing image of the Spirit that is *not* bound by buildings, rituals, or rules. The well becomes a sanctuary. The taboo becomes a temple.

Importantly, her transformation does not follow healing or repentance as traditionally defined. She becomes an evangelist not because she's "fixed" but because she's *seen*. "Come and see a man who told me everything I have ever done" (v. 29). This is not confession—it is testimony. Being known, fully and without shame, becomes her liberation.

Guide your congregation this week into their own wildernesses of longing. Encourage them to ask: What desires do we hide? What conversations are we afraid to have? Where have we built taboos that Christ would cross without hesitation?

This Lent, let us meet one another at the well—in the heat, in the thirst, in the messy middle. And may we, like her, find that being seen can be the first sip of living water.

Lent 4: María Sabina—The Wilderness of Healing and Plant Wisdom
Mark 1:35–39

In the morning, while it was still very dark, he got up and went out to a deserted place, and there he prayed. (Mark 1:35)

> I change myself, I change the world.
> —Gloria Anzaldúa, *Borderlands/La Frontera*

María Sabina whispered to the mushrooms, and they answered in stars. She was a Mazatec *curandera*, a medicine woman, who lived in the Oaxacan mountains of southern Mexico. Her healing practice centered on *veladas*, nighttime ceremonies of chant, silence, and sacred mushroom ingestion. But María Sabina was not a mystic of spectacle. Her work was quiet, relational, reverent. She called the mushrooms *los niños santos*—the saint children—and believed they were alive with presence, personality, and wisdom. She did not dominate them. She listened to them. Healing, for her, was never a product to be sold but a prayer to be kept.

When outsiders—Western ethnobotanists, seekers, and celebrities—discovered her practices in the mid-twentieth century, they came not with reverence but with conquest. They misunderstood her medicine, extracted her wisdom, and commercialized the plants without consent. Her village was overrun. Her sanctuary became spectacle. Her sacred knowledge was broken open and sold without reciprocity. And yet, she remained rooted—rooted in prayer, rooted in the forest, and rooted in the slow language of the Earth.

This week's Scripture from Mark 1:35–39 shows Jesus retreating to the wilderness *not* to escape but to pray, to return to his center, and to listen. Before healing others, Jesus goes to be healed by silence, solitude, and Spirit. What if this, too, is a kind of *curanderismo*—a sacred tending of the self so that one can responsibly tend to others?

The dominant culture likes its healing fast: a cure, a fix, a pill, a transaction. But María Sabina, like Jesus, teaches us another way: that healing begins not with doing but with listening. Not with ownership, but with consent. Not with extraction, but with reverence. The wilderness is not the place we go to escape our lives; it is where we go to remember the life that holds us, the life that pulses through cedar and stone, wind and worm, mycelium and memory.

Preachers might use this week to reframe healing as relational rather than transactional—a model we see reflected in many of the Gospel's healing stories. Who do we turn to for healing—and how do we approach them? Do we ask permission? Do we come with humility? In the church, we must confront how colonization has shaped our theology of healing. How often have we confused miracles with control? María Sabina reminds us: Some knowledge is not meant to be translated, only honored. Some healing cannot be mapped—it must be met with mystery.

Invite your congregation to explore this week: What is the medicine we've overlooked? What wisdom has been ignored because it does not speak in Western tongues? Where are we being invited to sit in silence and let the Earth teach us again?

This Lent, let us walk softly in the forest. Let us ask the plants what they know. Let us pray not to be cured but to be in communion. For the deepest healing does not fix us—it changes our relationship to all that lives.

Lent 5: Ruth and Naomi—The Wilderness of Migration and Chosen Kin
Ruth 1:1–19

When Naomi saw that she was determined to go with her, she said no more to her. So the two of them went on until they came to Bethlehem. (Ruth 1:18-19a)

> Belonging is not a given. It is an act of political imagination.
> —M. Jacqui Alexander, *Pedagogies of Crossing*

Two women walk across scorched land carrying grief in their bones and hope in their silence. Ruth and Naomi are not merely mother-in-law and daughter-in-law—they are kin by choice, bound not by blood but by love, survival, and sacred refusal. They are famine-walkers, grief-bearers, companions in the wilderness of unchosen loss. And in a world that expects women to disappear after men die, they choose each other.

The story opens with death and displacement. Naomi, once full, is emptied by famine and widowhood. Ruth, a Moabite outsider, should return to her people, to her gods, to the safety of the familiar. Instead, she makes a vow that stretches beyond cultural boundaries and legal obligations: "Where you go, I will go; . . . your people shall be my people and your God my God" (v. 16).

This is not mere sentiment. This is resistance.

Ruth's vow undoes the logic of empire and nationhood. It rejects the idea that kinship must follow bloodlines or borders. In a time of deportations, detentions, and family separations, Ruth offers us an alternate vision: solidarity that costs something. Kinship that migrates. Love that follows grief into unfamiliar terrain.

Naomi, bitter and bereaved, cannot yet imagine resurrection. But Ruth imagines it for both of them. She embodies what womanist theologians call *survival theology*—faith that grows out of the cracks in empire's foundation. She will later become the great-grandmother of David, ancestor to Jesus, but for now she is simply a migrant woman risking everything on a dusty road.

Preachers might linger this week in the tension between scarcity and loyalty. What does it mean to bind ourselves to another in the wilderness, not knowing what the future holds? This is more than a story about family—it is a story about *belonging in exile*. Ruth chooses not only Naomi but a different God, a different land, a different future. Hers is not a passive following but an active reimagining of home.

In Lent, we are called to ask: Who do we walk with? What does kinship require of us? Are we willing to be made uncomfortable for the sake of love?

The God of Ruth and Naomi is not a distant deity. God appears not in thunder or fire but in the gleaned corners of a field, in barley gathered by hand, in whispered promises passed from one woman to another. This is a God who lives in what is left behind—and makes it enough.

Your liturgies this week might carry the scent of migration and harvest. Prayers of the people can become prayers of the displaced. Communion might honor the gleaning: the grace of what remains after power takes its portion. Blessings can name chosen family, border-crossing loyalties, and the holy audacity of those who keep walking.

This Lent, may we be like Ruth: loyal to the widowed, attuned to hunger, brave enough to make a home where none exists. May we walk the road of sacred companionship, trusting that somewhere in the wilderness, belonging will bloom again.

Lent 6: Deborah—The Wilderness of Protest
Judges 4:1–10; 5:1–9

At that time Deborah, a prophet, wife of Lappidoth, was judging Israel. She used to sit under the palm of Deborah between Ramah and Bethel in the hill country of Ephraim, and the Israelites came up to her for judgment. (Judges 4:4–5)

> When women speak truly they speak subversively—they cannot help it.
> —Adrienne Rich, "When We Dead Awaken"

Palm Sunday is a day of tension. Jesus rides into Jerusalem not on a warhorse but on a donkey—enacting a protest of peace, a subversion of empire. The palms waved are not just praise; they are resistance. They say: Another kingdom is possible. Another story is rising.

Deborah, too, leads a protest. In the chaos of Judges 4–5, she rises not from a palace but from the wilderness—under a solitary palm tree between Ramah and Bethel. She does not wait for permission. She speaks the truth of God into a landscape ruled by violence, military might, and Canaanite oppression. As both prophet and judge, Deborah disrupts patriarchy not with spectacle but with sacred authority.

Her wilderness is not barren—it is alive with strategy, poetry, and courage. Her presence under the palm tree becomes its own procession: People come to her with questions, seeking justice in a time of collapse. She is not the warrior Barak, but it is she who summons him. She gives the command. She tells the story. She holds the tension between fear and faith, calling others into the holy work of resistance.

This week, as Jesus rides into Jerusalem and people shout "Hosanna," Deborah invites us to ask: What kind of protest do we embody? Where do we locate the sacred in political disobedience? Who do we imagine as prophets?

Deborah's leadership shatters theologies that confine women to silence or submission. Her presence is a protest against gendered power structures—then and now. Like Hagar and Mary Magdalene, like María Sabina and Sojourner Truth, she reminds us that wilderness is often the birthplace of prophecy. When systems collapse and the center cannot hold, it is often women who rise with fierce clarity, bearing both lament and liberation.

Preachers might reflect on Deborah's prophetic poetry in Judges 5, where she sings not just of victory but of the cost of war, the complicity of tribes who refused to act, and the surprising salvation that came through women. This Palm Sunday, her voice joins the crowd—lifting a song of defiant hope.

Let your congregation feel the pulse of protest this week. This is not a Sunday of sentimentality. It is a Sunday of holy uprising. From the palms of protest to the tree of judgment, the wilderness holds wisdom. And Deborah still speaks.

Lent 7: Mary Magdalene—The Wilderness of Witness
John 20:1–18

Jesus said to her, "Woman, why are you weeping? Whom are you looking for?" Supposing him to be the gardener, she said to him, "Sir, if you have carried him away, tell me where you have laid him, and I will take him away." Jesus said to her, "Mary!" She turned and said to him in Hebrew, "Rabbouni!" (which means Teacher). (John 20:15–16)

> The symbol of God functions. If God is male, then the male is God.
> —Elizabeth A. Johnson, *She Who Is*

In the hush before dawn, when the stone was still heavy and hope still buried, Mary Magdalene came.

She did not come expecting joy. She came bearing the weight of grief, the ritual duties of love after death. She came to anoint a body, not to see a risen Christ. But it is precisely there—in the wilderness of sorrow, in the fragile morning hours—that resurrection chose her.

Not Peter, not John, but Mary.

The one who stayed. The one who wept. The one who waited.

She is not named for her roles as sister, wife, or mother. She stands on her own, in a garden that echoes Eden—but this time, it is the woman who sees God first.

Mary Magdalene's wilderness is not geographic but emotional. It is the terrain of loss, of silence, of a love that outlives death. And still, she shows up. In a world that demands women be quiet, Mary speaks. In a theology that often casts women as secondary, Jesus makes her apostle to the apostles.

She is the first preacher of the resurrection, commissioned not in a pulpit but in the garden where tears still linger. Her sermon is just five words: "I have seen the Lord" (v. 18). And yet it is the entire gospel.

Mary's encounter is not spectacle; it is sacred intimacy. Resurrection is not announced with trumpets but with the whisper of her name: *Mary*. And she knows. She knows it is him not because of proof but because of presence. This is how God comes near—not always with answers but with recognition.

Preachers might linger this week in the subtlety of that moment. How often do we miss the holy because it looks like the gardener? How often do we cling, as Mary did, to what was, instead of receiving what is becoming?

This Easter message invites the congregation to hold both the wound and the wonder. Resurrection does not erase death—it transforms it. The risen Christ still bears scars. Mary carries that paradox in her body as she runs to tell the others: Grief is not the end of the story.

In a world desperate for resurrection but terrified of its cost, Mary teaches us how to stand among the tombstones and not look away. She reminds us that witnessing is not passive—it is costly. It means staying when others leave. It means risking your voice. It means letting love be louder than fear.

Let your liturgy this week be one of quiet fire. Let the alleluias rise gently, like the sun breaking over the horizon. Let your people imagine the garden. Let them hear their names called. Let them believe again that even the grave cannot hold back the One who sees them.

Mary Magdalene walks ahead of us, not triumphant but true. Her tears become testimony. Her mourning becomes movement. Her love becomes liberation.

Let us follow her.

Let us say with trembling joy: "I have seen the Lord."

What If?

A six-part Lenten series asking the church to embrace the possibility and hope of Jesus's challenging call on our lives.

JOY MARTINEZ-MARSHALL

Series Overview The Lenten season invites followers of Jesus to repentance, morality, charity, communion with God, and renewal. This Lent, let us imagine *what if?* What if we participated in Lenten traditions this year? What if we could be reminded why we believe? What if we identify places in our lives that feel like wilderness and ask God to bring about spring there? The *what if?*s of this series ask the congregation to consider embracing the life Jesus calls us to, in a variety of challenging ways.

Embracing the season's solemnity does not void Lent of the hopeful whisper of revival. Asking *what if?* implores Christians to hope, even at times to be foolishly hopeful, that the world, the church, and themselves can be made new in Christ. Asking *what if?* stands defiant in the face of apathy, obligation, and hopelessness. So, what if Christians considered the possibility of hope? What if we fail? But what if it transforms us?

	Sermon Title	Focus Scripture	Theme
Lent 1	What if we embraced the immigrant?	Deuteronomy 26:1–11	God invites us to welcome the immigrant among us.
Lent 2	What if we embraced lament?	Luke 13:31–35	Jesus models how to lament for us.
Lent 3	What if we embraced abundant life?	Isaiah 55:1–9	Abundant life is found not in things but in relationship.
Lent 4	What if we embraced restoration?	Luke 15:1–3; 11b–32	We are not in competition for God's love.
Lent 5	What if we embraced service?	John 12:1–8	Jesus invites us to serve him and our neighbors.

	Sermon Title	Focus Scripture	Theme
Lent 6	What if we embraced the politics of Jesus?	Luke 19:28–42	Sometimes, we must be political about peace.

Tips and Ideas for This Series

This series hopes to navigate the potential drudges of Lent by asking the preacher to confront and consider social justice concerns, political pandering, and overwhelming apathy. With the decline in church attendance, the closing of many churches, and the increase of Christian nationalism, many congregations are feeling burdened by hopelessness. At the beginning of Lent, groups can gather to create a "hope board" as a visual aid to identify places, situations, or relationships that need hope. Consider hosting a Prayer of Lament service that provides space to lament as Jesus did when overlooking Jerusalem. Images of rebirth, unexpected endings, and unlikely allies can serve as illustrations.

Lent 1: What If We Embraced the Immigrant?
Deuteronomy 26:1–11

"So now I bring the first of the fruit of the ground that you, O LORD, have given me." You shall set it down before the LORD your God and bow down before the LORD your God. Then you, together with the Levites and the aliens who reside among you, shall celebrate with all the bounty that the LORD your God has given to you and to your house. (Deuteronomy 26:10–11)

Our journey toward Jerusalem beings with a reading from the book of Deuteronomy, a book compiled of speeches given by Moses to the new generation of Hebrews preparing for life in the promised land after living in the wilderness. Often heard as a list of rules, laws, and ordinances only to be written off, at the heart of the book is a way to be in relationship. It mixes genres and extends to us an invitation into faithful relationship with God.

What is Lent but the opportunity to wander in the desert with Jesus? What is Lent but a time to make our way, covered in the dust of our rabbi as he moves toward the cross? With all this wandering comes a sense of restlessness like the Hebrews experienced. It brings with it a relentless push to put one foot in front of the other, no matter the aches, anxieties, or ambitions. Though we go knowing that the promised land awaits and the joy of resurrection meets us, the calling is to experience the journey. What if we, like this passage suggests, become people who give, remember, and foster a welcoming spirit for Lent?

Moses told the people that when they "come into the land that the LORD your God is giving [them]" (v. 1), they should take the first fruits that are from God's graciousness and offer back to God the best of what God has blessed them with. This hope of reciprocity and gratitude seemed far off in the desert, but Moses and the people know that God will honor the promises made. Lent asks us to do the same, to collectively, as a group, reenact and remember how God has been faithful in the past and let it illuminate the future.

This litany about covenant fidelity helps to ground the people lest they forget about God. With a home, a future, and hope, the celebration does not end. The bounty is not just to be celebrated in one community. Throughout Deuteronomy, the people learn what it is like to be in relationship with God and uphold the covenant. Such relationship with God asks God's people to welcome the stranger. In the Hebrew, *gar* means sojourner, a temporary inhabitant, a newcomer lacking inherited rights, a foreigner: in other words, an immigrant.

In our congregations and communities, we may not know about peoples' statuses, papers, or backgrounds. And yet, Deuteronomy asks of us to engage in hospitality to the immigrant, to welcome them into fellowship and the sharing of the celebration of provision. The invitation to give and remember must also lead to the ritual and practicing of welcoming all around us. Because the Israelite people knew what it was like to be exploited for free labor, God asks them to live as people of generosity. God asks them to honor their story by celebrating the bounty God graciously gives.

Immigration has been a polarizing issue in our world for ages. With changes in society, so, too, come shifts in people groups as they migrate. What if, when we welcome the immigrant among us, we find that there is much to celebrate? God has given plenty. In turn, we must share it with whomever we identify, even falsely, as a Levite or an alien to us.

Lent 2: What If We Embraced Lament?
Luke 13:31–35

"'Yet today, tomorrow, and the next day I must be on my way, because it is impossible for a prophet to be killed outside of Jerusalem.' Jerusalem, Jerusalem, the city that kills the prophets and stones those who are sent to it! How often have I desired to gather your children together as a hen gathers her brood under her wings, and you were not willing!" (Luke 13:33–34)

It is OK to not be OK. It is OK to be sad, mad, frustrated, disappointed, and a multitude of emotions. Emotions are a part of the human experience and something Jesus expressed fully. Too often, we in church ignore such truth. We come into the sanctuary with masks securely fastened, not letting the cracks of life show. You do not want others to know that you have struggled this month, that Lent has not really felt any different than the expected monotony of life. These intentionally curated masks might hide our hurt, but their cumbersome nature does little to ease the pain, the sadness, or the confusion one is truly experiencing.

One third of the psalms are songs of lament. Lamentations as a book lives up to its name. The biblical canon never offers platitudes like, "Suck it up, buttercup." "Life's tough; wear a helmet." "Get over it." Instead, the Scriptures tell us we are bade by a loving God to express our lament at the foot of the cross. To grieve to God knowing God will not leave us alone in the rubble left by divorce, infidelity, addiction, depression, fear, pain, seasons of darkness, seasons of light, joy, and great anticipation. God is there with us.

Jesus himself models lament, saying "Jerusalem, Jerusalem, the city that kills the prophets and stones those who are sent to it!" As the people dealt cruelly with the prophets before, the Messiah will be no exception to those he comes to offer salvation. Jesus is full of grief.

Day in and day out we hear: "How are you?" "How are things?" "How are you doing?" Only to reply, half-heartedly and quickly, "I'm fine!" "I'm good!" "Anyways, how are you?"—always attempting to turn the conversation. But Jesus can handle our truth, our laments. The season of Lent asks us: Are we really OK? After stripping away the distractions, being called back to faithfulness, self-denial, and almsgiving, and accepting our own mortality, why do we still allow masks to rule our lives? If not now, when will we come to accept where we really are? It is in this season of longing for resurrection and spring that we can explore these complexities of the human experience. In this exploration, we can find rest, solidarity, and wisdom from the experience of the one we call Lord and Savior.

The church must embrace the importance and place of lament in our world, our lives, and our churches. What if we had the audacity to acknowledge the things whispered only in the realms of our hearts to find hope in Christ's presence even there? What if we embraced lament this Lent?

What if we named what causes such grief and where wounds still ache? Only when we properly lament are we able to feel hope as we lean into Jesus.

Lent 3: What If We Embraced Abundant Life?
Isaiah 55:1–9

Why do you spend your money for that which is not bread
  and your earnings for that which does not satisfy?
Listen carefully to me, and eat what is good,
  and delight yourselves in rich food.
Incline your ear, and come to me;
  listen, so that you may live.
I will make with you an everlasting covenant,
  my steadfast, sure love for David. (Isaiah 55:2–3)

There are many messages that tell us what an abundant life might look like. We can be fooled into believing that an abundant life is the American dream of 2.5 children and a dog. An abundant life can be equated with "the good life," in which one has enough money in savings to qualify for a mortgage loan and upholds billionaires as examples. Our society seems to repeatedly teach us that money, success, and good vibes will lead to an abundant life. This kind of life is one of being content in material goods. It is reaching the finish line by achieving comfortability with lots of stuff.

This is never what Christians are promised. Last week, we explored lament, and this week we must now be confronted by Isaiah's words. Abundant life never appears to us as things but through relationship with God. God's people need not rely on money, labor, or being at the mercy of conquering nations. Thirsting no more and eating what is good is the new norm.

Ironically, the passage invites us to "delight [ourselves] in rich food," though in Lent so much onus is put on giving up something. Maybe the rich food we delight in is the spiritual feast of ridding ourselves of distractions in the Lenten season. The richness of life is being in communion with a God that restores, upholds God's promises, and is steadfast in love for us. In this richness, we are fed, full, and reminded of what really satisfies. We take our place as the beneficiaries of abundance and herald this good news for all people to come and taste the goodness of God.

In the Gospel according to John, Jesus extends this same invitation to abundant life. Jesus says, "The thief comes only to steal and kill and destroy. I came that they may have life and have it abundantly" (John 10:10). Thievery posturing as "the good life" is always afoot. Politicians want us to believe that marginalization and oppression of others is just a ramification of abundant life for some—those who the powerful deem worthy. Consumerism tells us that it is right and good to buy because it makes us feel something. Overconsumption hurts creation and creatures. It feeds the malpractice of payday-loan-lending sharks and the elite while ignoring those it hurts. The powerful experience abundance while making empty promises to the have-nots. None of this leads to abundant life but to destruction. The call of the Christ follower is to rest in the abundant promises of God. We must find peace with what has been graciously bestowed on us and work toward the good of our communities.

Imagine if we called out such lies about "abundant life" for what they are. There is more than enough for our neighbors to experience liberation through Christ, finding life in him, and abundant life at that.

Lent 4: What If We Embraced Restoration?
Luke 15:1–3;11b–32

"'But when this son of yours came back, who has devoured your assets with prostitutes, you killed the fatted calf for him!' Then the father said to him, 'Son, you are always with me, and all that is mine is yours. But we had to celebrate and rejoice, because this brother of yours was dead and has come to life; he was lost and has been found.'" (Luke 15:30–32)

Our reading forces us to run the risk of repeating ourselves. Because of the parable of the Prodigal Son's popularity and strong moral teaching, it is easy for us to skim it. Hit the highlights and go home. Read it again to say that we did as the lectionary instructed. Dust off an old sermon because no one even remembers what you said last week. Take this week off and let someone else do it. However, I think that with its familiarity also comes the opportunity to use a different lens. What if this time around we considered what feels overlooked? What if we have missed embracing restoration because it felt like competition?

The society in which we live breeds competition. Before we are even able to walk, we are being sized up against the baby in the basinet next to us. We consume reality television with the premise of forcing people to compete for money, clout, or attention. We rate everything all the time. We "like" posts or "thumbs down" messages without recognizing the spirit of competition that lurks in the undercurrent. Young adults are feeling commodified by peers as they are pitted against unrealistic body images, AI-generated photos, and algorithms.

What undergirds the parable of the Lost Son is the older brother's desire to be more cherished by the father. The heart of this competitiveness was a belief that both sons could not be beloved. When we consider the older son's anger, we find that it is rooted in indignation or jealousy. These emotions presenting themselves as anger force the brother to miss the celebration of restoration. Because the competitiveness of siblings can lead to broken relationship, we must be attentive to our own older-son emotions.

Unacknowledged emotions cause rifts in the faith community and can fester in times of change. When we constantly measure others' success through our own scale of fairness, which is often selfish in nature, we cannot see each other as beloved. People who have sat in the pews the longest or certain faithful members of the congregation can then become gatekeepers of the Father's house. Falling ill to the seduction of perceived belovedness can lead us to police other peoples' behavior, comments, and participation. This leads to exclusion and isolation. The church then becomes a place of judgment instead of acceptance. Instead of being siblings in Christ, we become self-proclaimed older brothers missing out on the Father's love, despite the fact that the Father's love can never be limited or manipulated. If only the older brother could imagine what it would be like for his father to love both sons, even if one had not lived up to societal standards. We surely do not want to miss out on what restoration can lead to: the lost being found, the isolated finding community, the church being a refuge and not a county club. What if we let ourselves name what we really feel—perhaps that we are not enough? Then we, too, could let restoration bloom in our chests. Even in the competitiveness of the world, the father's love restores both sons, and for that, we must rejoice.

Lent 5: What If We Embraced Service?
John 12:1–8

"Why was this perfume not sold for three hundred denarii and the money given to the poor?" (He said this not because he cared about the poor but because he was a thief; he kept the common purse and used to steal what was put into it.) (John 12:5-6)

Perhaps you hear this passage and think of how weird it is for Mary to wash Jesus's feet with expensive perfume. If you thought that was bad news, Judas, in John's rendition of the story, makes it worse. The bad news is not that Mary used something expensive but that Judas lacked contextual understanding. Judas does not stop to smell the roses, or in this case, nard. I imagine he does not ask softly and inquisitively but with judgment. The perfume cost about a year's worth of wages for a day laborer in the ancient Near East, and this sent Judas into a tailspin. The next verse clarifies for us that this question was not out of concern for the poor. Even now, people try to twist Jesus's words, claiming the poor will always be with us, so we do not have to be responsible for their care.

Could that be said of us? The bad news: It is easy for us to jump to conclusions like Judas, especially with the rise of extravagant wealth in churches and religious organizations. Modern-day parallels might be found when people ask, "How can they afford such nice shoes if they are getting government assistance?" or "Tariffs and budget cuts don't affect me personally, so who cares?" or "Can't they just go to a homeless shelter?" The bad news is that there are still the poor among us, not because it pleases Jesus but because of the brokenness of our world. We contribute to such wage gaps, resource restrictions, and greed.

The good news is that Jesus invites us to be like Mary by embracing the act of service as an expression of abundant and lavish love. Jesus is preparing to enter Jerusalem, situated in Bethany with his close friends: Lazarus, Martha, and Mary. Mary anoints Jesus with the perfume. He says, "She bought it so that she might keep it for the day of my burial" (v. 7). Mary, the same student we see in Luke's Gospel, is still sitting at the feet of Jesus as a disciple. She witnessed the raising of her brother, Lazarus. This was transformative to her understanding of Jesus, and she is the one who gets it right. She had been listening to the Messiah. The purpose of his incarnation was not missed by his faithful disciple. She washed his feet as a sign of love that foreshadows Jesus's own actions. The same verb used here for wiping his feet with her hair is used in the next chapter as Jesus washes the feet of his disciples. What if we had the boldness to do the same? To wash feet instead of accusing? To not be OK that there are poor people among us? Maybe there would be more good news to share.

Lent 6: What If We Embraced the Politics of Jesus?
Luke 19:28–42

As he came near and saw the city, he wept over it, saying, "If you, even you, had only recognized on this day the things that make for peace! But now they are hidden from your eyes." (Luke 19:41–42)

In 2020, George Floyd's death was a tragic moment that confronted the ethos of a divided nation. Instead of mourning the loss of life, many jumped to accusations. Instead of hearing stories of our Black, Brown, and Indigenous siblings, many White people put up their defenses. They discredited the family and ignored history's violent repetition of inequality. George Floyd Square remains a thin place of

God's tenderness haunted by the pain of what happened. Flowers line the sidewalk by a gutter. Its familiarity stares back at us, saying, "This could happen anywhere at any time." Floyd's murder was a terrifying reminder for people of color in this country, an injustice that reminded the nation that when there is no justice, there is no peace.

Protestors have been echoing this for decades, and the sentiment has been true for a millennium. We talk about Jesus entering Jerusalem with shouts of "Peace in heaven" (v. 38) only then to weep saying, "if you, even you, had only recognized on this day the things that make for peace!" (v. 42). The message of the triumphal entry is the revolution of the church asking: What if we embraced being political?

It is a band of tax collectors, women, fishermen, healed folk, and poor who come into the epicenter of the Jewish world to see Jesus riding on a colt, Jerusalem and its religious authority being challenged by outsiders who have started a parade fit for a king. It is a moment of such scandal and upheaval, such a political protest against the powers that be: the powers of Rome. Rome was known during this period for the Pax Romana, the peace of Rome. It was a peace achieved by violence, military coups, killing, rape, punishment, retribution, and power. This was a different kind of peace. The perception of peace, enforced by law and the appearance of order, is what Rome promised and Herod upheld. A political peace is what the Roman Empire offered.

Rome's peace is not dissimilar to the peace and politics we see in our world. It is a peace achieved by controlling the population with money, power, and limited resources. The peace we have in our county harms the marginalized, poor, and disenfranchised through systemic injustice.

During Lent, we must embrace Jesus's politics and call out the parades of our modern Rome. We must stand in disagreement with our Christian sisters and brothers "saying, 'peace, peace,' when there is no peace" (Jer. 6:14b). We must reflect on our own shortcomings and sins of racism, ableism, sexism, homophobia, classism, and selfishness. We must reject the parades of Christian nationalism as it distorts the political undertones of the triumphal entry.

Jesus did not come to make Jerusalem great again but to invite the people into a new reign, that reign of God where the first is last, where the hurting are comforted, where justice rolls down like rivers, where illness and death do not get the last word, and where there is forgiveness because the Jesus we know goes to the cross to make room for reconciliation and restoration of relationship. We must do something about the pain and suffering in the world, because if we do not, it will continue. Let us be willing to see the things that make for peace, on earth as it is in heaven.

Contributors

Gail Song Bantum has been a lead pastor, executive coach, and culture curator for diverse organizations for three decades. Gail is the coauthor of *Choosing Us: Mutual Flourishing in a World of Difference*. She is currently a board member of WomanPreach! Inc. and serves as an adviser for pastors and organizational leaders.

Shawna Bowman is an artist and pastor of Friendship Presbyterian Church and has been doing ministry with the creative and justice-seeking folks there since 2011. In 2019, the church launched Friendship Community Place, a neighborhood hub and collaborative space on the northwest side of Chicago. Shawna serves as the Executive Director.

Jia Starr Brown is an African American pastor, educator, author, and activist with more than three decades of experience advocating for underrepresented communities. Brown is ordained in the Christian Church (Disciples of Christ) and is the founding pastor of The Stable, an online anti-racism study church.

Carol Cavin-Dillon is the senior pastor at West End United Methodist Church in Nashville, Tennesee, and an adjunct faculty member in Methodist Studies at Vanderbilt Divinity School.

Benjamin R. Cremer has been serving in pastoral ministry since 2005 and has most recently focused on writing and ministering in digital spaces. He has been published in books and newspapers, and soon in a book of his own. You can find his weekly newsletter at benjamin-cremer.kit.com, his sermons on his *Into the Gray* podcast, and his presence on social media @brcremer.

Brandon Thomas Crowley is a pastor, scholar, public intellectual, and author of *Queering Black Churches: Dismantling Heteronormativity in African American Congregations*. Since 2009, he has served as Senior Pastor of the Historic Myrtle Baptist Church in Newton, Massachusetts, and has taught at institutions such as Harvard University, Emory University, Boston University, and the Episcopal Theological Seminary of the Southwest.

Amos Disasa is the senior pastor of First Presbyterian Church of Dallas, Texas, a historic congregation in the heart of the city. Previously, he served as the copastor of Downtown Church in Columbia, South Carolina.

Jill J. Duffield is the senior minister of First Presbyterian Church in Greensboro, North Carolina, and formerly served as the editor of *The Presbyterian Outlook*. She is the author of *Appreciate These Things: Eight Ways of Cultivating Compassion, Advent in Plain Sight: A Devotion through Ten Objects,* and *Lent in Plain Sight: A Devotion through Ten Objects.*

Roberto Che Espinoza, public theologian, pastor, and professor, is the founder of Our Collective Becoming, a space for decolonial imagination and embodied theology. Through writing, teaching, and community care, they cultivate ethical futures rooted in wonder, justice, and joy. Follow their work on Substack at Our Collective Becoming.

Mark Feldmeir is senior pastor at St. Andrew United Methodist Church in Highlands Ranch, Colorado, and author of five books, including *Life after God: Finding Faith When You Can't Believe Anymore.* Mark has served on the adjunct faculty at Claremont School of Theology, where he has taught homiletics, and he speaks frequently at conferences on topics from preaching to pop culture.

Brian Gerard is the senior minister of Middletown Christian Church (Disciples of Christ) in Louisville, Kentucky. You can find more of his sermons and thoughts on his socials and at www.middletownchristian.org.

Napoleon J. Harris V is proud to serve as the pastor of Antioch Baptist Church in his hometown of Cleveland, Ohio. He is happily married, father of two amazing daughters, and published across a variety of media. Connect with him on all major social media platforms.

Sam Lundquist is the associate pastor at St. John's Presbyterian Church in San Francisco. His creative worship projects have been featured in *The New York Times*, *BBC News*, and *Vice News*. Prior to ministry, Sam worked with renowned Hollywood brands like *Harry Potter* as a creative director in themed entertainment. Learn more at samlundquist.com.

Colby Martin is a pastor and author of *UnClobber: Rethinking Our Misuse of the Bible on Homosexuality* and *The Shift: Surviving and Thriving after Moving from Conservative to Progressive Christianity*. He currently runs a ministry on LGBTQ+ inclusion and travels the country preaching love and grace for all. Find his work at PerspectiveShift.co and on Instagram @colbymartin.

Joy Martinez-Marshall is the pastor of First Baptist Church of Ottawa, Kansas. She is delighted to serve on the board of directors for Baptist Women in Ministry. Joy loves to cook and values a perfect game-day snack. She and her husband, Austin, are avid sports fans and readers.

Matt Miofsky is the lead pastor of The Gathering, a thriving multisite congregation in St. Louis, Missouri. He is also author of multiple books, including *Let Go: Leaning into the Future without Fear*, *Fail: What to Do When Things Go Wrong*, and *Eight Virtues of Rapidly Growing Churches*.

Diane Givens Moffett, the first African American woman to lead the former Presbyterian Mission Agency, served as its president and executive director, overseeing 250 employees and mission coworkers across eighty countries. Prior to this role, she was a pastor for thirty-three years and authored *Beyond Greens and Cornbread: Reflections of African American Christian Identity*.

Rodger Nishioka serves as the senior pastor of the Village Presbyterian Church in Prairie Village, Kansas. Prior to his joining the saints at Village Church, he served on the faculty of Columbia Theological Seminary in Decatur, Georgia.

Jonah P. Overton is the lead and founding pastor of Zao MKE Church in Milwaukee. A writer, speaker, pastor, and podcaster, Jonah works at the intersection of faith, mysticism, and liberation inviting people into deeper relationship with God through radical inclusion, biblical storytelling, and spiritual disruption.

Bethany Peerbolte is dedicated to assuring the queer community that God made them as they are on purpose. Her community, Our Tapestry, is where her 290,000 followers can go to declutter their faith from toxic theology. Find her on any social media platform @RevBethany.

Josh Scott is the lead pastor at GracePointe Church in Nashville and the author of several books, including *Bible Stories for Grown-Ups: Reading Scripture with New Eyes*, *Context: Putting Scripture in Its Place*, and *Cross-Examined: Reading the Bible in Times of Division*. You can read his latest thoughts at joshscott.online or on social media @josh_a_scott.

Tyler Ho-Yin Sit is a church planter and pastor based in Minneapolis. Learn more about his ministries, including his book *Staying Awake: The Gospel for Changemakers*, at TylerSit.com.

Adriene Thorne is the eighth senior minister of the historic and history-making Riverside Church in the City of New York and the first African American woman to hold the position. Find her on Instagram and Bluesky @revadriene.

Joseph Yoo is the vicar of Mosaic Episcopal Church in a suburb of Houston, Texas. He has been a resident of Houston since 2016 along with his wife, Rahel, and son, Nathanael. He is the author of *When the Saints Go Flying In: Stories about Faith, Life, and Everything in Between*, and you can check out his other writings at JosephYoo.com.

www.ingramcontent.com/pod-product-compliance
Lightning Source LLC
Chambersburg PA
CBHW080757050126
37695CB00003B/6